Go West for Parrots!

A South American Odyssey

Rosemary Low

Rosemary Low

INSiGNIS
PUBLICATIONS

ISBN 978-0-9531337-6-5

Cover design and photograph: Hyacinthine Macaws in the Pantanal by Rosemary Low

Insignis Publications,
P.O.Box 100, Mansfield,
Notts NG20 9NZ, UK.

Printed by CPI Antony Rowe, Chippenham, Wiltshire

Contents

Acknowledgements

I am indebted to the many people I met on my journeys who provided help, information and pleasant companionship and who shared my love of the incomparable birds of the neotropics. Special thanks are due to all the dedicated ornithologists and bird guides who accompanied me in the field.

My thanks to the following who kindly provided photographs:

Thomas Brosset, Sweden (Austral Conure)
Fundación Loro Parque, Tenerife (Maroon-fronted Parrot)
R.& V. Moat, UK (Jamaican Conure, Coral-billed Parrot)
Priscilla Old, USA (Hoatzin)
Alonso Quevedo/ProAves, Colombia (Brown-breasted Conure)

All other photographs are the copyright of the author.

Threat Status
At least one in eight of all bird species is threatened with extinction. Where those species are mentioned in the text, their threat status is usually given in the list of species at the conclusion of each chapter. This is based on information in the monumental work *Threatened Birds of the World* published in 2000 (Barcelona and Cambridge, UK: Lynx Edicions and BirdLife International) but inevitably already out of date. The status of each country's bird species is from the same source.

Definitions are as follows:

Critically Endangered
The species faces an extremely high risk of extinction in the wild in the immediate future.

Endangered
The species faces a very high risk of extinction in the wild in the near future

Vulnerable
The species faces a high risk of extinction in the medium-term future.

Near Threatened
The species is close to qualifying as Vulnerable.

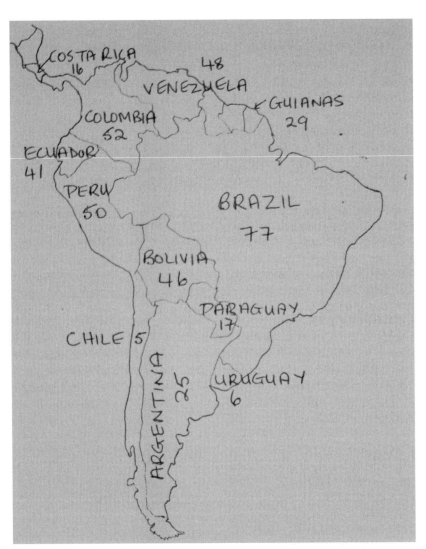

The numbers indicate approximately how many parrot species are found in each country, with Australia (52) and New Guinea (46) for comparison.

Introduction

Parrots have engaged and enchanted me since I was a teenager. But it was not until I was in my thirties that I had my first sightings of them in the wild. It changed my whole perception of these extraordinarily beautiful and intelligent birds. Once I had seen how and where they lived, my journeys throughout the tropics began. They were always longed-for interludes of two or three weeks, snatched time in a busy life, sometimes trips made as a speaker at a convention or, more rarely, in a professional capacity. It did not matter *how* I got there – the all-important factor was that it was a country where parrots occurred.

A particular nation or island might beckon me for one species only – Costa Rica for the Great Green Macaw, Bonaire for the Yellow-shouldered Amazon, Argentina for the Burrowing Parrot, but never Antigua, Guadeloupe or the Virgin Islands. There were no parrots there! In Rio I steered clear of Copacabana. In Mexico my destination was the mountains, not the beaches of Cancún. In short, I avoided resorts and theme parks and sought the wonders of rainforests and national parks. South America is incredibly rich in parrot species and drew me back again and again. That is why I often went West and why this book is devoted to my travels in that great and exciting sub-continent! It is home to more than one third of all parrot species in existence including the charismatic macaws, the adorable Amazon parrots and the captivating conures.

It was not only the parrots that intrigued me. The bird life is amazingly varied and beautiful and the species numerous. In fact, of the 9,800 or so bird species in the world, one third are found in South America. The sub-continent is also one of the most fascinating areas of the planet, with its extraordinary geography, diverse cultures and unique wildlife and, in the Andes, its haunting and evocative music.

All birds fascinate me and other species are not neglected in these pages – but parrots are my passion. I recount some of my journeys, spanning 30 years, along with the people I met and my concern for what was happening to the planet. There were memorable encounters with other life forms, from aggressive primates to pretty but poisonous arrow frogs. But it was the birds that held me spellbound. For me, there are no truer words than those of Mark Cocker who wrote:

Birding in the tropics isn't just the pursuit of a hobby or the fulfilment of an obsession; at times it seems like a quest for life itself as expressed through bird sound, bird movement, bird colour. For me it has no equal in all ornithology. – Birders, 2001, Jonathan Cape, London.

1. Jamaica 1975, Grand Cayman 1975 and 1988:

Naïve travellers in the neotropics

Outside Europe, we knew only the USA. In 1975 my husband, Bob, and I decided to be a little more adventurous and settled on a trip to the Caribbean. Now this might not sound very exciting by today's standards but at that time currency restrictions operated. Each person had a limited sum of £300 to take out of the UK and all overseas currency transactions were recorded in one's passport. Travelling outside Europe had to be carefully planned, especially as it was not possible to pay in advance for accommodation.

We flew from Heathrow to Kingston, Jamaica. That has a nice calypso ring to it. The reality was not so nice. We took a taxi to the hotel, gasping in horror at the road manners. The driver's remark: "Plenty bad drivers!" was somewhat superfluous. On arrival at the hotel, the Courtleigh Manor, we relaxed in the tropical surrounds of the garden, full of beautiful trees and a small fountain watched over by two plastic flamingos. Soon we were blasted by the sound of a blaring TV set and took off to our room. It had a stupendous view over the Blue Mountains. We sat on the balcony and watched a "John Crow" (Turkey Vulture) circling lazily overhead – perhaps the most conspicuous of the island's birds. Like me, Bob had enjoyed a lifelong passion for everything with feathers and wings.

A Mockingbird was running along the ground, and stopping every two seconds to open his wings like a giant butterfly, displaying white wing bars. This nocturnal (and diurnal) songster, an accomplished mimic, is known locally as the Nightingale.

Hungry for a good meal, as soon as the restaurant opened, we were there, along with a little bird that is quickly encountered by

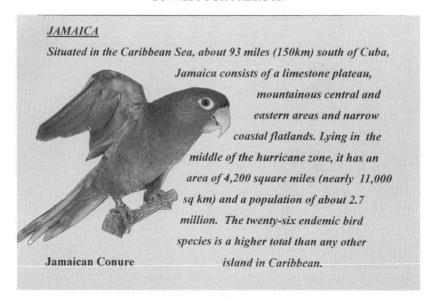

JAMAICA

Situated in the Caribbean Sea, about 93 miles (150km) south of Cuba, Jamaica consists of a limestone plateau, mountainous central and eastern areas and narrow coastal flatlands. Lying in the middle of the hurricane zone, it has an area of 4,200 square miles (nearly 11,000 sq km) and a population of about 2.7 million. The twenty-six endemic bird species is a higher total than any other island in Caribbean.

Jamaican Conure

most visitors to the northern neotropics, the Bananaquit. Bright yellow above and sooty grey below, it loves to hang out around sympathetic humans. In this respect it is a brightly coloured version of the homely House Sparrow, a common visitor to hotel dining tables, eagerly searching for sugar and tit-bits.

We sampled mango nectar, and snapper served with a slice of orange, carrot and artichoke. Then there was grapenut ice cream (what *is* grapenut?) or lemon pie. I ordered the latter. The pie eventually arrived with an apologetic waiter who said: "Sorry, no blueberry. I bring apple." It was lemon! Entertainment was provided at the side of our table by the ants rushing backwards and forwards carrying leaves. For ants, they were incredibly badly organised – Jamaican, of course! When I tired of watching them I made friends with a mouse by offering it bread.

Next morning we took a taxi to the Hope Botanical Gardens, part of the estate bestowed on Richard Hope. He had helped capture Jamaica from the Spanish in 1655. Dating back to the 1880s, the gardens were a haven of peace and mature trees, and displayed many of Jamaica's one thousand endemic plant species. Neat and well-kept, a stone-edged path ran through the lawns and circular flower beds, flanked by palms and other trees. The style would not have looked out of place in St James's

The nectar- and sugar-loving Bananaquit

Park. Exotic trees with extravagantly beautiful blossoms, such as the orchid flower tree, amaze first-time visitors to the tropics. Here, too, was ackee – named after Captain Bligh of the *Bounty*. Its yellow fruit is a popular local dish, served sautéed with cod.

A beautiful feature was a large pond, the surface of which was almost entirely covered with soft mauve and pink water lilies. It attracted Greater Antillean Grackles, large black birds with a violet sheen and weirdly shaped tails. A small flock divided their time between the trees bordering the pond and the large round lily leaves along the edge, from which they bathed with great enjoyment. Their tinny, plaintive notes were heard all over the island. These leaves are the true domain of the Jacana, here known as the "lily hopper". Its long narrow toes perfectly support its weight as it runs around, opening its wings to reveal bright yellow undersides. A couple of little Jamaican Euphonias, known locally as Bluequits, were searching a red-flowering hibiscus bush for insects and nectar. They have short, thick bills, grey-blue upperparts and yellow abdomen.

It was not long before we had seen all three species of hummingbirds. These included the Streamer-tailed (now classified as two species, Red-billed and Blackbilled), Jamaica's national bird, found nowhere else. It goes by the name of "Doctor". Supposedly its long bill was likened to the lancet which, in the 18th century, was used to cure most of the ailments of the local inhabitants. Common and unafraid, the Doctor is spectacular in flight, with his 9in (23cm) black tail streamers

3

with one serrated edge, floating behind him, as he hovers in front of colourful blossoms, sipping their nectar. His iridescent emerald green plumage glints with gold or blue as the sun catches it. With his black head and tail, and red bill, this is one of the most striking and handsome of all the hummingbirds.

Yet another endemic species is the 8g Jamaican Mango, boldly marked with greenish-bronze above, glossy purple on the sides of the head and outer tail feathers, and black below. In contrast, the tiny 3g Vervain Hummingbird, one of the world's smallest, is bronze-green above and white below, with a forked tail. All three species were common and a delight to observe. They were attracted to the Chinese hat plant, whose small orange flowers with scarlet trumpets were dripping nectar.

The gentle twittering of little Antillean Palm Swifts, less than 5in (12.5cm) long, soon became a familiar sound. In rapid, twisting, bat-like flight, their white rump and underparts were prominent. I watched the swifts at their nests at the bases of feathery palm fronds.

By late morning it was too hot to do anything but sit in the shade and watch the birds. These included the endemic Orangequit, a beautiful little nectar-feeder, named not for its colour but for its fondness for oranges. The male is blue with a chestnut throat patch; the female is brown. It feeds on an orange by making a hole in the side and sucking out the contents until only an empty shell remains.

Bob suddenly looked up into a large tree and saw a Yellow-billed Amazon Parrot, sitting quietly. This was a thrilling moment – the first parrot I had ever seen in the wild! However, this thought was almost immediately dispelled by the realisation that it was probably an escapee! Every year many chicks were stolen from their nests on the forested slopes of Mount Diablo to be sold at roadsides along with tangerines and orchids. When they matured and the novelty of being a parrot owner wore off, my guess is that the buyers released them. The single parrot we saw was later joined by another. They sat together, preening each other's colourful and mainly green plumage – white forehead, blue crown and rose-pink throat. Then they took off and were joined by three more which flew in at great speed from the Blue Mountains, calling in flight. Later, I was assured that there were no wild parrots in this area and that they were confined to the high, dense forest. This was probably true; however, I have since lost count of the times people in different countries have told me "There are no parrots here", while I have had them in view or within earshot!

The Yellow-billed Amazon had become a "protected" species. Only a few years previously it was on the "noxious bird" list and many were shot when they raided crops. Its raised status was difficult to enforce and trapping continued. In 1986 it was placed on Appendix I (the most threatened category) of CITES. Only two years later its numbers plummeted when Hurricane Gilbert hit Jamaica. There are almost 30 species of Amazon parrot, 15 of which are listed on Appendix I. This is mainly the result of their popularity as pets, resulting in immense numbers being illegally removed from nests, combined with habitat destruction. No other parrot genus has so many endangered species.

The Yellow-billed had already declined due to habitat loss as a result of deforestation and bauxite mining. A couple of days later we were shocked at the pollution caused by the latter. In the mountains we came across what appeared to be a red lake, unnaturally still. This was the waste from bauxite, the raw material from which aluminium is made. The acid was so strong, we were told it would dissolve any man who fell in… Bauxite mining occurs over large areas and the resulting loss of habitat is one of the biggest threats to parrots in Cockpit Country where the valleys between the limestone hills are filled with bauxite. Mining started in the 1940s, leaving pits 100ft (30m deep) in the landscape, central access roads and minor roads leading to various mines. Since the 1970s some effort has been made to reclaim the land that has been mined but it can grow only non-native invasive grasses.

That evening at dinner we were entertained by a steel band whose colourful members produced a heavenly sound. At 9pm the waiters got out a movie projector to screen a film on the wall of the hotel across the swimming pool. It took them half an hour to set it up. The film broke three times before the opening credits – and we retired to bed!

Next day we aimed to go into the mountains. We failed in our attempts to hire a car and, too late, we discovered the only train had left at 7am. So we took a taxi up the fabulous Blue Mountains, marvelling at their beauty. This was the first tropical rainforest I had ever seen. At St Mary, at 4,000ft (1,200m), we explored the ten acres (since expanded) of Castleton Gardens. One of the oldest botanical gardens in the Caribbean, they are known for the exceptional collection of cycads and palms.

The calls of parakeets alerted us to the presence of the endemic Jamaican parakeet or conure, a small emerald green species,

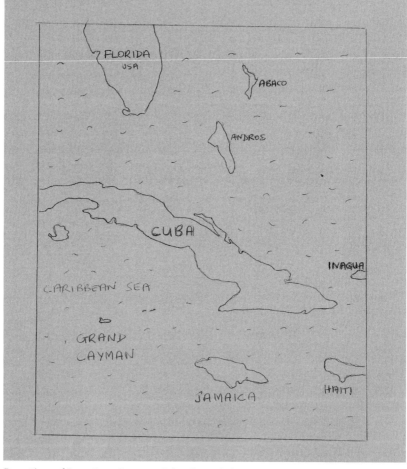

Location of Jamaica, Cayman Islands and the Bahamas (in relation to Cuba)

brown below. Its shade of green is more vivid than any other member of the genus. The conures were eating jackfruit, a huge dark green fruit the size of a pineapple, with an uneven surface. As we watched the parakeets feeding in this large tree, introduced from Asia, an elderly, friendly Jamaican man appeared and told us that they also consume star apples and cocoa beans. He pointed out the abode of a trapdoor spider – a small tunnel with a hinged lid! Full of botanical information, he showed us latex running from a rubber tree and gave us a piece of cinnamon bark. Then he slapped a leaf on his black hand to demonstrate that it left a perfect imprint in white.

At that elevation it was refreshingly cool, with a pleasant breeze. We relaxed near a stream with huge boulders and a tree full of pretty little Blue Mountain Vireos, a Jamaican endemic, olive green above with white iris and wing bars. Sharp and frequent bursts of song had alerted us to their presence.

We reluctantly left at 3pm. On arrival in Kingston we learned an important lesson: if the cab has no meter, agree the fare first. The driver demanded $60 in a menacing manner, more than three times the going rate. You don't argue with a big black man on an island where gun crime is rife! This expenditure made an unwelcome impact on our meagre allocation of dollars – and the hotel was expensive. Next morning we went to Barclay's Bank to request our bank to cable us some money. They could – but it would have arrived after we left Jamaica, so we did the whole day on $8.

Next morning a minibus took us and two other tourists to the Blue Mountains. It was raining. Cattle Egrets and "John Crows" were the only birds glimpsed from the bus. For the first time in my life I saw banana plantations (never dreaming one day I would live virtually in the middle of one) and the collection points to which the local people took bananas to be shipped to the UK. The driver proudly remarked on the primary schools whose children looked so smart in their bright uniforms. I later found this was typical throughout the Caribbean and could not help comparing these neatly dressed boys and girls whose families had only the necessities of life to the often carelessly dressed school children back home.

Our destination was a major tourist spot, Dunn's River Falls, where we paddled in a cove. The small size of the falls and their "improvement" with concrete made them rather disappointing. A Green-backed Heron and Little Blue Herons were waiting patiently or fishing in the river. The elegant blue heron is slate-coloured with a rich brown head and neck. An endemic species, a Jamaican Woodpecker was making his way up the trunk of a bare riverside tree, his orange-red feathers from forehead to nape, and whitish head, presenting a handsome image.

Jamaica is now a good destination for twitchers who can easily find fifteen of the island's 26 endemic birds in a half-day trip into the mountains. Such gems as the exquisite and tubby little Tody, with its green plumage, red throat and tiny dagger bill, would be easily encountered. Back then there were no bird guides and tourism had hardly taken off. Even making a local telephone call was a frustrating procedure! Many islanders were extremely hostile to foreigners and answered almost every query with a casual "Don't know". At the time of our visit a meeting of European heads of state was taking place. Queen Elizabeth was expected. A radio broadcast appealed to people to be nice to these strangers so that they went away with a good impression of their island. Its beauty has lived on in my mind but the attitude of the people, which perhaps has changed now, prevented me from making a return visit.

GRAND CAYMAN

The Cayman Islands lie at the extreme north-western end of the Caribbean island chain, 174 miles (278km) from Jamaica and 149 miles (238km) from Cuba.

Grand Cayman Parrot

The largest island, Grand Cayman, measures 23 miles (37km) long and averages five miles (8km) wide. The three islands are the tops of a submarine mountain range. England acquired them by treaty in 1670. The population originated from ship-wrecked sailors, freed slaves and immigrants.

From Kingston a 50-minute Cayman Airlines flight took us to Grand Cayman where we checked into the Holiday Inn. We were in George Town, the capital. It was evening. The sun was setting over the palm-fringed beach a few paces away. This was the world-famous Seven Mile Beach with sand like the finest sugar and few humans in sight. This flat little island was hot, very hot.

The people were so friendly and helpful. The ethnic mix had somehow produced a delightful race but their version of English, a distinctive patois, was sometimes difficult to understand. When we parked to watch birds, we were approached by concerned islanders who asked if we were in trouble. The concept of birdwatching was difficult for them to apprehend. After all, parrots were food, weren't they? Or killed for "sport". (Not until 1990 was the Cayman Parrot removed from the list of "game" species to be shot.)

One day we gave a lift to two Americans, one of whom was black. When we mentioned we had visited Jamaica he enquired how we liked it. I said: "It's very beautiful but..." He finished the sentence for me: "But the people are uptight. They are uptight to me and I could pass as Jamaican." Grand Cayman was like another world.

We were here to look for the Grand Cayman Parrot. Confined to this island, it is a sub-species of the Cuban Amazon. Other races are found on Cayman Brac, the smallest island of the Caymans group, Abaco and Inagua in the Bahamas, and of course on Cuba. All are readily distinguished from other members of the genus by their beautiful pink and white faces.

The morning after arrival we rented an Austin 1300 and set off to explore the island. It is dominated by the Central Mangrove Wetland (the name had yet to be coined) which extends over one third of the land. Taking North Side Road that bisected the swamp, we stopped by a clearing to walk over the rough ground. A pair of parrots flew low. One was very low – no more than 10ft (3m) above our heads, and peering down at us with interest. I experienced a rush of excitement that was to be repeated many times in the coming years, whenever wild parrots acknowledged my existence without fear.

The din being made by another pair was so great that it led us to a tree, after a ten-minute scramble through a dried-up swamp, in which a small group of parrots was perched. But their camouflage was so effective I saw only one before they took off. Cayman Parrots are easily recognised in flight by the rather blunt head, and as in all Amazons, by the rapid wing beat that is always below the horizontal. They differ from the Cuban Amazon in the slightly different arrangement of pink and white on the head. This is a striking parrot with snow-white forehead and cere, whitish beak and pink cheeks and throat. An estimated 300 Grand Cayman Parrots inhabited the island then but this figure was probably an underestimate.

We had many parrot sightings that day, then the totally unexpected occurred on exploring a dead-end road near Old Man Village. We sat for a while under a tree in a cool breeze from the sea. Casuarinas, almond trees and sea-grape lined the shore. It was so quiet and deserted we could have been the only human inhabitants of the island. As we made our way back we saw a lump of wood at the side of the road in the shape of a huge lizard and both jokingly cried "Iguana!" at the same moment. To our astonishment the iguana became alive! It had been basking in the fierce mid-morning sun. A 4ft (1.2m) beauty, it soon moved off into the scrub. We were amazed at its size, its huge dewlap and at its wonderful markings, blue on brown.

Cayman iguana

10

Having recovered from the surprise of a real live dragon, Bob reversed the car back to where we had been sitting in the hope that another might materialise. A black snake appeared, but moved off rapidly, then a smaller iguana, about 3ft (1m) long, moved onto the road some way ahead. On the way back we called in at the home of Mr Lyndburg, a friendly Bodden Town resident, to ask him how common the iguanas were. "Rare", he said. When we told him we had seen two he was astonished. "I have lived on this island for 30 years and I have never seen one!" he exclaimed. "Expeditions sent here have failed to find them." Lyndburg was not exaggerating. The Cayman blue iguana was even rarer than he had suggested and came perilously close to extinction. A few years later only five individuals were known in the wild.

We knew that throughout the Caribbean iguanas were killed for food and that the meat was said to taste like pork. More recently their enemies have been feral cats and dogs and loss of habitat. The Cayman iguana became the world's rarest lizard and is now a Critically Endangered species.

Grand Cayman, July 1988

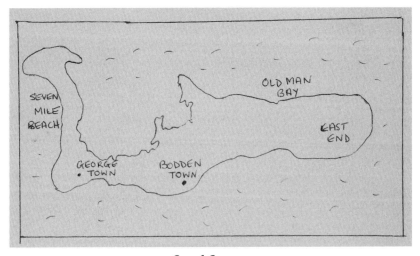

Grand Cayman

Poisonwood, with its toxic sap that causes severe skin irritation, buzzing mosquitoes and dense limestone thicket, stood between the path and the royal palms where we knew we would find parrots. We could hear their tinny but attractive calls ringing out. It was 5pm and the sky was becoming cloudy. Earlier in the afternoon there had been a sudden heavy storm and loud claps of thunder. I had returned to Grand Cayman 13 years later to see how the parrots were faring. In the intervening years there had been various reports. Most Caribbean island Amazons had declined, some of them seriously. Now as we picked our way across the swampy area, paying attention to avoid the poisonwood (an evergreen shrub or tree), the parrots' calls sounded closer and closer – a flock was present. Suddenly, a dozen birds exploded out of a royal palm and flew off noisily! There could have been 20 or 30 in all.

The Grand Cayman Amazon had increased not only its numbers, but also its range over the island. Why? I asked Ramon Noegel, the world authority on this parrot who was with me that day. Ramon and his partner Greg, both from Florida, had spent weeks on various occasions in the Cayman Islands studying the parrots. We considered the changes that had occurred since 1975. The most evident was the increased prosperity of the islanders, due to expansion of the tourist industry as indicated by the building developments along Seven Mile Beach – hotels, shops and condominiums. Islanders were no longer so dependent on farming and areas that were formerly cleared of poisonwood for cattle grazing, had reverted to scrub. There was still much suitable parrot habitat. I had not realised how much on my previous visit when fewer roads traversed the island.

One could go outdoors after dark, now that the mosquitoes were under control, adding to the island's popularity. This could, Ramon pointed out, have increased the parrots' breeding success rate, because mosquitoes can attack parrot chicks in the nest when the rains come, with fatal results. On the other hand, increasing development along the shore and mangroves, was eating into parrot habitat. Everyone wanted a home by the sea and some marshes had been reclaimed for building. At that time, mangrove forest covered one third of the island. Black mangroves are important breeding sites for the parrots who are opportunistic nesters and will utilise any suitable hole in a tree. Dead royal palms would be ideal.

The Frank Sound area provided the best parrot watching that day. Much depended on which trees were bearing fruit. In January, for example, the parrots feed in the sea grape trees along the coast. In July mangos are fruiting. We watched parrots at this, their favourite food source, climbing around the tree, tasting fruit after fruit and eagerly consuming the ripening flesh of the countless large orange mangos. Many trees were loaded and whole or partially eaten fruits littered the ground beneath them. We saw untouched fruiting guava bushes in parrot habitat which indicated that this fruit was not consumed so eagerly. We also watched the parrots feeding on a slim pod, containing flat, circular seeds, eaten in the green stage. The taste could perhaps be described as between a pea and a green bean.

On one occasion we located the parrots after hearing a young one making the bleating food-soliciting call typical of Amazon parrots. Pushing our way through the dense brush (and cutting my leg on some hidden wire) did not cause the parents to take flight until we were immediately beneath them. The two young knew no fear as yet, and swung upside down above us, exhibiting the exuberance so typical of youngsters. I hoped that they lived to breed and that the pink faces of these lovely parrots will forever be familiar to Caymanians.

Abaco, Bahamas, October 1980

The fearlessness of the young Cayman Parrots was in stark contrast to the fear of humans I saw in the sub-species of the Cuban Amazon from the Bahamas. Arguably the most beautiful race, it has a more extensive area of white behind the eye, greater intensity of red on face and upper breast and more conspicuous black margins to the green feathers. Once so numerous that passing flocks were said to darken the skies, by the 1980s it was confined to only two islands. Today parrots occur only on Abaco, almost the northernmost island and only 150 miles (240km) due east of Fort Lauderdale in Florida, and Great Inagua, the third largest and most southern of the Bahaman islands.

The Bahamas form a 750-mile (1,200km) arc through the Atlantic Ocean, creating a natural barrier across the eastern gateway to the Gulf of Mexico. It was a short flight from Miami, above sparkling turquoise seas, to the airport at Marsh Harbour on Abaco. As the plane came in to land I saw the curving chain of cays (tiny islands) that line its eastern shore and the flat island, covered in low vegetation and the white dots of small settlements.

From Marsh Harbour it was a 30-minute drive to Crossing Rocks. The Bahama Parrot lives in the southern part of the island, in the pine forest, with its open understorey and canopy, also in the taller, denser coppice habitat. In October 1980 I visited the forest with my husband, Ramon Noegel and Greg Moss. The pigeon-shooting season had started recently and as we made our way through the pines in the Crossing Rocks area I was appalled by the number of spent cartridges littering the ground. Even far from the road the earth was covered in them. It was not surprising, therefore, that distant glimpses of the parrots were, disappointingly, all that we gained.

The White-crowned Pigeon is the target of shooters but some are not fussy. The pigeon has a white crown and forehead, like the parrot, and is approximately the same size and shape – so that was a good enough excuse for a "sportsman". However, there was a much bigger threat to the parrot's future, whose significance had yet to be realised by myself. On this island unwanted kittens are simply thrown into the bush. As we walked through the silent pines, hearing only the calls of warblers and the coo of pigeons, we came across a scrawny feral kitten. Greg seized it, took it away and dispatched it. Cruel? No. Because there are no large trees on Abaco, the Amazons nest in subterranean limestone cavities – one of the world's very few ground nesting parrots. Within a few years it was realised that cats were entering the nest sites and eating the chicks. Without a cat eradication programme, the parrot could have become extinct as a breeding bird within a few short years.

There had been a notable decrease in the parrot's numbers in the 1960s due to widespread destruction of the Caribbean pine trees on whose green cones it feeds during the breeding season. Road construction, the passage of Hurricane Betsy and the illegal activities of shooters were other factors in its decline. Today the parrot's non-breeding habitat in the Crossing Rocks area is the site of new coastal complexes of apartments. The value of the land and its beautiful beaches is high. It seems that this parrot has to face one threat after another – almost all of them human induced. What will be its fate a century from now? Will it survive?

Updates

Hurricane Ivan in 2004 had a devastating effect on Grand Cayman, damaging much of the mangroves as well as 90% of the buildings. A census in 2006 indicated that the population of **Grand Cayman** Parrots was in the region of 3,400 individuals. Trapping still occurred and, of course, habitat destruction was ongoing. Despite being protected by law and even after becoming the national bird, parrots were still being shot by mango growers. It was suggested that the Cayman Brac population numbered between 400 and 500 individuals – a figure that some believed to be much too high. It has frequently been the case that estimates of parrot populations have been over-optimistic. The National Conservation Law, written in 2000, has yet to be passed. The law established a Conservation Fund but the accrued income has been used to balance the Government budget...

There is good news regarding the Cayman iguana. Captive breeding commenced in 1990. Since 2004 more than 200 captive-bred young have been reintroduced to Grand Cayman in a partnership that includes the National Trust for the Cayman Islands and the Durrell Wildlife Conservation Trust. Let us hope that the habitat of this handsome creature can be protected forever. For this blue dragon to disappear would be a tragedy. However, in March 2009 the Cayman Islands Government announced that 200 acres of government-owned prime dry shrubland habitat would be protected as a reserve for the blue iguana. The location would be in the eastern interior.

In the early 1990s attempts were made to control cat numbers on **Abaco** but even as late as 2004, after a decade of work, all the young in 22 nests out of 72 were killed. Sadly, sometimes the cats got the female as well. In 2005 a new pilot project to control cat numbers resulted in a decrease in predation of approximately 30%. This was funded by Parrots International and cost US$24,000. The high cost of predator control and irresponsible attitudes of local cat owners means that the battle against feline killers will continue for many years. In 2006 the total population of the Bahamas Parrot was estimated to be 2,700.

Bird statistics (year 2000)

Jamaica
Critically Endangered 2
Endangered 1
Vulnerable 8
Near-threatened 4

Cayman Islands
Vulnerable 1
Near-threatened 2

Bahamas
Vulnerable 4
Near-threatened 1 (the parrot)

Species mentioned in this chapter:

Mockingbird (*Mimus polyglottos*)
Bananaquit (*Coereba flaveola*)
Turkey Vulture ("John Crow") (*Cathartes aura*)
Yellow-billed Amazon (*Amazona collaria*) VULNERABLE
Greater Antillean Grackle (*Quiscalus niger*)
Jacana (*Jacana spinosa*)
Red-billed Streamer-tailed Hummingbird (*Trochilus polytmus*)
Vervain Hummingird (*Mellisuga minima*)
Jamaican Mango Hummingbird (*Anthracocorax mango*)
Antillean Palm Swift (*Tachornis phoenicobia*)
Orangequit (*Euneornis campestris*)
Olive-throated or Jamaican Conure (*Aratinga nana*)
Jamaican White-eyed Vireo (*Vireo modestus*)
Cattle Egret (*Bubulcus ibis*)
Grand Cayman Parrot (*Amazona leucocephala caymanensis*) NEAR THREATENED
Green-backed Heron (*Butorides striatus*)
Little Blue Heron (*Egretta caerula*)

Jamaican Tody (*Todus todus*)
Jamaican Woodpecker (*Melanerpes radiolatus*)
Bahamas Parrot (*Amazona leucocephala bahamensis*) NEAR THREATENED
White-crowned Pigeon (*Columba leucocephala*)

Cayman blue iguana (*Cyclura lewisi*)

Poisonwood (*Metropium toxiferum*)
Caribbean pine (*Pinus caribbaea*)
Orchid flower tree (*Amherstia nobilis*)
Ackee (*Blighia sapida*)
Chinese hat (*Holmskioldia sanguinea*)
Jackfruit (*Artocarpus heterophyllus*)

(Note: bold type indicates a parrot species not previously seen in the wild by the author.)

2. Colombian Andes 1976:

Tanagers and Tapaculos

Colombia is a country of startling magnificence and beauty. It also has one of the highest numbers of bird species within its shores of any country worldwide – believed, in 2008, to be 1,875. (Compare that with just over 300 species found in the UK!) Some indication of how its ornithological knowledge has advanced is given by the fact that, at the time of my first visit in 1976, only 1,500 species had been recorded there. The country's avian wealth is attributable to the many areas of endemism on its Andean slopes, and to its unique location and topography, and to the numerous migrants from North America. It is the only country in South America that has an Atlantic and a Pacific coast. It is also unique in stretching from the border with Central America to the Amazon River. In the east the habitats vary from lush rainforest and flat grasslands to sandy desert, while the west is mountainous.

Given this variety of habitats, it is not surprising that Colombia has the second or third highest number of parrot species worldwide, a total of 52. This is exceeded by Brazil with about 72 and possibly by Australia with 52 or 53 species. (DNA research is increasingly dividing one species into two).

Thirty-one hours after leaving our home in Barnet, on the outskirts of London, my husband and I arrived in Colombia, via a convoluted route that allowed us to examine the airports at Manchester, Amsterdam and Zurich, then Lisbon, Caracas, Maracaibo and finally, Barranquilla in the north of Colombia, on the Caribbean coast.

In 1976 travel agents chose the cheapest routes or airlines, resulting in journeys that, understandably, would not be tolerated by today's impatient travellers. (Today the chances of being reunited with one's luggage after such a complicated journey would be quite remote!)

COLOMBIA

Situated in north-western South America, with Panama to the north and Ecuador and Peru to the south, Colombia covers an area of 440,000 sq miles (1.139 million *sq km). It is divided geographically into three regions:* *the wet Pacific lowlands south of the border with* *Panama, the mountain ranges that extend over much* *of the western area, and the forested basins of the* *Amazon and Orinoco rivers. Oil and cocaine are its* *biggest industries.*

Male Cock-of-the-Rock

Viewed from a window in Caracas Airport, Carib Grackles were the first birds I saw in South America. Their glossy shiny black plumage, yellow eyes, *wee-ee* calls and busy way of walking about the rooftops with their strange big feet were to become very familiar.

An important fact absorbed by a bird lover visiting the tropics for the first time is the abundance of flycatchers. There is a very good reason for this! The huge populations of insects, especially in humid areas, is usually the second observation. On the first visit one is naïve enough to pack more shorts than trousers, is seldom armed with enough long-sleeved shirts (necessary even in high temperatures) or with an adequate supply of spray-on, roll-on and every other kind of repellent! But working hard to reduce the insect populations are approximately 150 species of flycatchers. They present an interesting challenge to the many bird watchers who are primarily interested in notching up another species for their "life list"! The most common include Tropical Kingbirds, Lesser Kiskadees and Great Kiskadees. The latter species, larger and more colourful than the other flycatchers, might be the only one you can distinguish. In fact, it will tell you its name! But do not curse the identification problems of this never-ending parade of grey or yellowish birds

19

because without them it would be impossible to survive there!

The room in the hotel in Cartagena was spacious with huge windows that looked out onto a Miami-beach type panorama. There was a wide sweep of shoreline of greyish sand with skyscraper hotels towering above it. This was the Caribbean coast and not at all typical of Colombia. At sunset I walked on the beach, looking out to sea at the breaking waves and the pink sky reflected in the wet sand. Magnificent Frigatebirds were sailing high overhead, their huge black wings and fork-tailed silhouettes making them instantly identifiable. The pirates of the bird world, they specialise in frightening seabirds into disgorging their catch – then collecting it.

It seemed that the location had been chosen by the tour company to appeal to the beach-loving tourist. Colombia had but a fledgling tourist industry. Few Europeans visited as the country was viewed as dangerous. This holiday was not one for – the word had yet to be coined – ecotourists – and no birdwatcher would expect this interest to be catered for. How different it is today! I might have asked myself why a small travel company would have organised this holiday. With hindsight I believe that it had a lot to do with the fact that our local guide was a luscious dark-haired Colombian girl named Marta. Here was an opportunity for the company's owner, who I will call Ken, to play away from home. And play he did!

There were 15 of us, only one other with an interest in nature. A hot and tiring tour of Cartagena introduced us to the perceived highlights – the convent with endless explanations by the guide about the saints. The unexpected appearance of a man holding a three-toed sloth, with a coarse brown coat like coconut matting, made me sad. I held the poor bewildered thing, now in an alien world, and scratched its throat. It had a round white face with wide apart eyes set in a dark mask. Incapable of moving fast, sloths spend most of the day apparently comatose, well disguised in the branch of a tree.

Cartagena would have appeared almost devoid of birdlife were it not for the Great-tailed Grackles. They were everywhere – displaying from rooftops, on the beaches and in the gardens. The

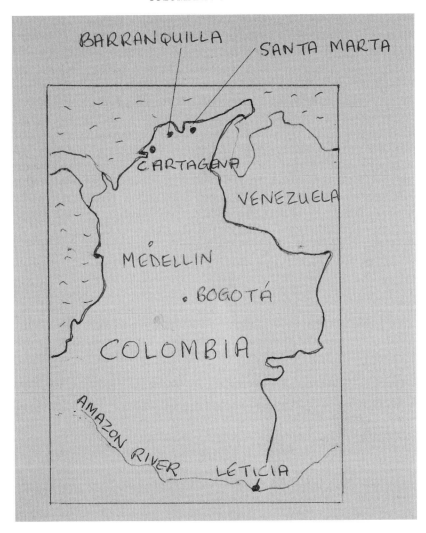

male is a handsome 16in (41cm) bird – black with purple and green reflections and a wedge-shaped tail that accounts for half his length. The much smaller female is brown and buff with a fan-shaped tail.

After lunch three of us took a taxi into the old part of the city and wandered around the market. The stench, activity and colour were memorable. There were hundreds of vendors, each with only one item for sale – perhaps yams or bananas, little fried things eaten with pieces of cheese and big things that looked like (and possibly were) naked, smoked dogs. More interesting than the wares were the sellers and buyers – a thousand colourful characters, their (mostly) brown faces making those of Europeans look lifeless in comparison. In the evening our group ate in a very smart restaurant in an old villa. The ancient city was romantic and beautiful by night. The modern hotels seemed less incongruous in the dusk, their lights shining against the darkness of the bay.

The next morning we departed in a boat called *Alcatraz* for a cruise to an island across the bay. The boat was named for the Brown Pelican, several of which flew alongside – majestic in flight with leisurely wing beats and head retracted. That evening, as dusk fell, I watched them fly in V formation over the beach, about a dozen birds forming each side of the V.

We arranged with the tour leader to visit the isolated mountains of Santa Marta on the following day, in the north-eastern part of Colombia. Four of us departed at 6am with two unlikely looking bird guides, female, and wearing 3in (7.5cm) wedge heels. Unfortunately, their knowledge of birds was non-existent. Worse still, the driver did not want to go to Santa Marta.

Our guides suggested that we should go to Barranquilla for lunch and return to the reserve when it was cooler. We pointed out that our purpose was to try to see some of the endemic birds of the Santa Marta area. Of course, this was terribly naïve. You would need days, not a couple of hours. In that era, however, there was virtually no published information to alert you to this fact.

It took two hours to drive to Barranquilla where we crossed the long, modern bridge over the River Magdalena. Six Amazon Parrots were flying not far from the road and, further on, a flock of Brown-eared (also called Brown-throated) Conures, small green parakeets with blue on the crown. Then the habitat changed to arid saltmarshes, small lagoons and mangroves. We visited *Ciénaga Grande* (big marsh), a bird reserve in Salamanca. From a long raised walkway we had sightings of two flamingos, Marsh Sandpipers, Black-winged Stilts, Anhingas and herons. Wattled Jacanas and Belted Kingfishers were more confiding.

In a leaky canoe the owner paddled us around the dense vegetation of the mangroves. There was a sudden explosion as 30 or more grebes took off from the water. After disembarking from the canoe we came across a small lagoon which was teaming with waders of six or seven species. My feet made a scrunching sound as I walked towards them on the parched, salty ground. At least 200 were feeding in the shallow water, the largest being Black-winged Stilts among the yellowlegs and sandpipers – winter residents.

We returned to the vehicle and one of our companions became decidedly fractious. We had been travelling for hours, he said, and had seen nothing. While I sympathised with this view, we had tried to dissuade the couple from coming with us, fearing they would be bored. Not long after we reached the Santa Marta Mountains – and he ceased to complain! The scenery, with giant cactus abounding, was incredibly beautiful.

We drove on to Tayrona and its national park, went three miles inside and alighted in a woodland area. There were birds everywhere! Within seconds a couple of conures (unidentified) flew over calling. To this day I wonder if they were the rare and endangered Santa Marta Parakeet. Blue and Yellow Macaws and Military Macaws occur here, but we saw neither. There were plenty of small birds, such as Black-faced Grassquit, Buff-throated Woodcreeper, Long-billed Gnatwren and various flycatchers. A marshy area revealed Greater Flamingos, Capped Heron, and Anhingas. Limpkins, widespread in the Americas, were probing the swampy ground for snails. These leggy brown birds, with a long, straight bill, are appealing to watch with their crane-like gait.

It was frustrating that we had driven all this way and had to return after a couple of hours without seeing manakins, of which there are three species, or the Black Antshrike that is found here, or the spectacular rocky coastline.

Next day Bob and I left the group and, departing at 6am, took a taxi to Lake Uruaco, one hour's drive away. The road was lined with groves of guava and banana, sugar beet fields and coconut plantations. Live obstacles such as mules, horses, cows, poultry and pigs were common. The memory of two shocking traffic victims still lingers: two horses rotting in the road, probably hit by a large lorry. About 50 vultures were feeding on their distended bodies. The stench was terrible.

The lake area was alive with grebes, coots, jacanas and a kingfisher. A pair of delightful Pied Water Tyrants were flitting about above the surface of the water or among the reeds, occasionally flying across the road and scolding us with a continual double note. Two Limpkins were wary, flying short distances with neck extended and legs dangling, on observing us. They have a very efficient method of dealing with the snails that are such an important item of their diet. They wedge a snail between the roots of a tree, insert a mandible at both sides of the shell and twist the creature free.

Brown-throated
Conure

An Osprey was fishing and a Grey-headed Kite was perched silently by the lake. We caught a glimpse of six Marbled Wood-Quail walking up a steep bank. Their buff-streaked plumage was effective camouflage against the parched earth. Feeding busily in a mango tree, a flock of green parakeets were enjoying the nearly-ripe fruits. They were Brown-throated Conures. By late morning the heat was intolerable and seeking shade in the restaurant was the only sensible plan.

Next day we flew to Bogotá, Colombia's capital, set at 8,500ft (13,600m) in the magnificent Andes. Three mountain ranges occupy the western part of the country. The Andes are, of course, the world's longest mountain chain, an immense granite backbone stretching approximately 6,000miles (10,000km). They extend from Trinidad's Northern Range all the way to the southern tip of South America at Cape Horn, a volatile region of earthquakes and volcanic activity.

Bogotá is a city of contrasts, its ultra-modern buildings, without any hint of nationality, stand but a stone's throw from stately Spanish-style colonial houses and narrow streets lined with balcony-hung dwellings. The shops were filled with exquisitely made leather goods. I had to leave behind the most beautiful boots I ever saw which were not available in my size. The city's Gold Museum was remarkable. Housed in a superbly modern building, the exhibits were displayed with taste and flair. I will never forget the room of pure gold where visitors are locked inside for five minutes – then released!

Our final destination in the region was in the Central Andes. During the 30-minute flight from the capital, we had impressive views of the great mountain ranges, like a dark quilt rumpled into a hundred folds, the tallest ragged peaks clothed in a mantle of snow. Medellin can boast one of the most beautiful residential areas to be found anywhere. Situated at a lower altitude than Bogotá, in the mining district of Antioquia, the town is spread out on a plateau totally surrounded by a mountainous backdrop. Outside the town centre this tableland is enhanced by attractive villas and gardens massed with flowers. These were the abodes of the wealthy.

A helpful and friendly guide, provided by the tourist office Granturismo, met us at the airport. To my dismay, as I had hoped for a trip into the mountains, Elizabeth had arranged for us to spend the afternoon with a local bird lover, watching the birds in the garden of a country villa. The setting was beautiful.

Blue-grey Tanager, a widespread species

25

A small stream flowed through the well-kept haven and a bird table in a tree on the lawn was piled with cut oranges from the nearby citrus grove, and swarming with Bananaquits, as many as 30 at a time. A pair of Spot-breasted Woodpeckers, with olive, crimson and yellowish underparts, flew busily in and out of their hole high in a dead tree. It was then that I discovered the delightful Spanish name for woodpecker: *carpintero.*

Two Blue-grey Tanagers perched conspicuously on the sun-bleached branches of a dead tree while a silvery-green Scrub Tanager was more reticent. The tanagers are one of the great groups of American birds that are impossible to miss. Colombia alone has more than 120 species. Related to the finches, but slightly larger, they are fruit- and insect-eaters. There is no such thing as a typical tanager: sizes, colour combinations and beak shapes are extraordinarily varied. Many species have wonderful, bright and contrasting colours.

By 5pm the garden was alive with birds. Rufous-tailed Hummingbirds were everywhere, their tails flashing chestnut as they darted about, and their bodies glittering with bronzy-green. A pair of Vermilion Flycatchers with a single offspring arrived as dusk fell and the insects became more numerous. The intense scarlet of the male makes him the most colourful of all the flycatchers. High above us dozens of large handsome White-collared Swifts were swirling about catching mosquitoes in the failing light, as the last rays of the sun slanted across the mountains.

A friendly local bird lover took us to his home where there was a tiny nest inside an orchid. He introduced us to his wife and five children as we drank Kol-Cana (the local equivalent of coke) and enjoyed being in the midst of a Colombian family. We were touched when they gave us a jar of honey from their bees.

Elizabeth arrived at our hotel early next morning to take us to a patch of waste ground. We watched several species of small seedeaters, such as the Southern Siskin and Yellow-faced Grassquit. When feeding on the ground, these little finches are extremely well-camouflaged with their olive-green upperparts. Next stop was the botanical gardens. The lake was massed with pink and white lilies and a large Ringed Kingfisher flew back and forth across the water, returning to a lakeside tree. A tiny wren-like Andean Tapaculo was creeping about nearby, its silver-grey and rufous coloration blending with its surroundings. Secretive little birds, tapaculos move around like mice, through the moss and tangled undergrowth. Non-tropical, they live in mountainous areas and the cooler parts of the continent. In contrast to these inconspicuous little creatures were the ever-present Ruddy Ground Doves, dainty and dressed in shades of brown and grey, with vinaceous feathers below.

The Botanical Gardens boasted an attractive aviary, the star of which was a male Andean Cock-of-the-Rock. We could enter the aviary and, as I focussed my camera on this riveting scarlet and glossy black bird, he suddenly landed on my hand, pecked at the camera and flew off! He had seen his reflection in the lens and, interpreting it as a rival in his territory, had come to confront it. This gorgeous bird flew to my hand several times and sat there quite contentedly. He even accepted a grape! I was captivated by his beauty and tameness.

Medellin is known as the orchid capital of the world. Orchid farms in the surrounding area send their blooms far and wide. It seemed ironic that they were producing them for the wealthy when most of Colombia's people were so poor. The poverty was not, of course, apparent at the destinations and hotels selected for our group. In Girardot we stayed in a hotel for millionaires built by a millionaire. It was the ultimate in luxury. Our room looked on to a man-made lake for water skiing, surrounded by a man-made beach. Tom Jones had performed at the night club. The gardens and surroundings were very beautiful – but manicured down to the last hibiscus bush. It seemed that we had endured the four-hour drive through the mountains, arriving at 10.30pm, and leaving after two days, just so that we could sample one of the country's finest hotels!

The gardens were inhabited by Saffron Finches, hummingbirds, euphonias, tanagers and ground doves. I discovered that *Forpus* parrotlets, such as the Spectacled, like to live around humans. These sparrow-sized parrots, with their brilliant blue wing coverts and rump, were usually perched on a tall post a few feet from the hotel. There must have been forest here a few years earlier. I wondered how many antbirds, cotingas and manakins had been displaced (or trapped) when it had been cleared to build this playground for the wealthy. It seemed that the tourist office wanted visitors to leave with impressions that were mainly far removed from the realities of life in Colombia.

The keen birdwatcher will read this chapter with incredulity or even scorn. Today it is easy, if you can afford it, to join a group with a company that specialises in bird tours and to cover the same ground in Colombia and see 300 species or more. Even in a country relatively little known to bird enthusiasts, there is ample information on where to go and what to see. Then it was so different. In a world with no internet and nothing published on birding in the neotropics, useful information was almost impossible to acquire. Only by coincidence or luck or by heading for the Amazon did the birdlife materialise before your eyes. Today's birders don't know how lucky they are!

2008 update

The forests and mountains of Santa Marta were recognised as an area in critical need of conservation. The 21 endemics include the Santa Marta Parakeet and the Antpitta also bearing the region's name. In the previous year a new owl species, the Santa Marta Screech Owl, was discovered. In January 2008 the importance of the region was recognised with the inauguration of the El Dorado Nature Reserve in the San Lorenzo Forest and a spacious ecolodge. One thousand seven hundred acres of forest had been acquired to help ensure that this area, that boasts the highest concentration of continental (mainland) range-restricted bird species in the world, will be protected forever.

Species not previously mentioned:

Great-tailed Grackle (*Quiscalus mexicanus*)
Carib Grackle (*Quiscalus lugubris*)
Tropical Kingbird (*Tyrannus melancholicus*)
Great Kiskadee (*Pitangus sulphuratus*)
Lesser Kiskadee (*Pitangus lictor*)
Magnificent Frigatebird (*Fregata magnificens*)
Brown Pelican (*Pelecanus occidentalis*)
Brown-eared Conure (*Aratinga pertinax aeruginosa*)

Marsh Sandpiper (*Tringa stagnatilis*)
Black-winged Stilt (*Himantopus himantopus*)
Anhinga (*Anhinga anhinga*)
Wattled Jacana (*Jacana jacana*)
Greater Flamingo (*Phoenicopterus ruber*)
Belted Kingfisher (*Ceryle alcyon*)
Santa Marta Parakeet or Conure (*Pyrrhura viridicata*)
    ENDANGERED
Blue and Yellow Macaw (*Ara ararauna*)
Military Macaw (*Ara militaris*) VULNERABLE
Black-faced Grassquit (*Tiaris bicolor*)
Buff-throated Woodcreeper (*Ziphorhynchus guttatus*)
Long-billed Gnatwren (*Ramphocaenus melanurus*)
Capped Heron (*Pilherodius pileatus*)
Limpkin (*Aramus guarauna*)
Black Antshrike (*Thamnophilus nigriceps*)
Pied Water Tyrant (*Fluvicola pica*)
Osprey (*Pandion haliaetus*)
Grey-headed Kite (*Leptodon cayanensis*)
Marbled Wood-Quail (*Odontophorus gujanensis*)
Blue-grey Tanager (*Thraupis virens*)
Scrub Tanager (*Tangara ruficapilla*)
Spot-breasted Woodpecker (*Chrysoptilus punctigula*)
Rufous-tailed Hummingbird (*Amazilia tzacatl*)
Vermilion Flycatcher (*Pyrocephalus rubinus*)
White-collared Swift (*Streptoprocne zonaris*)
Southern Siskin (*Spinus magellanicus*)
Yellow-faced Grassquit (*Tiaris olivacea*)
Ringed Kingfisher (*Ceryle torquatus*)
Andean Tapaculo (*Scytalopus magellanicus*)
Ruddy Ground Dove (*Columbigallina talpacoti*)
Andean or Scarlet Cock-of-the-Rock (*Rupicola peruviana*)
Saffron Finch (*Sicalis flaveola*)
Spectacled Parrotlet (*Forpus conspicillatus*)
Santa Marta Antpitta (*Grallaria bangsi*) NEAR THREATENED
Santa Marta Screech Owl (*Otus* sp.nova)

3. Colombia 1976:

Island in the Amazon

My first experience of a tropical rainforest was in Colombia. I was transported into a different world and felt as though I wanted to stay there forever. I had an amazing sense of belonging.

We had left the Andean region on a 1½-hour flight. There were awe-inspiring views, horizon to horizon, of forest canopy, and then the mighty Amazon, a wide ribbon of blue or brown snaking through the verdant forests. Just as the Andes is the world's longest mountain chain, the Amazon is the river with the greatest volume, pouring forth one fifth of all the river water on earth. Everything seems to be measured in superlatives here. The Amazon basin is immense, covering an area of two and a half million square miles (6.5 million sq km) in nine countries.

We landed in Leticia facing an invisible wall of hot, humid air as the cabin doors opened. Located in the very south of the republic, it is only two and a half miles (4km) from the town of Benjamin Constant in Brazil and the same distance from the Peruvian border. A finger of land reaches down to give Colombia the tiniest frontage on the north bank of the Amazon. On arrival at the hotel, the *Parador Ticuna*, the new guests were offered an iced whisky and ginger while the process of form-filling was completed.

Stepping outside we encountered various flycatchers, feasting on mosquitoes, and small finches, Black and White Seedeaters, feeding among reeds and grasses. I exclaimed in delight at the sight of a pair of Scarlet-crowned Barbets. Medium-sized and often brightly-coloured, barbets are found throughout the tropics – and this was my very first sighting. The male is striking with the red area stretching over the crown and nape, orange breast and yellow-olive abdomen. The female has the crown and

---

THE AMAZON

Its source is 17,000ft (5,200m) up in the snow-capped Andes of Peru, only 120 miles (192km) from the Pacific Ocean. From here it flows 4,000 miles (6,400km) eastwards to meet the Atlantic Ocean. Its length is second only to the Nile, while its volume is greater than that of any other river. Its mouth is 200 miles (320km) across; 1,000 miles (1,600km) upriver it is 7 miles (11km) wide in places.

Short-tailed Parrot

---

nape frosty white and her colours are more muted. Barbets have prominent bristles above the thick, strong bill with which they excavate nesting sites. The initial observation of a member of a well-known tropical bird family is always an exciting moment for the inexperienced observer. What might soon become commonplace is at this moment awesome.

We walked down to the waterfront. This was the hub of the town where its 20,000 inhabitants (the population has since doubled) bought and sold fish, fruit and vegetables. It was pulsating with life – with an unseen darker side of which we were innocently unaware but which contributed to the town's booming economy. Narcotic drugs were bought and sold with as little ceremony as rice and beans. Several cartel leaders grew rich there and built big houses. To move the drugs more easily they constructed eight miles (12 km) of a new highway to the town of Tarapacá before they were arrested and locked up. Their palatial homes were seized by the government.

In Leticia the river was paramount, with floating houses, and a floating petrol station. At the pier we embarked on the picturesque *Amazon Queen,* a small covered cruise boat, for an evening trip. For 50 minutes before the sun went down we chugged along, wide-eyed at the wonders of the huge river. Dusk fell and myriad bats were flying their rapid, zigzag flight, just above the water. As the sun streaked the clouds with gold and orange, and painted fiery reflections in the water, four macaws flew high, high overhead. My happiness was complete. What a setting for my very first macaws! We returned in complete darkness, the boat chugging through reeds so dense we almost lost faith in our crew. The last patch of colour in the sky had faded behind us.

Behind the hotel stood a large tree – the roosting site of Yellow-rumped Caciques. Every evening these glossy-black birds came streaming in, 50 or more together. I counted 800 birds! They were handsome with wing patch and under tail coverts of bright yellow, blue eyes and a whitish pointed bill. The noise and activity as they settled down for the night was remarkable! After the caciques came hundreds of White-winged Parakeets, stopping briefly in a large fig tree on their way to the town square.

Next morning we dressed by torchlight at 5am; our accommodation could not boast the sophistication of electricity at that dark hour! We walked purposefully through the streets to the town square. As we approached, two squawking clouds of parakeets flew in starling-like flocks towards the trees on the riverbank. We were just in time to see them depart their roost. The din they created was indescribable! Little 9in (22cm) green birds with longish pointed tails, the white wing patches flashed as they flew in tight, co-ordinated flocks.

Until Colombia ceased its legal bird export trade in 1973, thousands of these unfortunate little parakeets were trapped every year, especially in this area. Trappers would locate the roosting site in the dense cane thickets that line the banks of the Amazon, then cut lanes through the thickets. Here they would erect their mist nets. When the survivors of these trapping activities arrived in Europe and the USA there was little demand, they were sold for about £3 each and soon became unwanted when their harsh voices made them unpopular. It was, like so much of the trade in wild-caught parrots, based not on demand but on making money. Colombia had been one of the world's major exporters of live birds and animals, also crocodile skins. It was one of the first countries in South America to take an enlightened view and to end the legal trade. (The illegal trade flourishes almost everywhere.)

Late that afternoon three of us left the other members of the group. Dusk fell soon after the canoe pushed off. In the darkness, the three-hour ride to Santa Sofia (also known as Monkey Island), seemed endless. It became colder and colder and rain began to fall. We huddled together, listening to the nocturnal sounds, the unseen insects and the tree frogs. The night shift was very vocal. "What is that noise?" we asked, like all new visitors to a tropical forest. The main vocalists are the cicadas, winged insects not unlike grasshoppers. How could anything so small make so much noise, we wondered? But there must have been millions of them out there, drowning out the chorus of frogs and the cries of hunting owls.

The boatman's headlamp permeated the darkness for floating logs and other dangers. At last we arrived at the wooden lodge, a palm-thatched building on stilts, on the riverbank, to be served dinner by the light of paraffin lamps. In this idyllic spot, 240 miles (384km) south of the Equator, dusk fell and dawn broke at 5.30am.

This, my first ever experience of the rainforest, was paradise! To be in an environment not dominated by man is, in itself, a potentially life-changing experience for anyone from the concrete jungle of the so-called civilised world. After a couple of days England was forgotten, as remote as the moon.

The lodge on Monkey Island

Until man's impact, little had changed in the rainforest in 100 million years. Such a period of time is incomprehensible. In comparison, the temperate forests of Europe and North America are only 11,000 years old. Tropical forests occupy approximately only 6% of the earth's surface but they are believed to harbour about 50% of its biodiversity, that is, the plant and animal life. The neotropics contain approximately 57% of all remaining rainforest.

Tropical forests differ fundamentally from temperate ones in harbouring a huge number of species of birds and trees but with relatively few individuals of each. The nearer you go to the Equator, the greater the diversity. Except for the teeming insect life, including brightly coloured stink bugs and huge black rhinoceros beetles (so called for the impressive curved horns), you have to look carefully to find living creatures. Most of the birds and animals live high, high above but there is plenty to see from ground level. The newcomer to the Amazon rainforest needs to be quite still every now and then and examine the small details among the forest giants: the finely etched variegated leaves of a *Peperomia* vine (more familiar as a house plant) climbing up a trunk and the brown moth camouflaged against its bark. The huge buttressed roots can trip you up if your eyes are pointed skywards following the line of the trunk which might lack branches until it reaches the canopy. Tangles of lianas, like green velvet-covered ropes, make patterns between the trees and create highways for smaller creatures. We soon ceased to comment on the orchids growing on trees, no rarer than marsh marigolds beside an English river.

These forests tend to be quiet for long periods. Then suddenly the silence is broken by a troop of monkeys rampaging through the trees and stillness becomes frenzied activity when a dozen or more species of birds arrive calling and chattering to follow an ant swarm. The ants disturb small creatures that run for cover in the wake of the tiny predators. This is the moment that birders are waiting for. They become as frenetic as the feeding birds in trying to spot and identify antbirds, ant-thrushes and other species over the space of a couple of minutes. Then the forest reverts to a state of tranquillity.

Santa Sofia Island had been bought by animal dealer Mike

Tsilickis in 1967. There were reputed to be 25,000 squirrel monkeys there. Originally 6,000 were released, the aim being that the offspring would supply the dreadful trade in primates used for research. However, they had not been trapped for three years due to export restrictions on all native species.

There are no seasons relating to temperature on Monkey Island: only wet and dry. This was the time during which nearly all land was under water. The flood can extend for 25 miles or more on each side of the riverbed so bird watching took place from a motorised canoe. There was plenty to see. David, a young American who had been working at the lodge for 18 months, had identified 164 species.

With our boatmen Baptisto and Haroldo, we would cross the great expanse of the Amazon and enter a tributary, cutting the engine and drifting. In places the river looked like a meadow, tightly covered by a dense growth of tiny aquatic plants. Our boatmen struggled with one oar to get us through. Sometimes branches hung so low we had to flatten ourselves in the bottom of the canoe and might be showered with termites from the overhanging vegetation. But we were too excited by this wonderful new world to be discouraged by a few bites!

A common species seen among the reeds in small groups was the Yellow-headed Blackbird or Marshbird. The striking male is

The extraordinary Hoatzin

glossy black with head and upper breast bright golden yellow, while the female is brown and dull yellow. Another inhabitant of the reeds was the Black-capped Mockingthrush whose loud, monotonous song was often heard.

More spectacular inhabitants of the tributaries were the birds known locally as *kamungo*. My first glimpse, of a pair flying across the river in front of the canoe, gave the momentary impression of a huge eagle. Their plumage was mainly black with a green sheen, except for the white abdomen. Then the realisation dawned that they were Horned Screamers, apparently related to geese. The "horn" is a forward-curving spike on the forehead, which may reach 6in (15cm) in length. The powerful legs of these birds are bare of feathers so that they can wade through flooded forest. Their long toes support them when they walk on floating vegetation. They alone of living birds share with the primitive *Archaeopteryx* the distinction of lacking the small bony straps that strengthen the rib cage. The boatmen seemed bemused at our interest in what was, to them, a good meal. They told us that the water hyacinth is one of the screamer's principal foods. These birds often flew high, spiralling gradually upwards. Their honking and braying calls, said to carry for two miles, were among the most characteristic sounds of the area.

We had not been going for long when Baptisto whispered *"Cigano!"* – and pointed. All we could see was a dark shape perched among the branches. He eased the canoe forward and we had a perfect view. As we came closer, the bird displayed in threat, with rounded chestnut wings opening and closing and tail spread to reveal the white patches on the end of the tail. Then to the left we saw a pair. They were Hoatzins. My first sighting of one of the world's strangest and most primitive birds produced a great feeling of elation. The red eyes set in the tiny head are surrounded by bare blue skin and the tall spiky buff-brown feathers of the crest give them a slightly rakish look.

They flap clumsily around in vegetation, flying little, and usually only to the nearest tree. They are said to feed entirely on leaves but in Haroldo's view the diet consisted only of new shoots. Their digestion is so poor that these stay in the stomach for two days. Bacteria in the greatly enlarged oesophagus and crop aid digestion. This process is similar to stomach fermentation in cows.

The Hoatzin's best known peculiarity is the unique behaviour off its chicks. On hatching and until the age of three weeks they have two well developed, functional claws at the tip of each wing – like the *Archaeopteryx*. This intriguing fact has led to the speculation that the Hoatzin might be a link in the evolution of birds from reptiles. It all sounds like a tall story but the chicks can swim and if they fall into the water below the nest, either accidentally or perhaps evading a predator; the claws enable them to clamber along branches back to their platform of sticks!

Watching Hoatzins gave me a strange sensation that I never felt before or since, as though the clock had been turned back tens of thousands of years when these ancient birds perhaps lived among dinosaurs.

Palm trees with a multitude of long, vicious spines grow along the waterlogged riverbanks, interspersed with a thick tangle of riverine undergrowth. As we rounded a bend I saw a cluster of conures feeding in a smooth-trunked palm close to the water's edge. I called to Haroldo to stop. He edged the canoe right under the palm and I could recognise Black-tailed Conures, so engrossed that they seemed oblivious to our presence. Also called Maroon-tailed Parakeets, they are green with breast feathers scalloped in greyish-white and rosy-red wing coverts. White-winged Parakeets were feeding with them on the fruits of a *Euterpe* palm. There were about 35 parakeets in all, some sitting in small groups mutual-preening, others clinging to the trunk of the palm where they had gnawed away two large areas of bark, too low down to be protected by the overhanging fronds. We watched them for several minutes until a small parrot flew over at great speed and, with much shrieking, the whole flock took to the air in alarm.

Flocks of parakeets – usually *Aratinga* species such as the Dusky-headed and the White-eyed – were everywhere. The most common small parrot was the Short-tailed which resembles a miniature Amazon. We soon learned to recognise their double call note. Blue-headed Pionus and Mealy Amazons were often seen, also the most common Amazon, found only in riverine habitat, the Festive. Late one afternoon, as dusk was falling, a flock of about 25 flew across the river towards the island, heading for their roost. I was intrigued to see one detach itself from the flock and return to the mainland. Perhaps it had just remembered its mate!

It was rewarding to explore the tiny creeks. Occasionally we would encounter a native family, crammed into a tiny canoe with a dog. They were paddling so close to the water-line, you wondered how they kept afloat.

Sometimes we had to duck or lie low as we negotiated the hazardous branches hanging over the river. Baptisto and Haroldo laughed with us. They invariably saw birds before we did, so attuned were they to this watery environment. Boating in a flooded forest is an experience to be recalled again and again – a unique adventure in a fascinating landscape where fish swim among trees. The scenery has an indescribable beauty, especially when lit by the sun. The tall, gnarled, white-barked trees made an incongruous contrast to the lushness elsewhere. They were not dead. When the waters receded they would come back to life as the oxygen once again penetrated their roots.

On the first afternoon we identified 30 bird species; this would

Blue-headed Pionus

be a derisory total for real birders! As dusk fell and the bats came out from their roost, a nightjar with white-banded wings darted past.

Early morning was the best time for birds. Canoeing slowly through the creeks and searching the trees, we were rewarded with a handsome Crimson-crested Woodpecker, colourful araçaris (small toucans) and a Slaty-tailed Trogon sitting quietly, waiting to pounce on a moth. Trogons, typical and widespread birds of the tropics, are colourful and elegant, with metallic shining blue-green upperparts and, in this species, carmine underparts, set off by a long, broad tail. Suddenly encountering a Black-necked Red Cotinga was enthralling. A study in crimson and black, he had a short silky crimson crest, crimson body and tail, and velvety black mantle and neck. A flock of fifteen Blue and Yellow Macaws were leaving their roosting site and the calls of raucous Festive Amazons rang out through the forest.

At the lodge there was a resident Festive, completely reliable in temperament, who could be handled by anyone. This parrot species is an exceptional mimic. "Aurora" could spell out his name, laugh and repeat many words in Spanish. He was full-winged and spent most of his time in the trees outside the lodge or visiting the kitchen for tit-bits. It was a sobering thought that Aurora would almost certainly have ended up in the pot had someone not befriended him. The local people have no sentiment about the fauna they encounter. At the lodge we saw a snake (not a common event, as these reptiles avoid man) and were pleased to photograph it. Unfortunately, our activity brought it to the attention of two small boys who speared it and drowned it as soon as we walked away.

One day the lunch fare was not so good; apparently the cook was short of food. When the usual afternoon rains ceased at 3.30pm we canoed over to some floating homes with David to enquire after fish or eggs. There were none. Eventually David procured a chicken. It was tied by the legs and put in the canoe. I got out of the way while the cook killed and prepared the unfortunate chicken. It was very tough – but David ate his. The unspecified meat with which we were served on another occasion was, almost certainly, monkey. Most humans consider that a meal is incomplete without animal protein. While I can survive anywhere on beans and rice that view would not be popular with most diners.

One morning when the rain was pouring down, I was up at first light hoping it would cease. No one else had stirred. I sat in the dry, at the lodge door, and filmed the creatures that appeared before me: a gallinule, a kite, a snake and the friendly Black-fronted Nunbirds, dark with the bill red. My favourite was an antpitta, species unidentified, who rushed around, flinging aside leaves, in his search for insects. Antpittas are long-legged, short-tailed birds, the equivalent of the colourful Asiatic pittas but garbed more soberly in shades of brown.

The rain finally ceased and we ventured out in the canoe to visit an Indian village. It was called Arara after the large number of macaws in the area. Here lived Ticuna Indians, organised and artistic people who, even after 400 years of contact with white men, have preserved their identity through their language, religion and cultural art forms. They do, however, wear Western-style clothes. These river people rarely go far inland. They are skilled boat builders. In this village they grew most of their own food, plus rice as a cash crop. With the money they bought an engine for their communal boat and ran their own

The flooded forest

40

ferry service. To take a man to Leticia the charge was 10 pesos (61 pesos to the pound, at that time) for a man, two pesos for a woman and one peso for a child.

The village was situated in a clearing and the areas around the dwellings were clean and tidy. In one building their artwork was displayed for sale. It was apparent that they were talented basket makers, sculptors and mask makers. Using bark cloth they produced beautiful paintings and masks and dolls, all in their distinctive style. The soft whitish cloth has the appearance of paper and, for under £2, I bought a painting of birds and snakes made from this cloth and decorated using vegetable dyes. Animals were favourite themes; tanagers and owls were recognisable in the paintings and jaguars and alligators were the subjects of exquisitely produced funeral masks. These masks are worn during the funeral dance and represent the creatures that the deceased will hunt in the next life.

I learned that these hard-working people refused to be registered as Colombian citizens until they were provided with electricity and a school, which the children attend from the age of seven. Many aspects of their lives were quite sophisticated yet, I was told, girls have their hair pulled out at puberty and must wear a headscarf until it grows. Then they are married.

These industrious people contrasted in a striking manner with the Yagua tribe who we had visited on a previous occasion, after an hour's journey downriver by speedboat. Their village consisted of four open-sided abodes with only a thatched roof and a raised floor. Their appearance was more primitive. The men, with hair cropped short, wore skirts made of palm strips dyed orange with plant juice. They were pleased to demonstrate their prowess with blowpipes as long as they were tall. Skilful hunters, they use the poison that tips their arrows in a number of different strengths according to the size of the prey and whether it is to be killed or stunned.

The women were dressed in red cotton material wrapped around the waist. The children wore nothing or a cotton wrap. In one dwelling a baby and a small child swung in hammocks while a woman casually peeled some fruit while swinging in hers. Just by being there I felt as though I was intruding. An old man accepted the packet of cigarettes the tour leader brought as a gift. One might envy their simple life yet the women were old beyond their years: they carried young babies but their faces were lined and without the lustre of youth. The Yaguas seldom live in groups of more than about 30 people. Once this number is exceeded, a new village is formed. Unlike most tribes, their numbers were increasing, we were told.

When the canoe came to take us away from the lodge on the island I was sad. Living so close to nature, with the great Amazon river just 2ft (60cm) beneath my bed, I had forgotten everything about the developed world. Here nothing was important but one's surroundings. But back in Leticia running water (on the island, bucket showers were the order of the day), a toilet that flushed and fish for supper with fried potatoes, all seemed like the height of luxury. And here was a Fasciated Antshrike, who boasted no bright colours but was exquisitely barred and spotted in black and white. The female was chestnut and cinnamon. I was to meet this species or a closely allied one on other occasions, in different countries in the neotropics, and I always relished those encounters with these perky birds that have so much personality.

You would think that any writer would relish recounting a dramatic, life-threatening incident – or might even invent one to make the story more exciting. I did not need to invent one and I do not enjoy reliving it. Avianca flight 70 departed from Bogota on our return journey. Scheduled as a jumbo jet it was replaced with a Boeing 727 which, I later discovered, had already left the airport once that day but returned unfit to fly. The flight was delayed while mechanics repaired it for a flight across the Atlantic. As the engines revved-up for take-off, three hours late, I watched huge flames leaping from one engine. The aircraft lumbered into the sky but its obvious lack of power, jolting and shuddering progress, and failure of the air conditioning resulted in some anxiety (to say the least) among the passengers. Half an hour later once again the sight of flames shooting from one engine did nothing to reassure me of a happy landing. This engine, too, was shut off, with evident further loss of power. Most of the passengers were of Latin origin and panic and prayers to God were spreading through the aircraft.

Miraculously, a safe unscheduled landing was made at Barranquilla where the flight was delayed more than two hours while a new set of mechanics attempted to rectify the trouble. It was with no little apprehension that the passengers re-embarked. The engines were revved up for take-off and the aircraft taxied on to the runway. The take-off was aborted and the captain radioed to the control tower in a message that was live all over the aircraft. He was unable to take off due to "technical difficulties". It was 11.45pm. In order to avoid the expense of hotel accommodation for 200 people, delaying tactics were taken by the airline and it was announced that a meal would be served.

Due to the malfunction of almost everything on the plane, the food was inedible and the heat in the cabin became stifling. Tension among the passengers was mounting. Most people on board feared another take-off on an obviously faulty aircraft. What was the airline playing at? Our group intended to find out. Our leader Mrs Salt, a travel agent of 25 years' standing, asked a stewardess to bring the chief steward. She was told to sit down. That was too much! We did not take kindly to being addressed like naughty children.

I accompanied her to the captain's cabin (on reflection, it is amazing that we were not forbidden entry) where Mrs Salt told the captain she was appalled at the conditions under which passengers on the flight were being carried. I could not resist adding that I was a Fleet Street journalist (I omitted the word magazine!) and that Avianca could be getting some very bad publicity (assuming we lived to tell the tale). Evidently the captain had no wish for a further confrontation with two determined and irate British females and immediately the announcement *Cancelado* was made. Passengers were directed to leave the aircraft.

That was not the end of the ordeal. An unfortunate Avianca clerk then had to secure hotels for 200 people. Allocation for our group was (perhaps not unsurprisingly) left to last and it was well past 2am when we trundled tiredly to our accommodation. Without doubt it was the worst I have ever seen. The beds were so filthy we did not dare to sleep in them, the air conditioning unit was broken and the room was running with cockroaches and other insects. The captain's payback, perhaps? We finally reached London 23 hours late.

Apart from this incident, I was most impressed by the courteousness and kindness of all the people with whom I came into contact. It is regrettable that because the country's reputation is founded more on drug barons than on scenic delights and exceptional diversity of bird life, it is not better known to visitors.

2008 update

The Colombian government announced its plans to expand biofuel production with the opening of twenty plants within the next decade. A planned 7.4 million acres of "unused farmlands" would be converted to plantations of African oil palms. In fact they planned to use primary forests on the colonization frontier of the Chocó and Amazon regions. This will be a tragedy for the biodiversity of the regions and for many endangered bird species. The misguided demand for biofuels is accelerating deforestation throughout the tropics.

Species not previously mentioned:

Black and White Seedeater (*Sporophila luctuosa*)
Scarlet-crowned Barbet (*Capito aurovirens*)
Yellow-rumped Cacique (*Cacius cela*)
White-winged Parakeet (*Brotogeris versicolorus*)
Yellow-headed Blackbird or Marshbird (*Agelaius icterocephalus*)
Black-capped Mockingthrush (*Donacobius atricapillus*)
Horned Screamer (*Anhima cornuta*)
Hoatzin (*Opistocomus hoazin*)
Black-tailed or Maroon-tailed Conure (*Pyrrhura melanura*)
Dusky-headed Conure (*Aratinga weddellii*)
Short-tailed Parrot (*Graydidasculus brachyurus*)
Blue-headed Pionus (*Pionus menstruus*)
Mealy Amazon (*Amazona farinosa*)
Festive Amazon (*Amazona f.festiva*)
Crimson-crested Woodpecker (*Phloeoceastes melanoleucos*)
Slaty-tailed Trogon (*Trogon massena*)

Black-necked Red Cotinga (*Phoenicircus nigricollis*)
Black-fronted Nunbird (*Monasa nigrifrons*)
Fasciated Antshrike (*Cymbilaimus lineatus*)

Three-toed sloth (*Bradypus variegatus*)

4. Bonaire 1979:

Antillean Interlude

Bon bini Bonaire! (Welcome!) This is how you might be greeted in the expressive dialect of *papiamentu* on arrival at Flamingo Airport. Also known as *papiamento*, the spelling can vary as in the language itself, which is a mixture of Spanish, Portuguese, Dutch, English and French, with some Arawak Indian and African influences thrown in for good measure! Is this the world's most extreme hybrid language?

Bonaire is part of the Netherlands Antilles – a little known group of islands to those from the UK. They are sometimes known as the ABC Islands, after the initials of the three that make up the group. In 1979 even reaching Bonaire was an adventure for its small airport could not cope with jet aircraft. You travelled in a 30-seater plane from Aruba or Curaçao.

We had flown to Amsterdam with instructions to pick up our onward tickets. It sounded easy enough but the airline staff could not locate them! After a lengthy search, during which panic was beginning to set in, the tickets were produced. Bob and I were rushed on a luggage cart to the departure gate and ushered on to the flight just as it was departing. Examining one's tickets and documents after the cabin door has closed and finding that you are *en route* for the wrong hotel on the wrong island is not the ideal start to a trip! However, on arrival on Curaçao we were able to take an onward flight to Bonaire and to transfer our hotel accommodation. Curaçao, the largest of the Netherlands Antilles, is an industrial island dominated by oil refineries. In contrast, Bonaire was unspoiled. Only four hotels existed and, apart from the emergence of supermarkets, little had changed during many decades. Later, scuba diving became popular and Bonaire landed on the tourism map.

Our hotel was in Kralendijk, which was little more than a village

– and notable for the pineapple ice cream at the Neptune Restaurant! Gorgeous little Ruby-topaz Hummingbirds hovered around flowering trees, their foreheads glittering ruby and their throats gleaming gold. The second hummingbird species on the island is the Common Emerald so named for its dark green plumage. The male's crown is brilliant iridescent red. Both species seemed quite numerous and were conspicuous at dawn and dusk. Early one morning we picked a couple of scarlet hibiscus from the hotel garden and took them to an area with a wealth of low vegetation which was inviting to nectar feeders. Red is very attractive to hummingbirds so we tied the blooms to a low plant, focussed our cameras and sat back to await the arrival of our photographic subjects! Our blooms were ignored. The Ruby-topaz continued to feed on its favourite pink blossom!

It pleased me to see one of Bonaire's most colourful birds, the Yellow Oriole. Boldly marked in yellow and black, the orioles usually inhabited thickly-foliaged trees. Their pendulous woven nests were conspicuous structures, attached to the end of a branch. The island's strong trade wind never ceased to blow, giving the incubating bird a rough ride as the nest swung incessantly to and fro.

We soon discovered the fascination of Bonaire's scenery. This arid island is dominated by mesquite (a small spiny shrub). A prominent part of the vegetation are the tall candelabra and

Ruby-topaz Hummingbird

cadushi cacti, growing like a forest of spaced out trees, and the better known prickly-pear cactus with its spreading branches and ripe red fruits – perfect food for parrots. At that time a flight over Bonaire revealed large areas of scrub and rather few signs of settlement. With its wind-bent, stunted divi divi trees and weird limestone rock formations, it is perhaps the strangest island one is likely to encounter in the Caribbean region.

Drive to the southern tip and the landscape is bizarre: pink lakes and ice-white miniature mountains. Here are located the solar salt works, side by side with one of the most important colonies of the Caribbean or Greater Flamingo in the southern Caribbean. Plans announced to reactivate the saltpans in 1962 would have resulted in the loss of the flamingo breeding area. After four years of negotiations, tragedy was averted when the salt company and the conservationists reached an agreement. A breeding area of 55 hectares was set up in the midst of the condenser area of about 2,000 hectares. The Pekelmeer Sanctuary was born. Today it is one of the largest flamingo sanctuaries in the Western Hemisphere, with between 3,000 and 7,000 birds in a good year.

I was enchanted. Honking like geese, these big birds waded into the depths, keeping a wary eye on us distant humans. When they took flight, their black wing feathers made a striking contrast to the deep pink body plumage. They would fly low

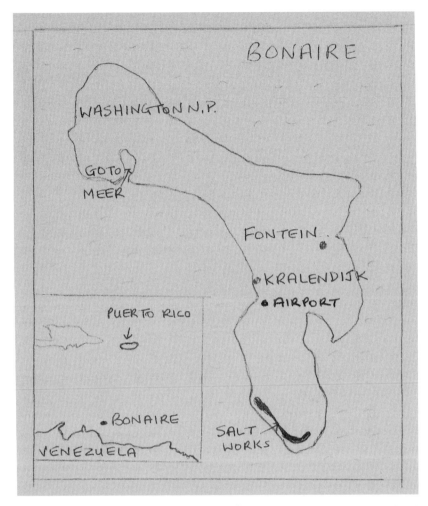

against the deep blue of the ocean then drop down again to feed among the saltpans. The correct conditions for their diet of algae, brine shrimps and larval brine had been destroyed by the salt works; the flamingos were feeding on small molluscs. Slowly walking forward as they fed, their graceful necks moved to and fro as their beaks sieved out the water.

Food supply was not their only problem. On at least one occasion, in April 1973, a catastrophic event occurred. At the time there were between 500 and 1,000 young in the colony. Two low-flying aircraft resulted in 400 nests being deserted. Two hundred chicks died and many others were scattered and abandoned. It was estimated that only 300 to 400 young survived. How can such stupidity be perpetrated by someone who has the responsibility of flying a plane?

Flamingos and slave houses are the main tourist attractions in the southern part. For a short while the island belonged to Britain, who leased it to a New York merchant, inclusive of 300 slaves, for an annual payment of $2,400. The stone-built slave houses, almost on the stony shoreline, still stand today, shelters for the workers in the saltpans until the abolition of slavery in 1863. These dwellings were only 5ft (1.5m) high.

At the south end of the island the beaches were rewarding places to visit. Various plovers could be approached within a few feet as they fed on insects and small crabs. Oystercatchers were foraging along the shoreline, among the boulders and big stones. Two white-phase Reddish Egrets were so engrossed in their comical courtship capers that they took little notice of human intruders. This common egret has two colour phases. The white one can be distinguished from the Snowy Egret (also present) by its partly black bill, flesh-coloured at the base. I can still recall one of the dark phase egrets standing on a rock on the beach, close to the incoming tide. It was silhouetted against the brilliant blue of the sea, which made a dazzling contrast to the white coral debris of which the beach was formed.

Laughing Gulls and lone Brown Pelicans flew overhead. We always hoped to see a pelican capture a fish, plunging into the sea with nearly closed wings after plummeting suddenly from a considerable height. Sometimes we watched an Osprey spiralling high above or flying along the coast, occasionally diving for fish. One day, lazily observing sandpipers and yellowlegs in the warmth from a cloudless sky, there was an exhilarating sighting from the beach! A ray that must have been at least 5ft (1.5m) in length was swimming close to the shore.

It was the northern end of the island that held the most attraction for us, especially the beautiful land-locked Goto Meer. In the distance, orange dots against the blue water turned out to be the long-legged flamingos, found on most inland waters. Various ducks and waders were present. The island attracts many migrating birds, just as much at home on a European estuary as on a Bonairean salt flat. There were always four or five Black-winged Stilts at the edge of this picturesque lake, towering over the sandpipers on their long red legs and shrieking angrily whenever they considered their territory had been invaded. Two species of plover, Kentish and Thick-billed, would take off without warning, flying low over the water and twittering in alarm

Half a dozen Bahama Pintail lived along the edge of the meer, where the overhanging rocks provided shelter and protection. They were perhaps the wariest of all the birds we encountered. The very sight of a car sent the ducks swimming rapidly away. No doubt they were hunted – along with, surprisingly, Brown or Common Noddies, terns found only in tropical waters. So called because of their elaborate nodding display, they spend most of the day at sea, returning at night to the rocky shore on the north coast. Apparently, their livers were considered a delicacy, free meals for the less well-off inhabitants. Food was expensive because almost all of it was imported. Even the tiny Common Ground Dove with its rufous wings, so conspicuous in flight low to the ground, was said to be fair game. No wonder the big pigeons were so wary …

In the Goto Meer area we encountered the most beautiful sub-species of the Brown-throated Conure, found only on Bonaire. This noisy, common, colourful parakeet, is bright yellow-orange on the sides of the head. I feel sure that if a few were released into the swamps of the southern United States, rumours of the miraculous survival of the extinct Carolina Parakeet would soon be circulating! Whether these desert-adapted birds could survive in a watery world is another matter. Relating voice to size, this parakeet must be the noisiest bird on the island. It is not afraid to draw attention to its presence by its loud, harsh calls and a pair heard but not seen might lead the uninitiated to believe that a small flock was responsible.

It feeds on cactus. It has always been a source of wonder to me how parakeets and parrots can alight on cactus without puncturing their little feet! The parakeets could land repeatedly on them with apparent impunity although it was impossible for them to avoid the treacherous looking spines. Parakeets might be immune to the stiff needle-sharp spines because they weigh only 100g or so, but we discovered that the small soft spines were almost impossible to remove if embedded in a finger. Touching a cactus as lightly as possible resulted in a fingerful – so how did the conures escape them?

We observed these parakeets eating not only the fruits but also the actual cactus, especially the datu, a tall, erect species, perhaps the most numerous of the island's flora. Except in the southern part, one could hardly find an area without it. Always interested to learn about the *taste* of items that parrots eat, I sampled a piece of datu on which a pair of conures had been feeding. In taste and texture it was much like cucumber.

The flight of these lovely birds is fast, erratic and often swerving. They were usually quick to take to the wing. However, one day we encountered a pair that was so busy preening and feeding each other, in the most affectionate manner, that they allowed us to approach within about 10ft (3m). Perched in a tree that was devoid of leaves, their golden heads were outlined against the unbroken blue of the sky. Next day we returned to the same spot and saw them leave their nest – a termitarium placed in the wide fork of a gnarled tree at a height that was only just above eye level. This symbiosis between parrots and termites occurs in Africa, Australia and South America. Once the parrots have excavated their nest site, the wall is apparently repaired by the termites and the two species live in harmony.

One traveller who enjoyed the presence of the parakeets was Robert Porter Allen who wrote about them in *Birds of the Caribbean* (1961). He found them to be ubiquitous "…in desert-like areas atop giant tree cactuses, in low half-flooded stretches where the deadly machineel grows in thick clumps, in plantations with their cactus fences, and even in scrubby goat pastures on the outskirts of Kralendijk… They are one of the many delights of this attractive island."

The entire northern end of Bonaire forms the Washington Slagbaai National Park. It covers an area of 6,000 acres and came into being in 1969. A former plantation, its owner, who had died two years previously, had the foresight to offer the land to the Bonaire government to prevent its development. This large, untouched area with a wild beauty will thus be preserved for posterity. Visiting it was an experience not to be missed, despite two punctures in two days over 21 miles (34 km) of unpaved trails of reddish soil. We should have rented a four-wheel-drive – if one existed. It was a photographer's paradise. In the foreground were huge tree cacti and mesquite and in the

The author points out the conure nest in a termitarum

Bonaire Brown-throated Conure at the nest

background limestone cliffs of the weirdest formations imaginable. These cliffs, varying in height from 10ft to 40ft (3m to 12m) are the exposed remains of former reefs. Scan them carefully and you might see the large, shy Red-necked Pigeon hiding in a crevice.

If you were very lucky you would catch a glimpse of sun-basking iguanas. Considered a tasty source of food by the islanders, the big reptiles were also wary. Not so the thousands of small lizards, brightly marked in blue and brown and spotted with white. At one point we had fifty of them scuttling around our feet by the simple strategy of offering an apple core.

One factor detracted from the appeal of this location – the thousands of sand flies that swarmed around our faces, aiming for eyes, mouth and nose. The only way to escape their attentions was to keep moving – which was not conducive to good birdwatching.

At Boca Cocolishi, a small bay formed by a deep cleft in the rocky cliffs, the crystal clear water was decorated with tiny colourful fishes. I dangled my toes from a rock to have them gently nibbled by deep blue and yellow fish. To those who dive, a miraculous marine world is revealed in what has been described as the best reef diving this side of Australia's Barrier Reef, complete with sunken wrecks.

But it was not parakeets or flamingos or the diving that had brought us here but the Yellow-shouldered Amazon. This parrot occurs elsewhere only in some coastal areas of Venezuela, and on the Venezuelan islands of Blanquilla and Margarita. Bonaire must have changed a lot since my visit – but one fact remains the same. The area called Fontein in the north is still one of the best places to find the parrot.

Our first sighting, in the national park, was memorable. A pair landed on top of a tall cadushi cactus not far away. We approached quietly and they took to the air in total and uncharacteristic silence. This time they landed in a tree that was completely covered in bright yellow blossoms. Here they were superbly camouflaged. These green birds have yellow faces and cheeks, yellow at the bend of the wing and red wing speculum.

Avoiding the searing heat of midday, we watched them there twice daily, soon after first light at 6.30am to 7am and at about 4pm. A disused plantation at the foot of limestone cliffs, containing sapadillo, almond and mango trees, was a popular feeding area. The parrots drank at the water tanks that had once served the plantation house. Water was pumped up from beneath the rocks and there was one point where it spilled over. At certain times of the day, dainty little Yellow Warblers were especially abundant, bathing and drinking and darting about. They were common all over the island and on a few occasions even appeared at the breakfast table (set in an open-sided structure on the beach), a role normally assumed by the even more abundant Bananaquits. The deftness with which some of the latter had learned to open packets of sugar was (to us) a delight to watch! There are no sparrows on Bonaire and the Bananaquit has taken over the role of companion to man.

But I diverge! High above, the cliffs at Fontein were riddled with the holes and tunnels that made perfect parrot nesting sites. A flock would fly low above us and swerve away when they discovered our presence. Noisy in flight, they called and chortled in typical Amazon fashion. On one occasion four parrots flew over, swerved back in curiosity, and two hovered with beating wings, actually peering down at us and calling. Two parrot-watching people were looking at two people-watching parrots!

In April the pale yellow foreheads of some birds were dirty –

almost black. The parrots must have been excavating their nests. During the first days of our visit they kept together in a flock of up to 19 birds. On the last day, April 17, it seemed that the flock was splitting up into pairs, prior to breeding. Trees are sometimes used, but large trees are not common and most such nests had been vandalised to remove the chicks for pets. But there were also avian vandals! When I first saw a bird that resembled a thrush but with a pointed beak I was struck by its malicious-looking light-coloured eyes. I later discovered it was the Pearly-eyed Thrasher, which is given a wide berth by small birds. It is also an enemy of the parrot, whose eggs it will steal if it can enter the nest.

We wanted to find out more about the breeding habits of the parrot which was a little known bird at that time. Who could tell us? "Frater Candidus!" was the universal reply. One of the good things about having a passionate interest in a subject is that it is likely to bring you into contact with knowledgeable and renowned people. When we met Frater Candidus, middle-aged, modest and very friendly, I had no idea of his revered status. Born Arnoldus Cornelius van der Linden in the Netherlands, he had been a member of the congregation of Brothers of Our Lady, Mothers of Mercy, since he was 19 years old. He had come to Bonaire in 1967 and was to play an important role in the education of Antilleans there and on neighbouring Curaçao. During his time on Bonaire he acquired a profound knowledge of its birdlife. Countless amateurs and scientists learned from him, as did Bob and I.

He combined education and the acquisition of ornithological knowledge in a way that was then unique and has seldom if ever been replicated. To find out about the nesting habits of the parrot he had sent questionnaires to schools, enlisting the help of children and impressing on them to write "Don't know" where applicable. He showed me some of the forms that the children had completed. Some of the answers indicated that their knowledge of the parrots' habits were more than superficial. To the question: "In which month do the parrots start to breed?" the replies in one batch of answers I examined were: March (1), April (7), May (15), June (2), July (3) and October (3).

This confirmed what we now know that April and May are the peak laying months but I was unaware that occasional eggs are laid in October, just before the start of the rainy season. Unfortunately, this knowledge regarding egg-laying was mainly related to the fact that so many young were taken out of the nest to be reared as pets.

Frater Candidus went on to gain distinction in two different spheres. His educational contributions in the Netherlands Antilles had already been recognised by the Queen of the Netherlands who appointed him a Knight of the Orange-Nassau in 1975. In 1991 he received the Silver Carnation from the Prince Bernhard Fund for Nature. In 1995 the Brothers' House on Bonaire was closed and it was with sadness that the people said goodbye to him as he moved to California. Frater Candidus died there in 1998, aged 79. The Antillean newsletter recorded: "The mark he made on the people and nature of Bonaire is indelible."

As he had told us, the population of the Yellow-shouldered Amazon fluctuates dramatically according to rainfall. In times of drought mortality is high. Frater Candidus had told us that in 1978 starving parrots flew into Kralendijk looking for food. Many died and others were shot.

I was sad to leave Bonaire, with its unique landscapes and wonderful parrots but when I reached Flamingo Airport I had to smile. The destination of our departing flight was listed as "Europe"!

Set in the Caribbean Sea, within its width of 1,500 miles (2,400km) and its depth that exceeds 16,000ft (5,333m) in places, are many islands that writers have eulogised for centuries. Some of these still have steadily encroached areas of rainforest with their unique native Amazon parrots – a different species on each island. I have seen the magnificent, colourful St Vincent Parrot in the mountainous forests of that island, the big St Lucia Parrot in a similar setting and, most memorable of all, the largest, the rarest and the shyest of the genus on Dominica, the appropriately named Imperial Parrot, with its purple underparts. All are hard to observe among the depths of the forests, wary of man after generations of persecution. But for me there was something special about observing Bonaire's lively and inquisitive parrot in the total contrast of a desert setting.

Update 2008

Today the Yellow-shouldered Amazon is better known, mainly due to the work carried out by two enthusiastic young Britons, Sam Williams and Rowan Martin. Sam spent each breeding season there from 2003 studying the parrots and educating the local people about their conservation and on the care of captive ones. In the 2007 breeding season, for example, 40 active nests were monitored with the help of volunteers. From 92 eggs laid, 23 young fledged but, causing great disappointment, ten chicks were poached for pets by islanders. This happened despite the programme to ring, record and legalise all captive parrots several years previously. Among a human population of 13,000 (an increase of about 5,000 from the time of my visit), there are more than 600 captive native parrots. Despite this sad statistic, the wild population has made an encouraging increase in recent years to approximately 650 individuals. A novel idea of Sam Williams raises money for parrot conservation on the island. Cameras in parrot nests enable those who log on to the website and donate to observe the wild chicks being reared.

The news was less promising regarding the wonderful reefs that had attracted so many divers. Global warming and the rise in the temperature of the sea was damaging the corals. Brain corals were turning blue as the symbiotic algae reacted to the higher water temperatures.

Bird statistics (year 2000)

Netherlands Antilles
Vulnerable 1
Near-threatened 1

Species not already mentioned:

Ruby-topaz Hummingbird (*Chrysolampis mosquitus*)
Common Emerald Hummingbird (*Chlorostilbon mellisugus*)

Yellow Oriole (*Icterus nigrogularis*)
Reddish Egret (*Egretta rufescens*)
Snowy Egret (*Egretta thula*)
Laughing Gull (*Larus atricilla*)
Oystercatcher (*Haematopus ostralegus*)
Kentish Plover (*Charadrius alexandrinus*)
Thick-billed Plover (*Charadrius wilsonia*)
Bahama Pintail (*Anas bahamensis*)
Brown or Common Noddy (*Anous stolidus*)
Common Ground Dove (*Columbigallina passerina*)
**Bonaire Brown-throated Conure (*Aratinga pertinax
    xanthogenia*)**
Red-necked Pigeon (*Columba squamosa*)
**Yellow-shouldered Amazon Parrot (*Amazona barbadensis*)
    VULNERABLE**
Pearly-eyed Thrasher (*Margarops fuscatus*)

Cadushi cactus (*Cereus repandus*)
Datu cactus (*Lamaireocereus griseus*)

5. Mexico 1997:

Parrots in the Clouds

For almost a decade my travels in the neotropics came to a halt while I discovered the Pacific region. There were so many fascinating birds and new habitats to explore in Australia, New Zealand, New Guinea and smaller Pacific islands. It was Mexico that started me back on the route to the New World.

Mexico: the popular conception is of a land of colourful people, wearing big hats and eating spicy foods, influenced by ancient civilisations, such as Mayas and Aztecs. Or perhaps that has been replaced with the scene of an all-inclusive resort in Cancun. There again, if your interest is in parrot conservation, the picture is a very different one. Mexico's rapid population growth in recent years has resulted in much habitat destruction or degradation. The approximately (experts differ) 20 parrot species are threatened by habitat loss and trapping.

An invitation to visit this fascinating country gave me the

MEXICO

Sandwiched between Texas and California to the north and Guatemala and Belize to the south, Mexico is a large country of 756,000 square miles (nearly 2 million sq km) – larger than any South or Central American country except Brazil and Argentina. It has one of the fastest growing populations in the world – from 50 million in the 1970s to more than 90 million in the mid 1990s.

Maroon-fronted Parrot

opportunity to find out more, in September 1997. With my friend Val Moat I flew to Dallas, then on to Monterrey. Mexico is big – seven times larger than Britain – thus seven days offered little more than a taster. What made this visit so memorable was not the beauty of the country or even the appeal of the parrots, although both were outstanding, but the special people with whom we were privileged to spend our time at Fundación Ara in Monterrey. This organisation was set up in 1996 to rehabilitate or breed from illegally trapped native bird species confiscated by the Mexican Government. The team was led by a dynamic young veterinarian Dr Miguel-Angel Gomez Garza, and Daniel Garza Tobon, ornithologist (and photographer).

Miguel and his lovely, slim wife Carla met us at the airport. A happy young couple with a two-year-old daughter, they lost no time in taking us on a downtown tour. Monterrey, Mexico's third largest city, is situated in the north-east in the state of Nuevo Leon. Its magnificent plaza is the second largest in the world, after Moscow's Red Square. The governor's palace is located there, also the cathedral, painted in soft sand, with a beautiful exterior. There were real bargains to be had in the genuine Mexican shops but I was more interested in a Mexican wearing a huge sombrero and a red neck-scarf. For one peso, his

Fortune-telling Canaries and their trainer

61

three Canaries were telling fortunes by hopping out of their cage and removing folded messages from a little rack. He was doing a roaring trade.

But there was little time for sight-seeing. I was there with a specific purpose: to see Mexico's least known parrot species, the Maroon-fronted. At that time, few people had seen it in the wild. After I visited its habitat, I understood why. With a trio of dark, handsome young men, Miguel and Daniel, and Juan Julian Vargas, another Ara staff member, we set off at 6.45am, stopping briefly for a breakfast of tacos under the yellow awning of a brightly painted wayside stall.

Soon we were driving through impressive scenery. Towering mountains surrounded us, many of them sheer-faced, stark and impenetrable. They reached so high into the sky we could hardly observe the peaks from the car.

They stretched as far as the eye could see – high and wide. At an altitude of 7,500ft (2,300m) we left behind our 4WD vehicle and started to climb through the pine-oak forest. The oaks in this temperate region were heavily garlanded with air plants, and

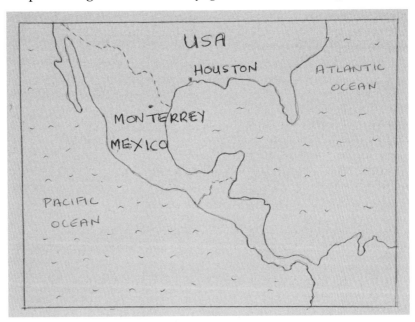

madrone trees (*Arbuthrus*) were covered with bright red fruits. Here and there fruiting prickly pear cactus were interspersed between the trees. Steep slopes and the thick layer of pine needles and small cones made the going slippery. It took us one and a half hours to ascend only 1,300ft (400m). Of course, the men alone could have got there in half the time! They had spent a lifetime on Mexico's mountain slopes.

Miguel had been watching the parrots since 1982 and Juan was an expert mountaineer. We climbed through an area where butterflies were plentiful but birds were scarce. We heard a Peregrine Falcon, and saw the occasional Scrub Jay and the wily crow. A large hummingbird, the Blue-throated, with a prominent white stripe from eye to neck and white markings on its tail, stopped us in our tracks, as we watched it searching for insects in a shrub.

Long before we neared the top we could hear the macaw-like cries of the Maroon-fronted Parrots. When we were as high as we could ascend, they were far above us, flying about the steep face of the mountain in which they nest. Even through the telescope the parrots were little more than black dots. Named *El Condominio* by scientists for its high density of nesting sites, no man has yet been able to scale the forbidding sheer face of the mountain. Striped with grey in places and covered in vegetation in others, the cliffs had the air of a fortress.

The habitat of this species is incredible in the true sense of the word. It must be seen to be believed. Although I had read descriptions and seen photographs, I was unprepared for the height and the inaccessibility of the nesting area. These parrots were quite literally living in the clouds. Who would have thought that parrots survived like this, protected by their habitat? Juan told me that if he asked the local people about them, they say "*No existe este especie*".

Most do not believe in the existence of any such parrot. It is so remote they have never seen it. There are a few exceptions. On rare occasions a young parrot that has fallen from the nest is found in the forest. There were six such birds at Fundación Ara, confiscated from local people. They were the only ones in captivity worldwide. With their large heads and bills (black) they bear some resemblance to a short-tailed green macaw. The forehead and lores are maroon and the underwing coverts are grey. This parrot is closely related to the Mexican Thick-billed Parrot which differs in its scarlet forehead and yellow underwings.

After listening to their calls for a couple of hours and seeing them only as dark specks moving against the face of the mountain, the calling increased. The clouds had closed in on us, blotting out the sun. Suddenly the parrots started to pass through – flocks of 30, 40, 20 and smaller groups. The estimate was of about 150 birds. My companions were elated. Miguel's mouth, half hidden by his short thick moustache, broke into a huge smile. Seldom had he seen so many Maroon-fronted Parrots together.

At that time it was believed that about 28 pairs nested in the central wall. The total population of the species was impossible to estimate but Miguel suggested that it might have been less than 1,000 birds. Its main problem is Mexico's rapidly growing population. Forests that were once protected by their remoteness are now being settled or used for cattle grazing. Illegal felling continues and we had seen a lorry loaded with ill-gotten logs. The appointment of two forest rangers was imminent – not sufficient, but better than none. The parrots depended on the pine-oak forest for food and could not survive without it – but neither could the human population because the preservation of the forests is vital for water catchment.

Only two large communal nesting sites of the Maroon-fronted Parrot were known. It breeds exclusively near cliffs with a good diversity of conifers. In addition to pine seeds, it feeds on the seeds and nectar of one species of *Agave*. Its numbers had suffered a great decline in the previous few years. Only two decades previously flocks numbering several hundred birds were reported. They had gone as the habitat was degraded, hastened by the grazing of goats in the forest. It was difficult to see what they could graze on, apart from a few succulents. Cutting the forests had inevitably led to drought (will Man never learn?). This meant that forest fires spread quickly, further eroding the habitat.

During my visit I was interviewed by a reporter from *El Norte*, one of the national newspapers. It was a good opportunity to emphasise the importance of preserving the forests and protecting parrots worldwide from illegal trade. The interview was published next morning.

Fundación Ara was owned by the extraordinarily wealthy Ramo family. (I use the past tense because the facility closed a couple of years later.) Very hospitable people, they kindly invited us to lunch. Pancho Ramo was a show jumper of fame and had his

The baroque cathedral in Saltillo

own indoor arena that was used for international competitions. The enormous picture window of the dining room looked into the arena with a distant view of the mountains. The room was dominated by a magnificent painting of two St Bernard dogs rescuing a man in the snow. Senor Ramo saw me studying it and told me it was painted by an Englishman. "Who?" I asked innocently. "Landseer" he replied and added casually that he had three more Landseers. I nearly choked on my prawn brochette!

After lunch we went to Monterrey's main shopping area, Calle Morello, which was pulsating with life. It was Sunday when many people come into town from outlying areas. A riot of colour, in preparation for the Independence Day celebrations, men with novelty balloons pushed their barrows in the street and children followed, as to a Pied Piper.

Contrast this bustling scene with some of Mexico's mountains where man has never trodden. Unfortunately, most parrots cannot survive in those areas because of inadequate food sources. On our way to Saltillo a couple of days later Miguel pointed out a stand of evergreens, *Pinus catarinae*, on a distant mountain range. The stand extended only about 4 miles (6km), yet every October the Maroon-fronted Parrots found their way there to feed on the seeds of these pine trees. The young fledge at the end of October to coincide with the greater availability of the nuts. With the exception of the Scarlet Macaw, now almost extinct in Mexico, the Maroon-fronted Parrot has the most restricted range and is the least numerous of all Mexico's parrots.

In 1995 Monterrey Tech started a long-term study of this parrot under its Ecosystems Sustainable Management Program (PMSE). Volunteers from around the world, mainly biology graduates and undergraduates, study the breeding habits, diet and habitat use. In 2007 the entire population was estimated at 2,000 to 4,000 individuals.

In the neighbouring state of Coahuila, we visited the old colonial city of Saltillo, founded in 1575 and an important cultural and educational centre. Many of the buildings are constructed of pink quarry and limestone. We admired the magnificent cathedral in this historic town, described as one of the most beautiful baroque buildings in Mexico.

Nearby is situated the *Museo de las Aves de Mexico* (the Museum of Mexican Birds). It had achieved the extraordinary in presenting most of Mexico's 1,010 bird species as mounted specimens in attractive displays. The country has 80 endemics, including five or six (depending on whether the Double Yellow-headed Amazon is classified as a separate species) endemic parrots. Five parrots are on Appendix I of CITES, mainly due to loss of habitat. This includes the Green-cheeked Amazon, a beautiful parrot with scarlet forehead and emerald cheeks. I

66

briefly glimpsed about 30 birds after waiting for two hours in a likely location not far outside the city of Monterrey. This was a feral population consisting of escapees and their young. The area contained many trees and gardens, and a large park where the Amazons often fed in the early morning, attracted to the ripening nuts of the pecan tree.

Green-cheeked Amazon in Arcadia

In 2004 the Ornithology Laboratory of Nuevo Leon University started to study the feral parrots breeding in Monterrey. They found 11 neotropical species plus the Budgerigar! Of the 22 nests recorded, 15 were of Green-cheeked Amazons and chicks were seen in two of them. The researchers (Peña and Gonzalez-Rojas) wrote: "Although these birds are not in their natural wild habitat, they are still protected by Mexican laws. We recommend that the authorities enforce our laws to protect the birds from illegal traffic, which is so visible in the streets of our cities".

Update 2007
Since 1996 a programme, co-ordinated by three organisations, has been initiated to understand the environmental and human pressures placed on the Maroon-fronted Parrot, in order to make a plan to preserve it. In 2007, 2000 hectares of its pine forest habitat were destroyed by fire, including an area protected for this species. The study confirmed that large fires destroy the

pine seeds that are the parrot's staple diet, causing a reduction in its numbers and late arrival at the two largest breeding sites. Late arrival means that fewer pine seeds are available to the parrots which can take the seeds only before they ripen and fall out of the cone. The Maroon-fronted Parrot is therefore one of the most vulnerable worldwide to habitat destruction in its small range. Its Vulnerable status will surely and sadly need to be upgraded before long.

Mexican bird statistics (year 2000)

Extinct in wild 1
Critically Endangered 8
Endangered 12
Vulnerable 19
Near-threatened 28

Los Angeles, 2007

Ten years later I watched Green-cheeked Amazons in the Arcadia suburb of Los Angeles. Here is a sort of Amazon heaven of beautifully manicured streets and lawns with hundreds of mature native and tropical trees from all over the world. They provided food and nesting sites. It was not entirely free of predators as Red-tailed Hawks were apparent – but apart from that I could not think of a nicer place for the Green-cheeked, and Finsch's (another endangered Mexican endemic) Amazons to have settled. I was told that hundreds, literally hundreds, come in to roost on winter nights. (California and Florida have thousands of introduced parrots, escapees or unwanted released pets.)

Flocks start to break up in March and to look for nest sites in the silver-leaf maple whose natural cavities are ideal for this purpose. It was April, thus I saw only a couple of males near their nests and a flock of eight in flight. Green-cheeked Amazons exist in big numbers in southern California – an estimated 2,800 in 2003. In Mexico the declining population is believed to number only about 3,000 birds. In this instance, feral populations might be the means of saving the species from extinction. Introduced species of any kind usually get a bad press but the fact is that most countries now hold hundreds of species of non-native flora and fauna. Globalisation doesn't only hold true for humans!

Species not previously mentioned:

Maroon-fronted Parrot (*Rhynchopsitta terrisi*) VULNERABLE
Scrub Jay (*Aphelocoma coerulescens*)
Blue-throated Hummingbird (*Lampornis clemenciae*)
Double Yellow-headed Amazon (*Amazona [ochrocephala] oratrix*) ENDANGERED
Green-cheeked Amazon (*Amazona viridigenalis*) ENDANGERED
Finsch's or Lilac-crowned Amazon (*Amazona finschi*) (CITES Appendix 1)
Red-tailed Hawk (*Buteo jamaicensis*)

6. Costa Rica 2000:

Ornithology's Patriarch

Politically the most stable country in Central America, since the 1950s Costa Rica has had no armed forces. It prefers to spend money on education. An amusing postcard depicts three pelicans with the caption: "The Army, the Navy and the Air Force." Another take on this theme says that ants are the Army, turtles are the Navy and Frigatebirds are the Air Force!

The countries of Central America are small. Costa Rica is only two and a half times the size of Wales (no bigger than the state of West Virginia). Despite its limited land surface, it has an extraordinary diversity of birds with more species recorded than in the whole of North America – more than 400 residents and 200 migrants. Its habitats are equally diverse, ranging from rich lowland rainforests, tropical dry forests and sun-drenched beaches to damp cloud forests and threatening volcanoes.

Firmly established as one of the world's top birding destinations, the reasons for its popularity are clear. This beautiful country receives many American visitors so the tourist industry is more sophisticated than elsewhere in Central America. In the most frequented areas, English is spoken in shops and restaurants. The people are friendly and most are well educated and realise that their avifauna attracts big dollars. They are not mystified by an intense interest in birds, as is often the case in the tropics.

Costa Rica is famous for its reserves, most of which have miles of trails. Some (such as Manuel Antonio National Park) are small and perhaps too crowded for enthusiastic birdwatchers. Nevertheless, this country has some of the world's most colourful birds, including macaws, toucans, tanagers and an incredible array of hummingbirds. The celebrated Resplendent

Quetzal, described by renowned ornithologist Alexander Skutch as "the most elegant bird of the Western Hemisphere", is on every birder's list of "must sees". There are 16 parrot species of which the best known and one of the rarest is the Scarlet Macaw.

In March 2000 Canadian friends Wendy and Horst rented an attractive villa and invited me to share it for a few days. I met them in Houston for the three-hour flight to San José, Costa Rica's capital. From the Hampton Inn (near the airport) I saw my first species – the ubiquitous Great-tailed Grackle. Seventeen inches (43cm) long, the male is glossy purple-black with a long broad tail, in contrast to the brown female. Both sexes have fearsome-looking beaks from which pours forth some joyful vocalisations.

The view from the hotel windows was of distant rolling mountains with cloud (absent elsewhere) hanging around their slopes. March was a good time to be there – just before the end of the dry season. On this trip bird-watching was incidental – thus the birds I saw were those that might be apparent to any casual observer.

COSTA RICA

Located in Central America, with Nicaragua to the north and Colombia to the east, Costa Rica has a population of about four million people. With a mountainous backbone and impressive scenery, it covers nearly 20,000 square miles (51,000 sq km). With a rich biodiversity, educated people and stable politics, it is a favourable country for ecological and conservation research. It might be the only country on Earth with an organization dedicated to conducting an inventory of its entire biota (plant and animal life), probably one million species.

At an *al fresco* breakfast on the first morning, I spied a tiny owl sitting beneath the broad sculptured leaves of a papaya tree. It was a Ferruginous Pygmy-Owl, only 6in (15cm) long, and a widespread species throughout the Americas. He was soon joined by his mate. We watched the pair, lazily opening and closing their yellow-globe eyes, as we ate our *gallo pinto* (scrambled eggs, beans and rice). Black Vultures, with their bare red and black heads and impressive wings, were common everywhere. Not exclusively carrion feeders, they also dine on palm fruits, bananas and, sadly (for these endangered animals) hatchling turtles.

Quepos, where we were staying, was about an hour's drive to the south, on the rugged Pacific coast. To reach our villa we climbed 101 steps and gradually the sea view and the Manuel Antonio National Park unfolded below. Next morning I arose at first light, 5.40am, and looked across the curve of the bay, with its thickly tree-clad promontory. The dawn chorus was muted against the sound of the thundering surf. The sky was streaked orange, tingeing the surrounding clouds with rose-pink. As this colour turned to gold, people started to stir and dogs to bark. What I thought was a grackle was revealed as a large black fruit.

The chorus became louder than the surf and I took my binoculars onto the deck. The early birds out looking for food included a pair of Scarlet-rumped Tanagers, the male glossy black with intense red rump and silvery bill. (The females of the Costa Rican sub-species can be very colourful, with orange breast band and rump, yellow underparts and dark brown plumage above.) The tanagers were sallying forth after flying termites. Hummingbirds and Squirrel Cuckoos, their long tails banded below with black and white, were also active. A handsome Golden-naped Woodpecker, with red crown and a silver line down his black back, clung to the top of a silvery-barked trunk. I watched this omnivorous beauty searching for figs and insects as he made his way jerkily around the trunk.

A delightful pair of Masked Tityras could usually be seen from the deck. They often landed in a dead tree trunk with silvery bark – on the one surviving horizontal limb. Gender was easily distinguished – the male with his black and white plumage and red facial skin and base of bill, the female more brownish than white. (Once classified as a cotinga, the species is now controversially considered to be closer to the flycatchers.)

Twenty minutes later the sun came up and a group of six little Orange-chinned or Tovi Parakeets flew over. They prefer open country with scattered trees, so their range is expanding as the forests are cut. Unfortunately, deforestation is a huge problem in Costa Rica. On another occasion, near the famous La Selva reserve (two hours from San José) I watched a flock of 15 or more Tovis feeding in a fig tree on the tiny reddish fruits. The parakeets landed with much shrieking but at that moment they seemed to disappear. Their camouflage is exceptional, as they blend into the leaves.

My friends were looking for a property to buy. Near one possible site we came across a pond that was overflowing with long-necked, long-legged Black-bellied Whistling Ducks. At least one hundred were crammed onto a small area of water. This species is described as generally uncommon and local in Costa Rica.

From Quepos we took a boat to Damas Island. Mangrove swamps occur around estuaries, where the fresh water of the

White-faced capuchin monkey in the mangroves

73

river meets tidal salt water. The water's edge was lined with red mangrove trees with spreading roots like stilts, partly above the water level, and a tangle of creepers and shrubs in the undergrowth. Perched on a white-bleached dead tree in the river, were several Elegant Terns, handsome with their orange bills and black occipital crests. Ibis, herons and egrets abounded and Ospreys were overhead.

As we approached the island, a troop of white-faced capuchin monkeys swarmed over the boat looking for the bananas that the guides offered them. I do not enjoy seeing wild animals behaving in this way. They would even drink water offered from lids, peering around like thieves with their evil, too-human faces! Fearless creatures, capuchins soon become aggressive if they do not find what they want. The black crown, light-coloured facial hair and sideburns remind me of a little old man wearing a black skullcap. In contrast were the shy and lovely little red-backed squirrel monkeys observed in another location. Only 12in (30cm) long, they are prettily marked with reddish-orange back and legs, black head and white markings around the eyes. To watch a troop moving through the trees gave much pleasure.

A couple of days later a chance encounter led to a memorable meeting. In casual conversation Horst discovered where Alexander Skutch lived. The author of nearly 30 ornithological books, he was the patriarch of tropical ornithology. An American by birth, he had devoted his life to studying the breeding biology of neotropical birds. Indeed, he was the co-author of the book I was carrying around with me, *A Guide to the Birds of Costa Rica.*

We had only the sketchiest idea of how to find his home; in fact, it consisted of a piece of paper with three words written in capitals: *SAN ISIDRO* and *QUIZARRA*. We decided it was worth a try, although I was doubtful that we should just turn up unannounced. Leaving before 8am, we took the unpaved road from Quepos to Dominical. Driving to San Isidro we had an exciting sighting of three King Vultures soaring overhead. An extremely handsome bird, it is the largest and least common of the four vultures found in Costa Rica. Its wattled head is brightly variegated with orange, yellow and black bare skin, and its bill is orange. The white undersides of the wings distinguish it in flight from other vultures.

We drove through the mountains, where the clouds were hanging low and coffee plantations lined the road. It was such a contrast to the tourist traps of Quepos and Jáco. We followed the bus to Quisarrá – and then the way was uncertain. I asked directions of seven or eight people and each one seemed to direct us to a different place. After apparently driving round in circles, we finally reached the Tropical Sciences Center in the valley of El General at about 2,500ft (822m). We knocked timidly on the door of a building at the entrance. A young man called Julio told us (much to my surprise) we would be able to meet Dr Skutch one hour later when his siesta was over.

We sat quietly near his old house, his home for nearly 60 years. *Finca Los Cusingos*, a modest wooden structure with green window frames, lacked electricity or telephone. Suddenly we saw the figure of a man bent double shuffle past. After a few minutes we entered his house and introduced ourselves. He sat at his desk, in a room lined with books and journals. Carefully and distinctively he signed my *Birds of Costa Rica*, the x in his first name

Alexander Skutch at 95 years

descending with a flourish. Then 95 years old, with neat silvery hair – certainly not sparse – and almost smooth skin, he told us that he had been a vegetarian from the age of 16. I (as a non-meat-eater) like to think that this accounted for his good health. He grew corn and yucca on his property.

Making us very welcome, he went off to find a banana. He invited us to sit on a green-painted wooden bench outside his house – and the banana set off his train of thought about how he became interested in birds. After achieving his doctorate in botany from John Hopkins University, he took off for Jamaica, Panama and Honduras to study banana crops for several years – and became totally fascinated by the avian gems around him. He did not want to leave Central America and in 1941 he purchased the 76 acres where he still resided.

Why was the property called *Los Cusingos*? I wanted to know. "Ah – that's another story!", he responded. "It is the local name of one of my favourite species, the handsome Fiery-billed Araçari. These small toucans are fascinating to watch and disprove the generally held view that birds do not play. On occasions I have watched them engage in a strange kind of contest. Two birds will perch, facing each other, then grasp the other's long bill until one is forced backwards and hangs momentarily beneath the branch. The defeated bird then withdraws and a third member of the flock comes forward to challenge the victor. The procedure is repeated: their bills are knocked together and grasped and they try to push each other off the perch. There is no aggression, no threats or pursuing the loser. It is just friendly sparring!"

As we watched the tanagers come in to feed, I reflected on the lifetime of unique experience that had resulted in such observations. The tanagers included Speckled, Golden-hooded and Western, also the Buff-throated Saltator, a large finch. Tanagers were his great favourites; he had found more than 200 nests of the Scarlet-rumped.

Dr Skutch told me about the birds and mammals associated with the red poró tree at Los Cusingos. "At the end of the rainy season", he said, "when the trees are dropping their leaves and flowering, the Orange-chinned Parakeets arrive early in the morning to breakfast on their nectar. Each bird will pluck a long, slender 'sword' [flower] then bite through the thick calyx [the flower sepals] and drop the flower to the ground. We used to have horses and they would eat the flowers if the cook did not first gather them to cook as a vegetable. The flowers that the parakeets missed were visited by Long-billed Star-throated Hummingbirds. As the seeds began to turn red the White-crowned Parrots came by. They removed the thick pods and ate the seeds."

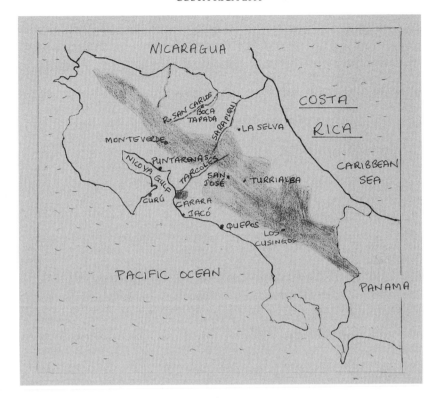

A casual visitor would look at the poró trees and see – just trees. His passion for and keen observation of nearly all living things was demonstrated in this simple story. I said "nearly all" because raptors were excluded from his beneficence. He tolerated the little Laughing Falcon because it eats snakes – but he hated the bird-eating species.

Then he told us a little about the personal side of his life. In 1950 he married Pamela Lancaster, a naturalist with whom he could share his passion for wildlife, and who was prepared to live in a house without running water until this modern convenience came to his isolated retreat in 1990. We were saddened to know that she was in hospital on the other side of the mountains and, due to high blood pressure, he was unable to travel there.

Sitting close to the house, watching the birds and listening to Dr Skutch reminiscing, somehow felt unreal. For one brief hour I was part of the history of this endearing and remarkable man,

77

once described as "one of the most famous unknown men in science" – known worldwide to ornithologists yet to comparatively few others. It was an occasion I will never forget and I feel deeply privileged to have met him. On my return I had received a letter from him, now carefully preserved, the product of a typewriter whose ribbon should probably have been changed several years previously! How thankful I was that he had not embraced the modern age. An e-mail would not have had the same cachet!

We headed back to Quepos, happy that our trip had been successful. But it was not over yet. About half an hour out of town we were halted by a short bridge at road level. It had been made from metal railway rails (not sleepers), most of which were not welded into position. The bars were prone to move, leaving a huge gap. Several vehicles were waiting to use this death trap. Fellow travellers put the metal bars back into position after each vehicle crossed over. Then they stuck part of a tree on the bridge to indicate that it was unsafe. I *walked* across – for fear of meeting a watery grave!

Update
Dr Skutch died four years after my visit, one week short of his 100th birthday. His seminal books will survive him to give future generations an insight into bird behaviour. His wife died in 2001.

Costa Rica bird statistics (year 2000):

Endangered 3
Vulnerable 10
Near-threatened 9

Species not previously mentioned:

Resplendent Quetzal (*Pharomachrus mocino*) NEAR THREATENED
Ferruginous Pygmy-Owl (*Glaucidium brasilianum*)
Black Vulture (*Coragyps atratus*)

Scarlet-rumped Tanager [*Passerinus*] (*Ramphocelus passerini costaricensis*),
Squirrel Cuckoo (*Piaya cayana*)
Golden-naped Woodpecker (*Melanerpes chrysauchen*)
Masked Tityra (*Tityra semifasciata*)
Orange-chinned or Tovi Parakeet (*Brotogeris jugularis*)
Black-bellied Whistling Duck (*Dendrocygna autumnalis*)
Elegant Tern (*Sterna elegans*)
King Vulture (*Sarcoramphus papa*)
Speckled Tanager (*Tangara guttata*)
Golden-hooded Tanager (*Tangara larvata*)
Western Tanager (*Piranga ludoviciana*)
Buff-throated Saltator (*Saltator maximus*)
Fiery-billed Araçari (*Pteroglossus frantzii*)
Long-billed Star-throated Hummingbird (*Heliomaster longirostris*)
White-crowned Parrot (*Pionus senilis*)
Crowned Woodnymph Hummingbird (*Thalurania colombica*)
Laughing Falcon (*Herpetotheres cachinnans*)

White-faced capuchin monkey (*Cebus capucinus*)
Red-backed squirrel monkey (*Saimiri oerstedii*)

Red poró tree (*Erythrina berteroana*)

7. Costa Rica 2000:

A Green Snake and an Orange Dragon

I had enjoyed my "taster" of Costa Rica so much that I went back in November of that year, flying in from Toronto, where I had been speaking at a convention. On arrival in San José, the representative of the tour company failed to meet me at the airport. It was dark and late and the place was bustling. It seemed threatening and unfriendly. I had to take a taxi to The Hampton Inn and the unsavoury-looking driver led me to a beaten up vehicle with no number plate. There was a woman inside. I asked suspiciously: "Are you a licensed taxi?" He showed me a piece of paper that could have been a parking ticket, for all I knew. I am not often scared but I was then. I had visions of them taking me somewhere, robbing me and dumping me. Or worse… Before we had even left the airport the driver hit another vehicle and laughed like a maniac. Five minutes later I was relieved to find myself in the welcoming atmosphere of the hotel.

At 8am next day the tour company's driver arrived to take me to Selva Verde Lodge where I would meet up with friends. Ron and Val, keen photographers, had already arrived from the UK. It took 50 minutes on crowded roads to crawl out of San José, past the shabby suburbs. We were heading for Puerto Viejo, near Chilamate in Heredia. Our progress was slowed by countless huge lories. One lay crumpled on an outcrop where it had fallen over the edge of the mountain road. The highway climbed up into the rainforest, literally into the clouds. Eventually we came out into brilliant sunshine where the forest was impressively high and dense.

Selva Verde Lodge, built in 1985, consists of individual lodges raised up amid dense vegetation. The tranquil grounds were crowded with exotic plants, such as the red ginger whose long waxen red bracts look like showy scarlet flowers. Reptiles were numerous: green iguanas, little basilisks and slender anoles. Crowned Woodnymph and Long-tailed Hermits fed at scarlet passionflowers. Unlike other hummingbirds, hermits are not territorial. They patrol a foraging line that might be one kilometre in length. The common Rufous-tailed Hummingbirds zoomed around the vivid red of shrimp plants. This species has a huge geographical range from central Mexico to western Ecuador, and an unusual altitudinal range from sea-level up to 8,200ft (2,500m).

After a delicious lunch we went to an area of the lodge grounds that had provided exceptional birdwatching that morning, with over 40 species. A flash of red proved to be the head of a gorgeous Red-capped Manakin. The male is a little gem, 4in (10cm) long, with short legs and bill and mainly black plumage. The display of manakins (see Chapter 13) is one of the wonders of the bird world and I wished I had seen more of him.

But now it was early afternoon and most birds were taking a siesta. Suddenly we heard a scream from high in a tree. Through binoculars a dramatic scene unfolded. A green parrot snake had captured a Clay-coloured Robin by the leg. The robin was flapping violently, trying to free itself from the snake's lethal grasp. Lots of birds, mainly smaller ones, also other robins, gathered around to see what was happening. The snake transferred its coils to the robin's neck. For minutes the poor bird thrashed about in vain. We were saddened that it took so long to die. Strangely enough, this common, dull-coloured species that looks like a brown Blackbird, is the national bird of Costa Rica. It is not even an endemic but it is well known.

Not far away stood a *pejibaye* or peach palm. This common introduced tree has a spiny trunk, and its large red fruits attract various birds. I saw the handsome Chestnut-mandibled Toucan swallowing them. Next day, at the same tree, a pair of White-crowned Parrots was feeding. These small, mainly green, parrots were soon frightened away by the fruit-eating Montezuma Oropendola, a large chestnut bird with yellow in the tail and a dagger-like beak. The woven, pendulous nests of oropendolas, a typical sight of the neotropics, could be seen in clusters, hanging from trees.

Small toucans in the form of Collared Araçaris, whose duetting calls carried long distances, were much in evidence. Their rumps and upper tail coverts flashed red as they flew. There were brief glimpses of Mealy Amazons, distinguished in flight by their large size and broad, rounded wings. In contrast, a Slaty-tailed Trogon sat quietly, as trogons do, waiting for insect prey. The male is a long-tailed beauty: vivid scarlet underparts and shining green head and breast. The female is grey above. Trogons excavate their own nests, usually in decaying tree trunks. Dr Skutch had observed a pair of these trogons at Los Cusingos. Suitable nest sites are so rare that the pair was attempting to excavate a nest hole amid the ferns, other epiphytes and accumulated debris just below the massive crown of feathery fronds of an African oil palm. Eventually they abandoned the site that probably swarmed with ants and other stinging creatures.

From the lodge it was only a 20-minute ride to the world-famous biological reserve at La Selva, founded in 1963 and operated by the Organization for Tropical Studies. We arrived at 8.30am to start a guided tour. These brief tours are good for people with no birdwatching experience but not always worthwhile for others; they start too late and in an assorted group of people you will find some who do not know how to watch wildlife and spoil it for the others. Two bored American teenagers fell into this category.

Crossing the swaying bridge into the reserve, we observed magnificent large iguanas resting in the trees, ready to splash into the river below at the first sign of danger. At 6ft (1.8m) long, full-grown adults are modern-day dragons, with a series of orange-brown spikes from nape to tail. The emerald green young are hardly recognisable as the same species, but they have a similar brown-banded tail pattern.

A fruiting fig tree was attracting many birds whereas inside the forest few were seen. A colourful and vocal exception was a Red-lored Amazon Parrot. The birds here are intermediate between the nominate race and the sub-species *salvini*. Handsome with their red foreheads, lilac-edged crown feathers and prominent area of white skin circling the eye, they are deeply suspicious of humans. Trapping them for the domestic pet trade (illegal) is rife and sadly is accepted by all.

Red-lored Amazon Parrot

The highlight was a Keel-billed Toucan (page 71) – whose multicoloured beak was reminiscent of pastel abstract art: soft skyblue below and yellow, orange and red above, complemented by the sulphur-yellow breast, black body and red under tail coverts. Toucans are fascinating birds to observe – gaudy, noisy and inquisitive. Recent research has revealed why the toucan's elongated bill is so useful. Filming these birds with heat-sensitive cameras showed that the bill is used to control body temperature by adjusting its blood flow. By opening or closing vessels in the beak, the bird can lose as little as 5% or as much as 100% of its body heat through the bill.

In contrast to the unmissable toucans were fleeting glimpses of agoutis, green poison-arrow frogs, and a huge blue and white damselfly. A hairy-legged tarantula waited at the entrance to its burrow. The hairs have a purpose: to detect the location and movement of their prey. Once captured, the unfortunate creature receives a lethal injection of venom which liquefies its internal organs, thus making it digestible for the spider.

The afternoon was memorable for a boat trip on the Sarapiqui (pronounced *sara-p-kee*) River. The three of us were the boat's only occupants and *Capitain* Carlos had eagle eyes. He swung the boat around when he caught sight of a spectacled caiman basking on a sandbank, and of two Northern Jacanas displaying at the water's edge, flashing yellow as they opened and closed their wings. An incredibly beautiful bright green lizard, the basilisk, was resting on the bank. Its form and colour were spellbinding. The shade varies from brown to green in individuals. Also called the Jesus Christ lizard, it has the ability to skim across the surface of water. It was exciting to see enormous green iguanas, the males almost orange when in breeding condition, close to the riverbank, usually stretched along a fallen branch. High up in the trees, mantled howler monkeys were moving about. This endangered species is blackish, so-called for its mantle of pale brown or chestnut hair on its back and sides. One female had a tiny baby clinging to her.

Carlos pointed out a three-toed sloth in a *Cecropia* tree, with big silvery leaves. Sloths hang upside down from branches and seldom come to the ground (except to defecate). Moving probably only a few feet in their entire lifetime, their speed is less than one sixth of a mile per hour. In Spanish the sloth is sometimes mockingly called *perico ligero* which translates as swift parakeet! I saw a female with a baby clinging to her in one *Cecropia* and another adult, perhaps the male, in the next.

It was a joy to watch the tiny, bluish-green Mangrove Swallows skimming and diving all around us. Small Amazon Kingfishers, green above and white below, sat quietly in the mangroves. Handsome Anhingas, with black and white wings hanging out to dry, were common riverside inhabitants. Slender birds with dagger-like bill, their facial skin becomes bright blue-green in breeding condition. A Boat-billed Heron, so called for its broad beak, stood solemnly on a branch overhanging the river. Reluctantly we ended this delightful relaxation, and the light was fading when we stepped onto the shore.

The key to successful birdwatching in the neotropics is to find a fruiting tree and to sit quietly and wait. In the hills above Tuis, at 3,000ft (900m) I observed a flock of about 30 Finsch's or Red-fronted Conures as they sped noisily by, to land in a fruiting *Inga* tree with bright green compound leaves. A young conure (easily identified by the narrow brown band on the forehead) clumsily removed the black seeds from the pod. An adult was eating the white pulp around the seeds. As suddenly as these parakeets had arrived, they departed *en masse*, as though at a given signal. Bright green specks, they sped off through the low clouds that were hiding the distant volcanoes.

I was watching the conures from the deck of a private house (east of Turrialba) in the Talamanca Mountains; it is famous among birders. This location was a three-hour drive from La Selva, through areas of little habitation and groves of bananas and up into the mountains, past coffee plantations. We had been shaken like jellies on the unmade road, the driver skilfully weaving around the potholes. The air grew cooler as we climbed higher until the driver pointed into the mountains and declared "Rancho Naturalista!"

On arrival we were greeted by the proprietress and by Matt Denton, a young bird guide from Oklahoma. We soon discovered two facts. The food was outstanding and Matt was extremely knowledgeable. We were offered delicious banana bread, hot from the oven, and hearts of palm. Apparently the Ticos (as the people of Costa Rica call themselves) have found a way to harvest hearts from the *pejibaye* palm without killing the tree.

It rained incessantly for the two full days we were there, pouring down unrelentingly. But all was not lost! Feeders on the balcony, bird tables down below and fruiting fig trees attracted an interesting range of visitors, whatever the weather. Eight of Costa Rica's nearly 60 species of hummingbirds included the widespread Green-crowned Brilliant, and the Green Thorntail with a narrow, stiff-looking tail held above the horizontal as he fed. The Green-breasted Mango with a purple tail, and the handsome and conspicuous White-necked Jacobin, with boldly marked blue, green and white plumage, were prominent at the feeders.

There is a special hummingbird here that everyone wants to see: the Snowcap. The most unforgettable bird I saw in Costa Rica, I gazed with delight at its diminutiveness and its extraordinary colour scheme. The male has a crown of the most dazzling white in nature; it might have been painted on! You would think that he had been flying among mountains with snowy-peaks and a blob of snow had fallen upon his head! His body is a unique wine-purple colour. At rest he tends to sit with his straight beak angled upwards like a thorn sticking out of a hawthorn branch.

A trip into the dripping forest below the house brought its rewards: two or three males buzzing around the feeders with several other species. It was an entrancing spectacle. We sat there for more than an hour, mesmerised by the buzzing and humming of these whizzing wonders. After spending most of the day watching rain falling, it lifted our spirits – but soon the rain recommenced.

Back at the house, the bird table was attracting velvety black and red Passerinus Tanagers (formerly called Scarlet-rumped) and Yellow-faced Grassquits, pretty little olive finches, who were feeding on rice on the bird table. Thirteen Grey-headed and one Black-faced Saltator were eating the bananas there. Countless colourful tanagers were hopping around. The handsome Black-cheeked Woodpecker also has a liking for fruit and sometimes visited the bird table. The male's red crown and nape distinguished him from the female. Both sexes have the wings and back pleasingly striped with black and white.

Ctenosaurs were common and ran about near the bird tables, probably hoping to pick up some tasty fruit. These big lizards

A boldly marked Ctenosaur

(genus *Ctenosaura*) are also called black iguanas but the colour is variable, including the handsome dark yellow specimens seen here.

One of the most remarkable creatures in the vicinity was an owl butterfly. I have often seen a member of the genus (*Caligo*) in butterfly houses but this was a different species with an extraordinary appearance: like the head of an owl peering through two brown leaves. Its visual mimicry was a true wonder of nature's art.

Sixteen parrot species occur in Costa Rica, of which the most flamboyant is the Scarlet Macaw. Deforestation and trapping have brought a huge reduction in its numbers in Central America. Dr Skutch had told me that when first he moved to Los Cusingos in the early 1940s, large flocks would pass overhead early in the morning, calling noisily, with the rising sun behind them. He said they had gone "decades ago".

This spectacular macaw is now rare near human habitation. A well-known place to see it is the Carara Biological Reserve, about 2½ hours from San José on a main highway. We stayed at the famous Tarcol Lodge, in the central Pacific coastal region, on the estuary of the river of that name. From the balcony we observed Black-necked Stilts and small waders feeding on the

Yellow-crowned Night Heron

sandbars. I watched a Wilson's Plover catch a small crab with its stout bill, and swallow it. Roseate Spoonbills fed on the mudflats, glowing pink in the early morning light. They were joined by White Ibis, flying down in shallow flapping flight on black and white wings. Yellow-crowned Night Herons in abundance – forty or so – stood solemnly surveying the scene. (Yellow crown is an exaggeration – buff would be more precise.) A grey and white Belted Kingfisher sat on a dead branch by the shore. Pelicans were visible on the horizon.

On the first afternoon, on the trail that led to the beach, a pair of Scarlet Macaws flew low overhead, their long tails fluttering like gaudy streamers. They shrieked their disapproval at seeing us on the newly-cut trail. Then they silently returned and, to my surprise, one of them perched low to observe us. I was on the balcony daily before 5.30am to watch the macaws leave their roosting site in the distant Guacalillo Mangrove Reserve. On the last morning 16 came streaming out together. Half an hour elapsed then two late-risers followed them. The flyway between the mangroves and Carara has made it possible to assess the population. The counts made between 1990 and 1995 revealed a decline.

At 10am a boatman took us into the mangroves, and turned into a small tributary. The squawking of macaws echoed through the forest. Through the trees we could see the scarlet plumage of a pair. They continually returned to the same tree, lunging with open wings and yelling at the trunk. We watched them for twenty minutes, uncertain as to what was going on. Perhaps a snake was threatening their nest...

In the forest not far from the lodge I noticed a most beautiful spider, illuminated by the sun in his large web. His body was spotted with red, yellow and black and his legs were striped with yellow and blue. When I was sitting quietly on a log, a little skink appeared on a nearby fallen tree. He had an olive-brown head, black body and short black tail that looked as though it was made of plastic. Slender lizards, with a prominent yellow stripe from head to tail tip, were running about in the leaf litter. They were Central American whiptails. Walking through the forest you see few reptiles, but sit soundlessly and watch and they will appear.

A striking forest inhabitant was a large woodpecker with a pointed crest like a red dunce's cap. It was the Lineated. His loud *weep weep weep weep* call rang through the trees. Like our Green Woodpecker, this species feeds mainly on ants.

On the waterfall trail three Crested Guans were moving about in the top of a tall tree and there was a fleeting glimpse of a Great Curassow, as big as a turkey, running along the forest floor. Both these cracids are hunted as game birds, especially curassows which are wary and difficult to observe. Heard but not seen, a Great Tinamou was calling its deep whistled notes, described as one of the most stirring sounds of the tropical forest. We stood under a tree where Scarlet Macaws had been feeding and picked up some brown seeds, like beans, on which they had fed. Dusk was falling as we left the forest to the happy, chuckling calls of Red-lored Amazons going to roost.

In the evening we stood on the bridge over the Tarcol River and watched the alligators below us. Dozens and dozens of them were lying, hardly submerged, in the muddy water at the river's edge. They reminded me of giant fat slugs. A solitary egret walked among them.

That night our American hostess, Kathy Erb, had generously prepared a wonderful Thanksgiving dinner. Next morning I departed alone for the Monteverde Cloud Forest in the Cordillera de Tilarán to the north. This is one of the most famous birdwatching sites in the neotropics. In 1972 scientists and local people collaborated to establish this 2,500-hectare reserve. Now owned by the Tropical Science Center, it supports more than 500 species of trees, 400 bird species, 300 orchids and one hundred mammal species. Additional nearby reserves now total more than 10,000 hectares. The celebrated Resplendent Quetzal is the reason why many people go to Monteverde. My friends had excellent views and photographic opportunities in early November, just before I arrived. Alas, by the end of November these gorgeous birds, the male with iridescent bluish-green plumage and one of the longest tails in the bird world, had almost certainly moved to lower elevations.

Passing fields of sugar cane and deforested slopes, it took three hours to reach Monteverde. Half of that time was spent on a bumpy dirt track, after leaving the Pan American Highway. It is rumoured that the road is so bad because local people want to deter visitors! When I arrived the rain was pouring down and my room was not ready. I changed into warmer clothes and went to the near-deserted hotel restaurant. An American couple told me about the atrocious weather. A fallen tree had cut off the power supply. They had been wet for three days, they said. Yes, we were in a cloud forest area that receives 4-5ft (120-150cm) of rain per annum!

Workmen were hammering and drilling all over the place, trying to repair the storm damage. The noise was like a construction site. Inside my room the howling wind was rattling the windows. The table was so rickety I had problems writing. I hated the place and made an instant decision! Taking my airline ticket with me I went to Reception and phoned American Airlines. For $100 I could change my flight and depart the next day. Relieved, I then went for a walk and saw a Brown-hooded Parrot – my first ever sighting of this species. As the sun finally emerged and struck the red and blue underside of the wings, its colours were breathtaking!

Early next morning I was watching a toucanet and some large dull-plumaged Brown Jays. At 7am I went with a small group of quiet and well-behaved people to the cloud forest at 5000ft (1,500m). The noisiest person was the guide who, three days previously, had used his scope to protect himself from a falling tree. His knowledge was botanical and bird identification was not his strong point. There were few birds about after the storm. The most striking were dark blue Azure Hooded Jays with the nape skyblue. Common Bush Tanagers, brown and greenish, and a couple of American Redstarts were searching for insects.

Despite my four layers of clothes, I was cold! The cloud forest is cooled by the high altitude and the mist that veils the sun. The lack of sunlight and the low temperature breed stunted trees, with a lower canopy, festooned with air plants and epiphytes that absorb moisture from the atmosphere. They don't need roots. Mosses, ferns and lichens grow from every surface, dripping in the mist that can give an eerie feel to the forest. Its dampness seeped into my bones. I hate cold damp.

After 3½ miserable hours, we came out into the open – a different world! It was like stepping from a grey winter's day on to a sun-drenched Mediterranean beach. Around the feeders there was a hive of whizzing hummingbirds. The colour! The speed! The ceaseless activity! There was every size from the large, gorgeous Violet Sabrewing with his shimmering amethyst plumage down to the tiny but aggressive Stripe-tail just 3¼ in (9.5cm) long. My heart leapt! The glittering emerald and violet of the male Purple-throated Woodnymph dazzled me and transformed the morning into something wonderful. I almost regretted the decision to leave and could have spent two days among these little gems.

This trip had not lived up to my expectations. The weather had been bad – but in November you take a chance. I had not seen the Great Green Macaw – but something much more important had happened. When I was at Selva Verde I had sought out Olivier Chassot and Guisselle Monge Arias who were devoting their lives to its conservation. Their story was one of desperation. After meeting them I resolved to help. Thus I returned to Costa Rica two years later – my mission accomplished.

Update

The Scarlet Macaw was the subject of intensive conservation efforts, starting in 1996. From 1990 to 1995 the count of three fly-routes from the mangrove roosting area to Carara National Park varied between 190 and 220 individuals. Between 1998 and 2006, numbers counted varied between 200 and 280. There was an increase and the population was deemed to be stable in 2007. Captive-bred Scarlet Macaws had been released at several sites and were doing well. Some were nesting and in 2008 young hand-reared at *Amigos de los Aves* near san José, fledged young of their own into the wild.

Species not previously mentioned:

Scarlet Macaw (*Ara macao*)
Long-tailed Hermit (*Phaethornis superciliosus*)
Red-capped Manakin (*Pipra mentalis*)

Clay-coloured Robin (*Turdus grayi*)
Chestnut-mandibled Toucan (*Ramphastos swainsonii*)
Montezuma Oropendola (*Psarocolius montezuma*)
Collared Araçari (*Pteroglossus torquatus*)
Mealy Amazon (*Amazona farinosa*)
Red-lored Amazon Parrot (*Amazona autumnalis*)
Keel-billed Toucan (*Ramphastos sulfuratus*)
Northern Jacana (*Jacana spinosa*)
Mangrove Swallow (*Tachycineta albilinea*)
Amazon Kingfisher (*Chloroceryle amazona*)
Anhinga (*Anhinga anhinga*)
Boat-billed Heron (*Cochlearius cochlearius*)
Finsch's or Red-fronted Conure (*Aratinga finschi*)
Green-crowned Brilliant (*Heliodoxa jacula henryi*)
Green Thorntail (*Discosura conversii*)
Green-breasted Mango (*Anthracothorax prevostii*)
White-necked Jacobin (*Florisuga mellivora*)
Snowcap Hummingbird (*Microchera albocoronata*)
Yellow-faced Grassquit (*Tiaris olivacea*)
Grey-headed Chachalaca (*Ortalis cinereiceps*)
Black-cheeked Woodpecker (*Melanerpes pucherani*)
Black-necked Stilt (*Himantopus mexicanus*)
Wilson's Plover (*Charadrius vociferus*)
White Ibis (*Eudocimus albus*)
Yellow-crowned Night Heron (*Nyctanassa violacea*)
Lineated Woodpecker (*Dryocopus lineatus*)
Crested Guan (*Penelope purpurascens*)
Great Curassow (*Crax rubra*) NEAR THREATENED
Great Tinamou (*Tinamus major*)
Brown-hooded Parrot (*Pionopsitta haematotis*)
Brown Jay (*Cyanocorax morio*)
Azure Hooded Jay (*Cyanolyca cucullata*)
Common Bush Tanager (*Chlorospingus ophthalmicus*)
American Redstart (*Setophaga ruticilla*)
Violet Sabrewing (*Campylopterus hemileucurus*)
Stripe-tail Hummingbird (*Eupherusa eximia*)
Purple-throated Woodnymph (*Thalurania colombica venusta*)

Green parrot snake (*Leptophis ahaetulla*)
Ctenosaur (*Ctenosaura similis*)

Mantled howler monkey (*Alouatta palliata)*
Basilisk (*Basiliscus basiliscus*)

Red mangrove tree (*Rhizophora harrisoni*)
Pejibaye or peach palm (*Bactris gasipaes*)
Red ginger (*Alpinia purpurata*)

8. Trinidad, 2001 and 2006:

Swamps, Turtles and Oilbirds

Just before sunset our boat came to rest within sight of a small tree-covered island. Settling in the treetops like vivid red blossoms, Scarlet Ibis were coming in to roost. I was in Trinidad's Caroni Swamp, watching its national bird. This important coastal wetland extends over 5,000 hectares and contains more than half of the island's mangroves, rooted in brackish water. Earlier I had climbed up an observation platform to view an extensive area of tidal lagoons, mangrove forests, and grass and sedge complex. It was revealing: from swamp-level, one has no comprehension of the immensity of the Caroni.

Now the ibis were coming in greater and greater numbers, the setting sun lighting up their wings as though they were on fire. The long-necked, curved-beaked, stream-lined silhouette in flight is unmistakable. There were big groups and small family parties, the young birds conspicuous in their brown and white plumage. They sped overhead, all going to the same small patch of mangroves, alternating wing beats with gliding. When perched, the brilliant, uniform scarlet makes them candidates for the title of the world's most colourful large bird. Much more intense than the colour of a flamingo, it is derived from the same food sources – crustaceans, including crabs.

The Scarlet Ibis occurs mainly along the coasts of the tropical (northern) part of South America, southwards to Colombia, also in Central America. In the Caroni swamp breeding usually starts in April and continues until August. The flimsy nests, containing the clutch of three dull green eggs, are packed closely together in the mangroves. In some parts of South America breeding colonies number thousands of pairs. However, their range has been reduced and existing populations are fragmented remnants of the formerly abundant species.

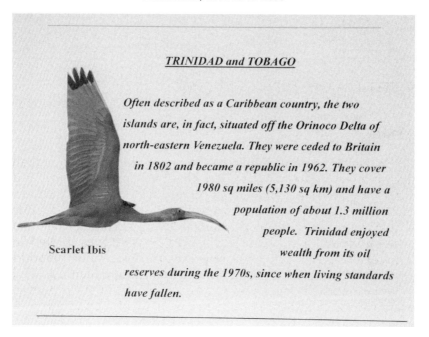

TRINIDAD and TOBAGO

Often described as a Caribbean country, the two islands are, in fact, situated off the Orinoco Delta of north-eastern Venezuela. They were ceded to Britain in 1802 and became a republic in 1962. They cover 1980 sq miles (5,130 sq km) and have a population of about 1.3 million people. Trinidad enjoyed wealth from its oil reserves during the 1970s, since when living standards have fallen.

Scarlet Ibis

The Caroni Swamp, on Trinidad's west coast, became a wildlife sanctuary in 1953 yet the 150-plus species of birds there are still not totally protected. Illegal hunting continues and, sadly, the coastal areas are polluted with industrial waste. But this is not apparent to the tourist, for whom Caroni continues to provide one of nature's most magical shows. Ibis numbers there have increased in recent years after three decades when breeding rarely occurred due to disturbance. But today the ibis's value as a tourist attraction has never been more obvious. Daily boat tours take nature lovers to see these brilliantly coloured birds flying in, making a glorious contrast to the blue of the sky.

If a poll were taken among birders of the best birdwatching spots in the neotropics, Trinidad and Tobago would surely be very close to the top. These two islands have the lot! They can boast a wide diversity of bird species, ease of watching them, beautiful scenery, and one of the world's most famous nature centres.

However, it was the Blue and Yellow Macaw that took me on my first visit to Trinidad in 2001. South of the chain of Caribbean islands, Trinidad lies only about nine miles (14km) off the coast of Venezuela. Strictly speaking, it is not a Caribbean island but a geological extension of South America. Its fauna reflects this with mammals that originated in the Amazon region – howler monkeys, agoutis and crab-eating raccoons. With nearly 400 bird species recorded, Trinidad exceeds the total of any island in the Caribbean region. Tobago, 21 miles (34km) to the north-east, is a detached piece of the Northern Range.

Due to its proximity to South America, Trinidad is the only island in the region where the Blue and Yellow Macaw was found. A few other islands had large species of macaws but sadly they are now extinct. This macaw was found in Nariva, a freshwater swamp in the central-eastern part of the island, five or six miles long and just inland from the coast. This vitally important habitat was declared a protected wetland under the Ramsar Convention in 1993*. It possesses characteristics found nowhere else on Trinidad and was formerly ideal habitat for a large parrot.

In the 1960s the macaw was trapped to extinction there. At the same time, 20% of the swamp, which covers about 23 square miles (60 sq km), was destroyed by rice farming. In September 1989 the part known as Bush Bush (about one quarter of its total) was declared a wildlife sanctuary.

In the early part of 2001 I read an article in an American magazine about a lady called Bernadette Plair. In 1992 she had conceived the idea of reintroducing the macaw to the Nariva swamp. She was born in Trinidad and when she left to attend college in 1963 the macaws were probably already gone. Bernadette became a scientist at Cincinnati Zoo; its support had been of crucial importance for the implementation of her idea. Consultation occurred with a forestry officer on Trinidad, and it was agreed to attempt the reintroduction to Bush Bush through Cincinnati Zoo's Centre for Research of Endangered Wildlife (CREW).

There were several difficult problems to overcome but finally, in August 1999, eighteen wild-caught Blue and Yellow Macaws

* The Convention on Wetlands, signed in Ramsar, Iran, in 1971. This treaty, with more than 150 participating countries, provides a framework for national action and co-operation for conserving the world's wetlands. It includes 1,832 sites, totalling 170 million hectares.

Trinidad

Bernadette Plair

from Guyana arrived at the quarantine aviary within the reserve. The macaws were fed on the foods they would find outside, such as the large seeds of mahoe. Some macaws could not be released for several months until their flight feathers had grown. Four of them would never fly due to the barbaric way trappers removed their flight feathers – with a machete.

I was so excited about Bernadette's vision to see macaws flying again in the swamp that I contacted her. She invited me to participate in her next visit to Trinidad. I arrived on May 17. Bernadette met me and I was immediately impressed by her quiet and pleasant determination. When she made up her mind to do something, she overcame any adversity.

She wasted no time in introducing me to the diverse habitats found within the Nariva swamp. We drove east from Port of Spain towards the Atlantic coast. Going south through the town of Sangre Grande the road runs parallel with the coast for six miles (10km), where cocorite palms on the beach bend towards the sea. Near Manzanilla we met three of the macaw "guardians" who had a boat waiting for us to traverse a narrow channel lined with mangroves. Tiny crabs scuttled about in the mud. As we emerged into the grassy marsh a small flock of Wattled Jacanas flew ahead of the boat, their yellow underwing coverts contrasting with the green of the reeds and grasses.

The eastern side consists of a palm swamp, with fragmented stands of stately smooth-trunked royal palms and moriche palms. The small Red-bellied Macaws, that were flying overhead, breed in their cavities, along with Yellow-fronted Amazons, and the more numerous Orange-winged Amazons. The larger fauna includes manatees and giant anaconda, but I was realistic: we would see neither. Caimans also live here, plus eleven species of snake, three of which are poisonous. We scanned the horizon, and the freshwater swamp, without any sign of Blue and Yellow Macaws. Only the wind-battered remains of the release aviary testified to their existence.

Several small, poor villages, lacking some of the most basic facilities, are found on the edge of the swamp: Plum Mitan to the north-west, Manzanilla to the east, Kernahan to the south-east and Biche to the west. The swamp camp near Plum Mitan, manned around the clock by a remarkable group of men, was our next destination. Originally unpaid fire fighters, the men, mainly of Asian origin, kept watch, night and day, over the area that the macaws inhabit, preventing entry by strangers. Between January and May 2001 they had clocked up a total of 8,640 man-hours.

Smoke was drifting over the impoverished area, thwarting Bernadette's idea of going up in a small plane to look for the macaws. Here there were a few wooden shacks, some raised up on stilts. The men had nothing but a roof over their head and their families, and I was touched by their dedication to the macaw project under their leader Bim Rampaul. They welcomed Bernadette and I and cooked us a delicious camp meal of cascadoo fish.

The good work of these men was soon rewarded when the first young macaws for nearly 40 years fledged into the swamp. Bernadette's dream was succeeding against all the odds. The macaws were so well protected that between 2001 and 2005 twenty-six young macaws fledged, numbers gradually increasing annually.

In the community centre in Plum Mitan, close to the swamp, I attended Bernadette's workshop and witnessed conservation education first hand. I visited the village school and met

The swamp men – guardians of the macaws

Marissa, an enthusiastic young teacher who had incorporated an environmental education programme into the curriculum in an imaginative way that made it fun. I was greatly impressed by this. Every morning 140 children assembled to listen to an authoritative talk on the swamp or on environmental issues.

We took our seats for a touching and tuneful performance. Pupils sang a song they had written about the swamp: a girl played steel drum and there was a boy on the keyboard. I was elated when I left the school, confident that the young generation of swamp people had pride in the habitat and in the macaw. I could not help wondering how many teachers in British schools would initiate a programme to emphasise the value of their own environment. These people were so much closer to nature than we are in Britain.

Everywhere we went Bernadette was recognised and greeted with hugs or waves of the hand. She loves her native island and its people and her family. When we visited her sister I realised how Bernadette's fine mind had led her to a much more affluent lifestyle and to bring up her children in a different, more material, world. But she returns to Trinidad regularly, doing much to promote the protection of its natural resources.

April 2006

In April 2006 I revisited Trinidad to spend three days with Bernadette. Our base was the exotic sounding Coconut Grove Beach Resort, basic and pleasant – and the food! The young male cook called Junior produced some of the best meals I have ever eaten. We dined on such dishes as salmon chowder, white fish cooked in tomato, and pumpkin rice and pigeon peas, all exquisitely flavoured.

By then there were four teams of macaw "guardians", totalling 24 men. On the first morning we met Shortman the boatman at 6.30am. Once again we visited Bush Bush. A kingfisher flew ahead of us as we navigated past the mangroves. Now and then a Pied Water-Tyrant flitted through the branches. When we disembarked after the short boat ride through the channel, the forest was dry underfoot. We walked on the trail, stopping to examine items eaten by parrots, such as the big, black mahoe seeds. High above us red howler monkeys fed while huge blue emperor butterflies seemed close enough to touch. This was the location of the first release site. Suddenly there was a shriek and a pair of Blue and Yellow Macaws flew overhead. In a second they were gone. But I had seen them!

As we left the area I saw a bird that looked like a Pied Water-Tyrant but it was all black with a white head. I was puzzled. In Kernahan, a settlement in the swamp that I had visited five years previously, I was pleasantly surprised to find a new research centre. Staff gave me leaflets and posters relating to the swamp. One poster depicted, among other species, a White-headed Marsh-Tyrant. Mystery solved! A fledgling eco-tourist industry was developing. Near the building a strong steel observation tower had been erected. We ascended to view the wide vista of the flat landscape and, far away, three blue macaws, tiny specks in a distant palm tree where they were feeding.

The following day Bernadette and I drove off at 7am – and soon encountered problems. At 3am protestors had felled four trees to block the road. One tree took the power line with it, which explained the lack of electricity or water in the hotel that morning. Local people had been protesting against the absence of a basic amenity, piped water, in this neglected part of the island. They had to draw their water from huge blue plastic water butts at the roadsides. Finally we got through, passing local service workers who had been sent out to clear the road. One beautiful old tree that had been cruelly felled was covered in orchids and epiphytes. Bernadette carefully collected the orchids to take them to a member of the orchid society. Trinidad has an amazing 700 species.

When we arrived at our destination Mr Motilal from Biche and his four macaw guardians were waiting for us. They took us into the western edge of the swamp. It looks like an area of long grass but is, in fact, treacherous terrain. Deviate a couple of paces from the path and you could be up to your waist in the water that lies just below the surface. It would be foolhardy for a stranger to enter the swamp alone. Bernadette told me that she and I were the only women ever to have ventured into this area!

Formerly a large part of the swamp was covered in forest but now only small patches survive. The area is dotted with little pools in which the much prized cascadoo fish are breeding. The men of Biche pointed out a distant stand of trees where one pair of macaws had a nest site. They told me about a place that they call "Parrotland". It is eight miles (13km) from the nearest human habitation and inaccessible during the wet season. It would dry out later in the year, allowing access. On some evenings hundreds of parrots fly in to roost there, including Red-bellied Macaws. When I mentioned that a recent report had given the number as 234, Mr Motilal laughed, saying that there were many more. Unrecorded in most literature, Hahn's, the smallest of all macaws, also exist there, along with Orange-winged and Yellow-fronted Amazons.

The earlier road closure delay meant it was now too hot and too late in the morning to see parrots, but to be in this remote landscape and to listen to these enthusiastic and knowledgeable men talk about the macaws was experience enough. Among the grasses, ferns and reeds, water buffalo grazed. They were introduced from Asia many years ago. The presence of these animals reminded the men to tell me the story of Mr Brysie

Boodhai who, for decades, had tended his buffalo in the swamp, coming out here alone to do so. One day in July 2005 he did not return. The area was searched and searched but his body was never found. Some conject that he had fallen victim to a boa constrictor – but the truth will never be known.

That afternoon Bernadette introduced me to Penelope Beckles, the Minister of Utilities and the Environment. She was charming and very interested in the project. The meeting resulted in the government agreeing to pay a stipend to the macaw guardians. Later that year the largest flock yet was seen – 18 Blue and Yellow Macaws flying over the swamp where their species had existed for millennia. The reintroduction of a parrot to a habitat where it was extirpated by man is difficult to achieve and rarely attempted. Education is a vital factor. Without Bernadette it would never have happened.

Back in 2001, I had stayed at the island's most famous bird-watching site, eight miles (12 km) north of the town of Arima. Overlooking the valley of the same name, in the mountains of Trinidad's Northern Range, is the Asa Wright Nature Centre. A former cocoa, coffee and citrus plantation, it was reverted to secondary forest and became renowned, worldwide, as a birding destination. This legendary place was established in 1967 to promote the conservation of the wildlife of the valley and to carry out research. Education is a strong priority; 4,000 children visit annually and there are lectures and internships. Abandoned cocoa and coffee estates have been purchased to return the land to tropical forest.

During the dry season (January to May) the weather is perfect, with temperatures between 65 and 86 deg F (18-30 deg C). Ten or so species of hummingbirds came to the feeders and attended the flowering shrubs in the gardens. They were greatly attracted to the powder puff tree, so named for its round pink or red pompom blossoms. Another flowering spectacular in the garden was the yellow poui – like a great cloud of sunshine! It was a huge mass of blossom. The leaves appear only after the flowers fall.

The most gorgeous hummingbird was the Tufted Coquette, a fairy-tale gem weighing 3g with rufous-red crest and bill and rufous feathers covered in iridescent green spots that are erected from the cheeks. Blue-headed Pionus Parrots and Channel-billed Toucans visited the taller trees from where the Bearded Bellbird called. It is hard to *see* this mainly white member of the cotinga family, with its brown head, and a beard consisting of a multitude of narrow wattles hanging under his beak.

The birds that fascinated me most were the tiny black and white White-bearded Manakins, only 4in (11cm) long. I was alerted to their presence by the cracking and clicking sounds made by displaying males. They gather in small groups, then one will fly down to his "court", an area he has cleared of leaves. I was mesmerised by what followed. The little bird whizzes between four or five points, travelling in straight lines like a mechanical toy, almost faster than the eye can follow. It is an astounding performance. There are few birds in the entire world that I would rather watch than manakins!

Perhaps the strangest I had ever seen was a cave-dwelling creature with the habits of a bat. One of the few accessible breeding caves of the Oilbird is within the grounds of the Asa Wright Centre. A guide took me there. It was an extraordinary sensation to enter the cave and, as my eyes gradually adjusted to the darkness, to make out shadowy forms on the ledges within. The Oilbird, the only nocturnal avian fruit-eater, has huge eyes, a narrow hooked upper mandible and long bristles on either side of the beak. The fruits of oil palms, apparently located by their smell, form the main part of its diet. A series of clicks and the echoes emitted by Oilbirds enable them to navigate in their dark world and to locate their nests of plant fibres.

Now the Oilbirds are safe but a century earlier it was a different story. Men with hooked poles would prod the nests until a suitable-sized chick fell out. It would be taken to a fire burning at the mouth of the cave and roasted to obtain the grease from the palm nuts on which it had been fed. This grease, stored in earthenware vessels for cooking, would keep one year without going rancid.

Trinidad can boast of yet another extraordinary wildlife spectacle. One evening Bernadette took me to Matura beach to witness the age-old annual happening: leatherback turtles coming ashore to lay. This Critically Endangered turtle is the world's most widespread reptile and one of the largest, weighing up to one and a half tons. It is a truly imposing animal. Unlike other turtles it lacks a bony shell; its carapace is covered in skin.

To watch a female brushing aside the sand with her flippers to make a pit and then to see her eggs, surrounded in fluid, falling into the pit, was an extraordinary experience. A couple of decades ago it seemed that the days of this ancient creature might be numbered. Thirty per cent of the defenceless turtles would be slaughtered while they were laying and their eggs would be taken. Now a dedicated group of people protect the turtles during this vitally important process, and we were in their company. They got together in 1990, with support from the Government, to stop the cruel practice that was driving the turtle towards extinction. The population had declined by a catastrophic 80% in ten years. Matura Beach is among the five most important breeding sites on earth – probably *the* most important. As many as 150 turtles might be seen during one April night, all safely depositing their eggs. The slaughter has been reduced to zero but they are still at risk from ingesting plastic bags eaten in mistake for their sole food – the jellyfish. Plastic is the curse of the oceans. It even kills albatross chicks on an island as remote as Midway in the Pacific. The parents feed plastic in mistake for jellyfish and the albatrosses – already endangered by long-line fishing – die. I have never understood why people continue to use literally billions of bags annually at supermarkets when they could take their own reusable ones.

Update 2008

Thirty-three young Blue and Yellow Macaws had fledged from eight breeding pairs, to give a total population of 59 birds. Trinidadians can be proud of what they have achieved.

Species not previously mentioned:

Scarlet Ibis (*Eudocimus ruber*)
Red-bellied Macaw (*Ara manilata*)
Orange-winged Amazon (*Amazona amazonica*)

Hahn's Macaw (*Diopsittaca nobilis nobilis*)
Tufted Coquette Hummingbird (*Lophornis ornatus*)
Bearded Bellbird (*Procnias averano*)
White-bearded Manakin (*Manacus manacus*)
Oilbird (*Steatornis caripensis*)
White-headed Marsh-Tyrant (*Arundinicola leucocephala*)

Leatherback turtle (*Dermochelys coriacea*)

Mahoe (*Sterculia caribaea*)
Royal palm (*Roystonea oleracea*)
Moriche palm (*Mauritia sentigera*)
Powder puff tree (*Calliandra inaquilatera*)
Yellow poui (*Tabebuia serratifolia*)

9. Tobago, 2001, 2006:

Easy Birding in the Sun

One can fly between islands on the Tobago Express. Tobago lies in the sparkling aquamarine ocean 21 miles (34km) north-east of Trinidad. This beautiful location is famed for its reefs and its bird life although, due to its small size, Tobago has just 230 species (compared with Trinidad's 400). In 2001 I spent a couple of days there with Bernadette, staying in the popular little town of Speyside on the north-east coast. I was quickly enchanted by the island, ablaze with the flame-coloured blossom of the flamboyant trees and blessed with endless hours of sunshine.

Just across the bay lies Little Tobago. We reached it on a glass-bottomed boat, observing corals and fish as they passed beneath us. Bernadette pointed out a house built into the rocky shoreline. "That's where Ian Fleming used to live", she told me. Fleming was so interested in birds that he called his most famous hero James Bond after a well-known ornithologist!

Little Tobago rises steeply out of the ocean, its craggy sides clothed in sea grape, palms and cactus. A reserve, with limited access, this is one of the most important seabird sanctuaries in the Caribbean. In 1898 Sir William Ingram purchased the 450-acre cotton plantation with conservation in mind – before the word had even been coined. The island was presented to the British government by his sons, after Sir William's death, on condition that it should forever remain a bird sanctuary.

We stood on a high point and watched elegant Red-billed Tropicbirds swooping below us on black-tipped white wings, their long white tail streamers floating behind them. In tangled vegetation within the roots of a tree, a female was brooding a feathered young one. We passed close by but they did not move. Here they were protected, with no reason to fear humans. In contrast the handsome Laughing Gulls, with grey-black head

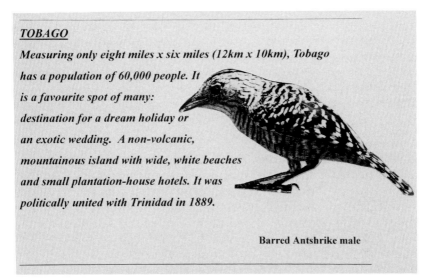

TOBAGO

Measuring only eight miles x six miles (12km x 10km), Tobago has a population of 60,000 people. It is a favourite spot of many: destination for a dream holiday or an exotic wedding. A non-volcanic, mountainous island with wide, white beaches and small plantation-house hotels. It was politically united with Trinidad in 1889.

Barred Antshrike male

during the breeding season, did not ignore our intrusion but protested loudly and aggressively, dive-bombing us repeatedly. Nearby was their nest, containing two brown-spotted eggs.

Close to the path was another incubating bird. Surrounded by leaves on the stony ground, her camouflage was truly remarkable. Look away and you could not find her again! She was a Common Potoo, mottled in shades of brown and buff, with black bristles on either side of her moth-catching beak. These nocturnal birds are closely related to nightjars.

Little Tobago was the site of a strange experiment in the early years of the 20th century. Sir William Ingram had acquired forty-seven Birds of Paradise from the Aru Islands in Indonesia. At the time he feared that the birds of paradise would be exterminated by the demands of the millinery trade. A hat decorated with the skin of one of these exotic creatures was the height of fashion. (Did the women who wore them have *no* compassion?) In the last years of the 19th century more than 50,000 birds of paradise had been killed for this purpose, and their skins exported to Europe. Even as late as 1911 more than 7,000 skins were exported from the German protectorate in New Guinea.

Reputedly Sir William had paid £1,000 for the birds and only £200 for the island! His intentions were good. It is said that some of these exotic survivors existed until 1963 when they were wiped out by Hurricane Flora. I find it extraordinary that they could have survived so long in habitat so different from the Aru Islands. Perhaps they fed on the fruits of palm trees and sea grape? The ruined cage dated from a post-hurricane reintroduction idea that fortunately never came to fruition.

The national bird of Tobago (not found on Trinidad) is the Rufous-vented Chachalaca, a large long-tailed fowl-like bird. Its raucous calls could be heard all over the island and, as the largest land species, it was very conspicuous. Its popular status does not protect it from being shot and eaten. The voices of the small group that dwelled around the hotel where I was staying echoed across the valley during daylight hours. Sometimes several were perched on the roof of the former sugar plantation

Red-crowned Woodpecker

Blue-crowned Motmot

house. On one occasion they were joined by a tiny young one. An adult plucked yellow flowers from a nearby tree and fed them to the chick. Chachalacas feed mainly on berries and young shoots – and could also be seen at the bird table, boldly helping themselves to leftovers from the kitchen.

In 2006 I stayed at the historic Arnos Vale Hotel in Plymouth, in the south of the island. Surrounded by coconut palms and tropical flowering trees, it is set into the lush vegetation of the hillside, overlooking the Caribbean Sea, a secluded sandy beach and a pristine coral reef. The location is idyllic.

Every birder who visits Tobago knows this hotel. It is famous for "tea with the birds". At 4pm the hummingbird feeders would be filled with sugar and water and the bird tables loaded up. The Bananaquits knew the hour. Within seconds the area behind the hotel, near the dining room, was alive with these little black and yellow birds that had been waiting patiently in nearby bushes. It was an avian rugby scrum, a dozen or more jostling for position. Even in the heat of the day the Bananaquits were busy, making their buzzing call notes as they flitted around, taking nectar. If you visit a hotel in the Caribbean and notice only one bird, this will probably be it – and it is most likely to be seen on a table, thieving sugar from a bowl or taking fruit from a plate!

Eared Doves monopolised the bird tables, squabbling among themselves and aggressively sending off other species. The most handsome diners were undoubtedly the Blue-crowned Motmots. The gorgeous blue and green plumage, the long tail and large size invariably drew gasps of delight from the guests. Motmots are unusual for the partly bare tail shaft. Sometimes there were five or six in evidence, patiently waiting an opportunity. They never used their size to bully other birds but flew in quickly, took some food and darted off. Their plumage repaid close inspection with its unusual black tear mark on the upper breast and dazzling turquoise and blue on the crown. They made low calls, reminding me of distant Ground Hornbills (in Africa). I saw one with an enormous black spider in its beak, just before it swallowed it.

At first I mistook the black male White-lined Tanager for a Shiny Cowbird – then I saw the flash of white as it flew. Its scientific name suggests that it was named from a female, who is an attractive rich-brown all over. The uninitiated would think they were different species.

Only the occasional hummingbird appeared before 5pm and most came an hour later. They did not enjoy competing with the rugby scrum! One of the larger species was the Black-throated Mango. Bronze-green above with black underparts and a purple tail, the male is very striking. As is usual with hummingbirds (except the hermits), the female is duller, in this case white below with a black stripe from chin to abdomen.

Arguably the most beautiful of Trinidad and Tobago's hummingbirds is the exquisite little Ruby Topaz, only 3½in (9cm) long. It is indeed a jewel! For a photographer trying to capture the ruby iridescence of the head and the golden topaz of the throat and upper breast, it presents an enormous challenge. In all hummingbirds, iridescence is apparent only when the light catches the feathers at a certain angle; on film you might capture one iridescent colour but not the other. These hummingbirds often perched on the feeder with the tail spread, showing the lovely chestnut feathers, tipped with black. The tail is the clue to identifying the female, who is white on the throat and underparts. Her chestnut tail is tipped with black and white.

Six species of hummingbirds are found in Tobago. One of the most common is the Copper-rumped. Both male and female are glittering emerald green, with a copper-coloured lower back and little white tufts on the thighs. The rarest, which I did not see, is the White-tailed Sabrewing. Hurricane Flora destroyed much of its forest habitat and it was slow to recover. The population has now stabilised and might be increasing.

Birds have a well-developed sense of time and a host of species would be waiting at the Arnos Vale Hotel in eager anticipation of a feast. At exactly 4pm a male Orange-winged Amazon, one of a pair, would zoom in from wherever he had been foraging and eye the plates of those taking tea. He would then fly on to the table of some unsuspecting guests and help himself imperiously to a fairy cake. He would proceed to sit at the same spot and consume the whole cake! I always felt the poor guests should have asked for a replacement!

The female would clip-clop along the terrace and climb the leg of a table where guests were eating. If they had not seen her coming there was some surprise when a little green head appeared over the edge of the table. It amused me to watch the reactions of different guests. These ranged from delight to caution or even fear and horror!

The male was full-winged and came and went as he pleased. The female, who seemed quite young, had one wing clipped. She had the sweetest temperament you could ever encounter. She liked to sit with me to have her head rubbed. No one could touch the male. He swaggered around, looking for mischief. Watching them together reinforced in my mind the difference in temperament that is typical of the sexes in Amazons. The male was much more assertive, the female more gentle and affectionate. She always wanted to preen the male, although sometimes he pushed her away quite roughly.

As the male was absent for long periods the female would amuse herself on the terrace, interacting with visitors or sitting quietly under an awning. I noticed that every day she would climb into a planter and take a little earth. She seemed to be eating it. One afternoon she nearly demolished a small bougainvillea, eating not only the pink "flowers" but breaking off the stems.

The female, or both Amazons, would share my breakfast. I would start off with papaya and croissants, both of which were greatly appreciated. The female enjoyed my omelette and beans and drank hugely from my glass of water. The male's favourite was scrambled egg. Hardly believing his luck, he rapidly swallowed great mouthfuls, no doubt believing he would be removed any minute (as the waiters normally did). But they could eat like kings at my table! Afterwards I did my best to clear up the chaos of their feast!

The Orange-wing is the most conspicuous parrot on both islands. Classified as a pest, landowners can shoot birds on their property. Sadly, it has earned this classification due to its liking for cultivated crops, especially cocoa, with its one inch (2.5cm) long beans. The very large dark red pod is thick and hard before ripening but the parrots relish the bitter green (unripe) seeds it contains. Other favoured food items are the fruit of the golden apple (Pomcaete) and the black seeds of the mahoe tree.

While in Trinidad I had the pleasure of meeting the renowned bird photographer Roger Neckles. His superb photographs line the walls of both airports. One depicted a lutino Orange-winged Amazon, that is, a yellow, red-eyed bird. It was a wonderful photograph! I asked Roger how he had obtained it. He had seen the lutino previously in a certain tree so he climbed the tree, then camouflaged himself with branches stuck in his belt and hat. His luck was in! The lutino returned and landed close by. Roger stayed motionless, suffering the stings of insects and the bites of mosquitoes. But he obtained two photographs before it flew off! He laughed at himself when he was recalling this episode. "Are these the antics of a perfectionist – or is it sheer madness, lunacy?"

Next morning the sky was just starting to lighten when the parrots exploded out of the forest, chortling and calling, flying over the road to the coastal side. More than thirty passed overhead during two or three minutes, their joyful Amazon calls filling the air. It was 6am on the edge of the Tobago Forest Reserve, an area that covers much of the island. This reserve was declared in 1764, shortly after Tobago came under British rule. Its central mountain range is the oldest protected reserve in the Western Hemisphere. But, explained my friend Wayne Gray, the forest is being cleared to grow bananas and plantains and the parrots are increasingly leaving its shelter to feed in gardens and plantations, especially on citrus and cocoa.

In the early 1990s a study sponsored by the International Tropical Timber Organization showed that almost none of the countries with tropical forest managed them sustainably. Trinidad and Tobago were exceptions. They realised the need to protect the forest reserves to prevent soil erosion and flooding and they had planted teak from Burma nearly a century earlier to provide a sustainable source of timber. Was the increasing human population placing all of this in jeopardy, I wondered?

We found a pair of Orange-wings perched in a *Cecropia* tree not far from the roadside. We moved gradually closer, to watch the male display in typical Amazon fashion, fanning his tail and chortling. To my surprise (for a species that is often persecuted), they seemed quite relaxed, preening themselves one minute, eyeing us the next. The sky was getting lighter. Now I could take photos. I could see that the Amazons' faces were dirty and I wondered on what they had been feeding. After ten minutes or so the male flew a few feet to sit beside the female, and they preened each other's heads, the male's "ruff" (longer nape feathers) standing up. The sun broke through and in the same instance they were up and away!

Knowing their fondness for the flowers of the mountain immortelle, Wayne drove to an area where the trees were in bloom. Immortelles are forest giants and the Amazons fed high, high above us, the sun catching the green of their plumage as they came in to land. It lit up the orange blossoms on which they were feeding and the brilliant orange of their wing feathers. This was Bloody Bay Road where an important battle was fought during colonial times. Here there were exquisite views over the rainforest of giant buttressed trees such as the kapok or cotton tree. Recognised by its thick trunk and creamy white flowers, the seed capsules contain the floss used to stuff pillows and upholstery. A sudden gust of wind brought down hundreds of leaves – and the parrots seemed to float with them.

The Amazons kept moving, rarely staying in the same tree for more than a few minutes. Wayne knew exactly where they would be at 8am. We drove to a cocoa plantation near Argyle Falls. The noise was loud! And there they all were in the tops of tall trees! Wayne pointed out the damage to the cocoa pods – so now I knew why the parrots had dirty faces. They eat ripe pods and green ones, also mangoes, even when they are green. No wonder they are not popular.

During the early morning or late afternoon a flock of these parrots visited the extensive grounds of my hotel. Wayne told me they usually fed on the huge red-orange blooms of the African tulip trees – but I never saw them there. This is one of my favourite tropical trees, widespread in the neotropics. I have seen various parrot species, down to sparrow-sized parrotlets (*Forpus*) feeding on them. The profusion of big, beautiful blooms on these trees can hardly be surpassed anywhere.

When the parrots did arrive they made so much noise I was immediately alerted. One morning I followed them, as best I could, for an hour and a half as they sampled various food sources. As the tops of the tallest trees were becoming sunlit, they ate the little seeds in the cones of casuarinas or ironwood – a favourite parrot food. Soon they were off again, shouting as they flew, then settling into a tree, most of them unseen. I might be watching five or six parrots but at an instant twenty or more would explode out from among the leaves. They stayed at length in a high tree with large, dangling seeds, swinging by one leg or leaning down from a slender, swaying twig to reach them. Sometimes a parrot would stop eating to fan his tail and converse with his mate.

Orange-winged Amazon eating pods of the immortelle

When the flock reached the immortelle tree it started to rain green beans. The beans fell thick and fast around my feet. The parrots were feeding on what looked exactly like French beans. Each pod contained two to six beans, nearly 1in (about 2cm) long. I removed one from a fallen pod that had been opened by a parrot. It tasted just like a fresh green pea. Here they fed for some minutes, nipping off a pod, opening it with deft bites on one side only, holding it in the foot and rapidly removing the beans.

Orange-winged Amazons are found in the northern part of South America, in Venezuela, Colombia, eastern Ecuador,

114

eastern Peru, northern Bolivia, the Guianas and Brazil. Their range extends over a larger area than probably any other Amazon parrot except the Mealy.

The grounds of the Arnos Vale hotel are large, hilly and attractive but what pleased me most was the deck attached to my room. By 10am it was too hot to do much but laze about, so I would sit there, overlooking the Caribbean ocean, watching the breakers foaming against the rocks and listening to the wind rustling the palm fronds and, in the distance, the faint calls of the Amazons. A huge immortelle tree, draped with gigantic bromeliads, would suddenly come alive with the twittering of Green-rumped Parrotlets whose light green plumage is decorated, in the male only, with violet-blue wing coverts. But, try as I might, I could not see them. They were invisible among the leaves – not much larger than a leaf and identical in colour. Giving their urgent double call note they would leave the tree and be out of sight in a fraction of a second. So fast! These tiny parrots (the equivalent in size and shape of lovebirds in Africa) are said to have been introduced to Trinidad and Tobago as there are no records of them occurring there before the 20th century. Their main stronghold is the northern part of South America.

The tree's branches overhung the ocean where leatherback turtles could be glimpsed in the depths. For me, this was paradise island. Its social problems (including at that time, the murder of tourists renting expensive villas) seemed oceans away. I could watch birds from dawn to dusk, feed them on my deck and gaze at hummingbirds hovering above colourful blooms, while the sun and the ocean's breeze alternately warmed and cooled me. I could not ask for more!

I would put crumbs on the deck or on the wooden railings and wait to see who would arrive. I looked forward most to the Barred Antshrikes. The male has a black crest and is completely barred with black and white. The female is a lovely cinnamon brown with brown crest and fawn head. These cheeky hook-billed characters, members of the antbird family, became my favourites, with their jaunty crests and confiding ways! They skulked around in ground cover but often flew up to my deck. Once the female flew towards me, plainly asking for food, as

Barred Antshrike female

there was none on the rail. I dropped a piece of bread at my feet and she took it and flew off.

The pair often went into a nearby shrub on a steep slope and I guessed that they had a nest there. After my absence of three days in Trinidad, I was delighted when the female came to the deck accompanied by a young bird, with similar plumage to her own. It was shy and stayed only a few seconds, resisting my attempts to photograph it. Several hours later the male appeared with the young one, but it quickly disappeared, much to my disappointment.

Three species of tanagers were much in evidence, flitting around in search of fruit, nectar and insects. The most confiding was the Palm Tanager, attired in shades of olive-green and brown. Probably the most widespread of all tanagers, it is found from Nicaragua to Paraguay. It nests around human dwellings, under the roofs of houses or in the crowns of the palm trees, and is a prominent visitor to bird tables. Throughout their range these tanagers are often seen in *Cecropia* trees where they feed on the catkins and fruits and search for insects among the underside of the leaves. Similar, except for its more retiring nature, is the Blue-grey Tanager. The Tobago birds are arguably the most beautiful with their indigo wing coverts, skyblue plumage and shiny black beak and eyes. A pair came to drink in the roof gutter just below my deck, and then helped themselves to crumbs offered on the wooden railing.

Most places in the neotropics can boast of more bird species but few are so accessible from the UK. After a nine and a half hour direct flight and a 35-minute drive, you can be sitting on a sun-drenched terrace with views of the sparkling Caribbean, surrounded by hummingbirds and motmots. What more could one ask?

Trinidad and Tobago bird statistics (year 2000)

Critically Endangered 1
Near-threatened 2

Species not previously mentioned:

Red-billed Tropicbird (*Phaethon aethereus*)
Common Potoo (*Nyctibius griseus*)
Rufous-vented Chachalaca (*Ortalis ruficauda*)
Eared Dove (*Zenaida auriculata*)
Blue-crowned Motmot (*Momotus momota*)
White-lined Tanager (*Tachyphonus rufus*)
Black-throated Mango Hummingbird (*Anthracocorax nigricollis*)
Copper-rumped Hummingbird (*Amazilia* [or *Saucerottia*] *tobaci tobaci*)
White-tailed Sabrewing Hummingbird (*Campylopterus ensipennis*)
Green-rumped Parrotlet (*Forpus passerinus viridissimus*)
Barred Antshrike (*Thamnophilus doliatus*)
Palm Tanager (*Thraupis palmarum*)

Flamboyant tree (*Delonix regia*)
Mountain immortelle (*Erythrina poeppigiana*)
Kapok or cotton tree (*Ceiba pentranda*)
African tulip tree (*Spathodea campanulata*)
Ironwood (*Casuarina equisetifolia*)

10. Ecuadorian Andes 2001:

Snow on the Equator and Hummingbird Heaven and Hell

The Equator is the imaginary circle around the earth, equidistant from the North and South poles. Associated with hot, tropical countries, it passes through Africa, Indonesia and South America. Yet in Ecuador – the Spanish word for equator – the volcanoes astride this line are so high, they are snow-capped for most of the year.

Ecuador is remarkable in many ways. Only twice the size of England, it shelters one sixth of all the world's birds. They evolved in an amazing diversity of habitats in only 0.75% of the earth's land surface. You can start the day birding in lowland rainforest, visit high elevation tundra and finish the evening in desert.

Robert Ridgely, the renowned American ornithologist whose two-volume *The Birds of Ecuador* was published in 2000, wrote: "Nowhere else is such incredible avian diversity found in such a small country". With more than 1,600 bird species, it has also been proposed as "the unrivalled centre of world birding" and "the Mecca for neotropical birds". Truly Ecuador is unique! I had to go there.

So, in 2001 I participated in a birdwatching tour. This was a new departure for me, usually an independent traveller. In a well-organised group, you see much more in a short time, aiming straight for the endemic species with the knowledge of local bird guides. An oddity among eleven people (plus tour leader), I was not a twitcher and I did not keep a life list. I was one of those strange beings for whom the enjoyment lies one hundred per cent in observation.

It was November. Our group flew via Miami to Quito, nestled in the Andes at 9,350ft (4,800m). The narrow hilly streets of Quito's old town are lined with small white houses with tiled roofs and little iron balconies. It boasts of 30 churches. Quito is ringed by volcanoes, including Cotopaxi, the highest active volcano on earth. To the south is Volcán Chimborazo, at 20,700ft (6,310m) the loftiest peak in Ecuador and, due to its situation on the Equator, the closest place to the sun on earth.

At 5am on the first morning, a quick look outside the hotel revealed the common Rufous-collared Sparrows, a honeyeater with the intriguing name of Cinereous Conebill and a spectacular Black-tailed Trainbearer in a nearby tree. The male of this hummingbird has a tail that accounts for about three-quarters of its total length of just over 10in (26cm). With its shining bronzy-green plumage and iridescent green gorget, it typified the beauty of the fifty-nine hummingbird species in the areas we passed through. Some of my companions saw in excess of forty of these! More than any other avian groups, hummingbirds and parrots are, for me, emblems of the neotropics, their sightings laced with excitement.

We climbed into the small red and white coach that was our means of transport for the next six days. Passing the airport, we saw colourful people along the perimeter, looking through the wire fence to wave goodbye to their loved ones. Pancho, the local guide, was very informative. He said one million

Ecuadorians live in Spain without the required permits, and work illegally. In Ecuador the wages are so low that families struggle to survive. Ten per cent of the nation's income is derived from money sent back by relatives overseas.

We drove from the Southern to the Northern Hemisphere, where the *Mitad del Mondo* (Middle of the World) monument marks the spot, then over the western ridge of the Andes. The scenery was arid; introduced umbrella trees had been planted on the eroded slopes. At nearly 13,000ft (3,900m) on the Nono road, with the snow-capped volcano Cayambe visible in the distance, our "target" species was the rare and local White-tailed Shrike Tyrant, an inhabitant of sparsely vegetated high altitude areas. The sighting of a single bird caused much excitement among those who kept a "life list" as, we were told, it had been seen by only a few hundred birders worldwide. A seemingly unremarkable little grey and white bird, its numbers have suffered a precipitous decline in recent years. At the same location, a Tufted Tit-Tyrant, intricately-marked in black and white, with long black crest and yellow abdomen, caused further excitement.

At our next stop we witnessed the poverty of a farming family. Their home was a single-story white-washed breeze-block house with a tin roof, in a tiny area enclosed by corrugated iron. The farmer was trying to plough the arid field with oxen. The ground was dust-dry. "What will they plant?", I asked Pancho, and he replied: "Maize to feed cattle."

The other members of our party were trying to identify distant brown specks; they turned out to be Ashy-breasted Sierra Finches and Plain-coloured Seedeaters. Near at hand a Southern Yellow Grosbeak singing in a dark green evergreen made a splash of sulphur against the bright blue sky. Eared Doves were perched above us and a large brown moth with two long tail streamers was nearly overlooked in the parched landscape. A Plain-breasted Hawk was flying over, scanning the ground for prey.

We passed through temperate forest where native bamboos and introduced eucalyptus stood together. The trail was tinder-dry, the roadside vegetation bore a thick layer of dust and the black shiny shoes of one member of our group (unusual footwear for a birdwatcher!) now resembled brown suede. The rain was two months late in coming and humans and bird life were equally affected. Birds were scarcer as a result. We saw the Rufous-naped Brush Finch, a member of a genus of larger finches that are found throughout the neotropics, and are mainly garbed in brown, black and white.

Further down the mountain it was much greener and its flanks were fully clothed. In the dense leaf cover we saw Red-headed Barbets, with orange-red head and breast and white collar, and softly coloured Plumbeous Pigeons feeding in a tree. I walked the path in a state of contentment. Lingering to look at the roadside shrubs and flowers, I was privileged to witness a sight the others missed. In a miniature rocky grotto in the mountain face, a tiny female Andean Emerald Hummingbird was taking a bath. Water was running down the grotto as she flew down to dip into it, returning to her perch (almost screened by vegetation) to preen. This enchanting little vignette was imprinted on my mind forever. Hummingbirds are rewarding subjects to observe because they show no fear of man, despite their frustrating tendency to zoom away just as you have them in your sights!

Each bend in the path opened up a fresh vista, the mountains towering above us on the left and a deep drop into the gorge below on the right. The banks were overgrown with ferns, bromeliads and vines that twisted here and there past tiny plants made more mysterious by my ignorance of their names. I looked with pleasure at everything that grew and this invoked in me a heightened interest in the world of plants that has delighted me ever since.

We continued our journey by road, past jagged mountain peaks, even the steepest of which bore scars of deforestation. Our next stop was at the remote home of a German lady, Barbara, and her American husband. They had turned their garden into an oasis for hummingbirds. Nineteen species, most of which we saw in the space of a few minutes, were attracted to the circular red nectar feeders. Among the most memorable were the Collared Inca, with its striking black and white plumage, the Booted Racquet-tail with snow-white leg puffs and ornate tail plumes, the Gorgeted Sunangel and the big Green Violet-ear. A male Long-tailed Sylph, with glittering green plumage and enormously lengthened shining blue tail (females have short tails), spurned the feeders and fed at a shrub covered in mauve flowers.

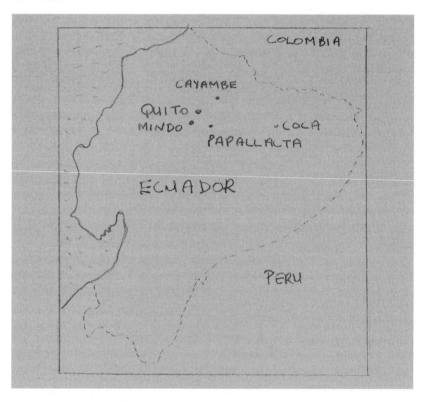

Ecuador is, without any doubt, the world's Capital of Hummingbirds. Of the 328 species (coincidentally, almost the same as the number of parrot species), 163 (50%!) have been recorded in Ecuador. Their breathtaking and fragile beauty always leaves me spellbound. Perhaps one day I will be able to sit and watch them for a week, without being dragged away to the next location!

Another hummingbird of north-west Ecuador, observed by our group, was the Hoary Puffleg whose small range is centred on the Equator. Mainly bronzy-green with white leg puffs, deforestation has caused a steep decline in its numbers. More than 40% of the Choco forests (those of southern Colombia and northern Ecuador) have been cleared or degraded and the surviving forests are rapidly being logged for settlements, mining, cattle grazing and the cultivation of oil palms also, of course, coca (for cocaine). Its future survival will be dependent on protected reserves.

When Barbara had finished refilling the numerous feeders with sugar and water, she told me that one White-tailed Hillstar – an endemic species – was so tame it would feed from a hand-held tube. Flower nectar, the main food of hummingbirds, is low in protein. A small amount of pollen (with a higher protein content) might be gathered but the main protein source is small insects. It has been calculated that most hummingbirds take nectar and insects in the ratio of 9:1.

We were in the Bellavista Cloud Forest Reserve, 600 hectares of knife-edged mountains and deep gorges. An attractive palm-thatched lodge at about 6,500ft (2,000m) in the lower montane forest was where we stayed. Here there were yet more hummers. The bronzy-green Buff-tailed Coronets visited feeders on the verandah. When taking nectar from flowers, hummingbirds of the Andes tend to cling to them; this is an energy-saving device more efficient than hovering. The Coronet sometimes also clings to tree trunks when searching for insects. It has the unusual habit of drinking sap from trees, at holes made by woodpeckers.

Another endemic, a White-whiskered Hermit, was feeding a few inches above the ground, inserting his red bill into red flowers. The hermits form a sub-family among the hummingbirds, consisting of 34 species. They are distinctive, all with a black patch through the eye, a white line above and/or below this patch and with little iridescence. Unlike other hummingbirds, hermits do not have territories and males gather at leks (communal display areas) to attract females.

Next morning we left Bellavista Lodge very early – too early to have enjoyed its wonderful location. I wish we had stayed longer. The main building was a stylish four-storey geodesic dome. I shared my room of varnished split bamboo construction, in a two-storey lodge, with Susan, a pleasant lady who had never been on an organised trip before and was quite apprehensive – needlessly, of course.

The morning was spent walking the old Nono-Mindo road that climbs up Pichincha volcano to an altitude of 11,000ft (3,400m) and then descends into the humid temperate and subtropical cloud forest of the West Andean Cordillera. The extraordinarily rich avifauna here is due to the fact that in the steep-sided valleys the flora changes with about every 200m of altitude, as do the species, thus the number of bird species found here rivals that of anywhere on earth. Starting to the north-west of Quito and almost traffic-free since the construction of a new road, this is perhaps the most famous area for bird-watching in the Ecuadorian Andes.

Unsuccessfully I looked out for Mercenary Parrots, Coral-billed Pionus and Lineolated (Barred) Parakeets that had been seen here during the previous November. The rest of the group were happily ticking off greenlets, vireos, various warblers and tanagers such as the Golden-hooded and Beryl-spangled. The beautiful Blue-winged Mountain Tanager lit up the bushes with his daffodil yellow underparts and crown, glossy black face and back and shiny blue wings and tail.

This area hosts species that are highly-sought by birdwatchers, such as the endemic Toucan Barbet. Named for its shorter but toucan-shaped yellow bill, this is one of the most charismatic of Ecuador's birds. Its multi-coloured plumage has a strong line of demarcation dividing the soft grey head from the red and yellow underparts. We were thrilled to find a pair – but their presence in a large tree was all too brief. Everyone crowded on to a tiny concrete platform overlooking a ravine for a glimpse but if you were at the back, all you saw were sunhats! Fortunately, this was not our only glimpse of this unusual beauty.

For me the most enjoyable sighting was that of a pair of Golden-headed Quetzals sitting calmly on a favoured perch, allowing prolonged observation. Lacking the long tail of the Resplendent Quetzal, the male is, nevertheless, an apparition of beauty with his scarlet underparts and gleaming green wings. Their bright appearance contrasted starkly with the poverty of the region. We were birding close to a tin-roofed shack, which was a typical family dwelling. Lines of washing hung outside in an untidy clearing. Living like this cannot be easy in the damp environment of the cloud forest.

We continued by coach to the little town of Mindo, at 4,000ft (1,250m) on the western slope of Pichincha. While the guides went to buy cold drinks, I walked along the main street, past its wooden houses, and into a little *Centro de Información*. Here a vivacious girl of 15 told me that she was a bird guide and that there were many Cocks of the Rock in the area. We stopped at a restaurant where Rufous-tailed Hummingbirds and White-whiskered Hermits were darting around the feeders. They simply mesmerised me and made my day!

The Mindo Gardens hotel, an attractive collection of cabins, rustic and comfortable, had been built five years previously to cater for birders. The setting, close to a stream, was beautiful. Fishtail palms, *Impatiens*, *Monstera* and tall forest trees crowded up to the lodge windows. When Susan and I walked into our room, my eye fell on a hand-painted cupboard depicting a Blue and Yellow Macaw. An oropendola design spilled down from the top. I coveted it! I looked out from my first floor abode straight into the face of a woodpecker! He eyed me cautiously and flew off.

A few metres away the rocky river with foaming white water was home to a bird with intricately marked plumage: the unique Sunbittern. The only member of its genus, we don't yet know what it is related to. It looks something like a brown heron – but is transformed in an instance. In threat display it appears many times larger, extending its wings and spreading its tail to resemble a fan of the most complex design imaginable. Marked with lines and spots of brown, buff and white, its primary and secondary wing feathers have large panels of chestnut brown and black, a theme that is reproduced near the tip of the tail.

Three beautiful Lemon-rumped Tanagers searched a tree for insects, the male glossy black and the females brownish above and yellow below. I noted the numerous intact hands of ripe palm fruits in the locality. One glance told me that there were no toucans or parrots here. Parrots peel off the outer orange flesh and toucans swallow the fruits whole and regurgitate the stones.

The intricately marked Sunbittern

That evening dinner was served to the group at a long table. I left the "chicken" to the others. I did not enlighten them that it was guinea-pig, farmed for the table. Talking to our friendly coach driver, Jorge, I discovered just how hard life is in Ecuador. Jorge worked twelve hours daily, seven days a week, earning the equivalent of US$40 (about £24 at that time). He was separated from his wife who lived in Italy with their two children. In Ecuador, schools sat for only three hours a day on two or three days a week. All the good teachers had gone overseas. The Government gave little help to poor families.

Next morning the noise of a chainsaw jarred over the sylvan sounds of small birds moving around and feeding. Five minutes later a crash reverberated through the forest. Another arboreal giant had been felled. Illegally, of course. I asked Jorge, if this was a protected reserve. Yes, he replied, this was part of the Bosque Protector Mindo-Nambillo set up in 1988 to preserve the subtropical and montane cloudforest – but men with chain saws came into the forest. There was no-one to stop them.

This is an IBA (Important Bird Area) and one of Ecuador's most famous locations for endemic birds due to the many small and unique areas of habitat. These are being eroded so fast that there is grave concern over their future. The forests around Mindo contain a higher number of species than anywhere else in Ecuador: 360 plus, including 33 hummingbirds.

A typical cloud forest dweller is the Green-crowned Brilliant. The glittering blue-green males prefer the middle strata and the canopy, whereas the females, white below, spotted with green, are more often seen feeding low down. They often perch on the conspicuous *Heliconia* in order to feed. Among the best known of all tropical plants, the "lobster-clawed" heliconia lights up the forest understorey with its large unusually-shaped red bracts. Many hummingbird species have slightly curved bills so that they can more readily take its nectar.

Next morning we departed at 5am for the threatened Choco forest which occurs in this area of north-western Ecuador and in south-western Colombia. Our first stop was a quarry near Maldonado. As we alighted from the coach a flock of a dozen Coral-billed Parrots flew over. This was to be my one and only sighting of this species, with muted green and greyish plumage which contrasts with the red bill and red under tail feathers. A Blue-headed Parrot was perched on a bare tree. I was elated with my first ever sighting of four distant Bronze-winged Parrots on a leafless branch. When they took off I discovered that there were at least eight. To see three *Pionus* parrots within five minutes helped to compensate for the scarcity of parrots thus far. This is an interesting genus, medium-sized, and distinguished by their scarlet under tail coverts. The Blue-headed is the most widespread (found over much of the northern half of South America) whereas the other two are mountain species with a limited range.

In quick succession came a handsome pair of Chestnut-mandibled Toucans, several Pale-mandibled Araçaris (smaller toucans) and – a first for this tour company – a Blue-chested Hummingbird.

When we arrived at our destination that morning we found a scene of devastation. The forest had gone in the four months since the tour guide had last been there. Oil palm seedlings were being planted in the newly cleared area. There were also mature oil palms and piles of harvested palm fruits. Sadly, this scene is

127

being repeated all over the tropics, at the ultimate cost of extinction for many species. The destruction was heartbreaking – but so was the poverty of the few people we saw. One family apparently lived in a room formed by a tarpaulin stretched over a frame. We spoke to the three mop-haired children. They had nothing but they were happy and friendly. I could not help contrasting them with children from wealthier societies who have so much and are always carping for more.

We sought the shade of a small forest patch in which to take a break and eat our sandwiches. Suddenly a group of Maroon-tailed Conures sped through the trees screeching *kree kree*. I scarcely had time to take in their dark green plumage, barred breast and the red bend of the wing. Parakeets of this genus are difficult to observe, being fast and wary and flying in tight formation. Unlike the *Aratinga* conures, more than a fleeting glimpse is exceptional.

Earlier the cloud had hung low for some hours but by midday it was very hot. We drove back the way we had come, through lush and degraded forests, past quarries and few settlements. High in the mountains at 5,900ft (1,800m) we were in the clouds

Poor but friendly, these children dwelt in forest recently cleared for oil palms.

again and stopped at a shack where there was a sign indicating an orchid reserve. We followed a steep trail up the cloud-shrouded side of the mountain clothed in tall, moss-covered trees. With the river burbling below, we stopped opposite a rocky outcrop and Pancho focused his telescope on a dark ravine.

When I looked through it, and my eye gradually adjusted to the shadowy view, I could scarcely believe what I was seeing. Here was a female Cock of the Rock, her reddish-brown plumage visible on top of the nest! The nest was in the apex of an inverted V-shaped rock, with a thick tangle of vegetation above and below it. What a privilege to see such a rare sight! I was enthralled. I wanted to feast my eyes on her and imprint the scene of my memory forever. Some other members of the group looked through the scope for a couple of seconds, and then walked away. I was surprised when one commented: "Anyone seeing a Cock of the Rock for the first time here would be very disappointed." For me it was the highlight of the tour thus far!

Our bird guide told us that this female had used the same site for the previous ten years, always laying two eggs – *twice* a year in June and November. Both hatch. He would see two little heads over the edge of the nest – but only one chick would survive. He assumed it was the same bird as her red-brown plumage deepened in colour each year. As in all cotingas, the male does not attend the nest so the female must depart every two hours to collect food.

We drove back into Quito to find the streets unusually quiet. Football fever had gripped the nation! Everyone was glued to their TV sets as Ecuador played Uruguay in their penultimate World Cup qualifier. They needed only a draw to reach their first ever World Cup final. A late equaliser for the home side sent the capital into a riot of colourful fiesta!

We had a 6am start next morning. The drive up over the eastern ridge of the Andes was spectacular with a view of the 19,342ft (5,897m) Cotopaxi. Its eruptions destroyed the town of Latacunga on several occasions, the last in 1877. The great German explorer and naturalist Alexander von Humboldt wrote in 1802: "Cotopaxi's shape is the most beautiful and regular of all the colossal peaks in the high Andes. It is a perfect cone covered with a thick blanket of snow which shines so brilliantly at sunset it seems detached from the azure of the sky."

Ecuador has a wealth of natural beauty but it is perhaps the volcanoes that etch themselves most indelibly on the memory.

On our first stop, in temperate forest at 10,500ft (3,200m) we saw an Andean Condor soaring high above us and heard the melodious calls of the Tawny Ant-Pitta. In the far distance Quito appeared as sprawling patches of white, dwarfed by the towering majesty of the brown slopes of the Andes.

The road wound its way over the Papallacta Pass. Here, in the páramo region, the hummingbird species changed along with the scenery. In stark contrast to the lushness of the cloud forest was the open tussocky grassland above the tree-line, dotted with low shrubs and giant puya bromeliads. The ground cover of tiny mosses and delicate little flowers was miniaturisation at its most exquisite. Here, in the Reserve Ecologica Cayambe-Coca, we seemed to be close to the snow-capped cone, stark white against the bleak green-brown of the stony ground and mountainsides. The daytime temperature does not rise much above 50 deg F (10 deg C), and the wind chill factor makes it feel a great deal colder. Frosts are common and brief snowfalls can occur.

Yet hummingbirds live here! A typical species is the Ecuadorian Hillstar, the male with purple head, olive green upperparts, snowy white underparts and white panels in the tail. Its comparatively large feet assist it in clinging to flowers when feeding. This species is found right up to the snow-line at 16,000ft (5,000m). At this altitude the spiky puya, a strange relative of the pineapple, is the only tall plant. One species, *Puya raimondii*, can grow up to 30ft (9m) high and is, reputedly, the world's largest herb. There can be as many as 8,000 flowers on a single stalk. This abundance explains how hummingbirds can survive in a region where nectar-producing plants are rare.

At night and during hailstorms the Hillstar roosts in caves and crevices. It is one of the miracles of nature than a tiny 8g bird can exist in such a harsh climate and survive icy nights. This would be impossible but for its ability to become torpid, a sort of overnight hibernation. In this state, a hummingbird's body temperature is adjusted to the ambient temperature, with a huge saving of energy.

We crossed the Papallacta Pass, at over 13,000ft (4,000m), one of the highest passes in the Andes. Leaving the coach for a while, headgear and thermal gloves gave some protection from the fierce, icy, howling wind while we searched for an elusive bird, the Rufous-bellied Seedsnipe. We were all elated to see a pair. All too soon they hurried away, walking down the slope. The beautiful intricacy of their markings was unexpected in this bleak yet haunting landscape. As we watched them, we were pelted with flying ice from the communication pylons. But that was a small price to pay! As our guide said: "Just think of the legions of birders who have spent fruitless, freezing oxygen-starved hours on this mountain to no avail!"

This was still the páramo zone, grey-green and windswept with low vegetation clinging to the mountainsides. Flanked by tussock-clothed mountains, the landscape unexpectedly revealed a lake. We scrambled down the hillside for a closer look.

The lake at 13,000ft within the Cayambe-Coca reserve

A little lower down was elfin forest, where the trees have twisted trunks and rarely grow above the height of a man. Growing on rocky slopes were small patches of gnarled *Polylepis* trees, once the predominant vegetation, now endangered throughout much of its wide range. A distinctive high altitude tree with flaky reddish-brown bark, we had seen only a couple of small remnant patches. A century ago *Polylepis* was felled to extract the resin used as a wood preservative. More recently the trees have been cut to make charcoal.

We drove on towards the town of Papallacta, where the hot springs brought fame to this otherwise unremarkable and bleak settlement. The hydro-electric plant provides power to the region and its pure waters are piped all the way to Quito. We spent an hour on a hillside where, shivering, I watched Turquoise Jays and studied the nearby town and the intrusive pipelines above us. I took an instant dislike to the place, described in our itinerary as "a paradise in the Andes".

Our accommodation was a collection of low wooden lodges situated around the hot thermal springs, connected by neat paths of crazy paving. The partly denuded mountainside loomed above us. It was very cold – almost as cold inside our room as outside. Eventually, still shivering, I went to reception and asked for a heater. Outside, in the fading light, the steam was rising from the "sculptured pools" (brochure talk) over the thatched roofs of the chalets. The pools were empty. Everyone had gone inside to shiver. I was thankful we were there for only one night. I wondered what it was like to be born in this town, at over 10,000ft (3,200m), and never to leave it.

Here I discovered how hard life can be for hummingbirds. When we walked into the lodge one of the workers handed our tour leader a Shining Sunbeam that had been lying on the floor. Unmoved, he placed it outside. I wrongly assumed that it had flown into a window and would fly off when recovered. However, it seemed that it was suffering from cold and hunger. Pancho and I made up a solution of sugar and water and fed the hummingbird from a plastic spoon. It drank an amazing amount.

As we placed it in a quiet spot to recover, I watched two more

Shining Sunbeams. One dived aggressively at the other, defending its food source, a puya. I watched the subordinate bird fly off and suddenly plummet from the sky to the ground. It sat there fluffed up, with eyes closed. Once again we administered a sugar solution. After 15 minutes or so both the hummers that we had tended flew off. The first seemed very strong but I had doubts about the survival of the second one, a male – sexed by the greater area of iridescent feathers on the rump.

The late afternoon was spent climbing up the freezing mountainside in search of the Sword-billed Hummingbird whose main food source is the long trumpet-shaped red and yellow flower of *Datura*. One glance showed that it was ideal habitat. The Sword-bill has evolved in synchrony with this plant and is probably its principal pollinator. Half of its total length of 9in (23cm) is made up of the long, straight bill, which must be longer in proportion to its body (50%) than that of any other bird in the world. The beak is so long that, when perched, the hummingbird's head must be tilted upwards in order to maintain balance.

Several of my companions had a split-second glimpse of a Sword-bill as it zoomed away. I was disappointed that such a wealth of flowering *Datura* had not produced a sighting for me. I did see a hummingbird that had learned to cheat the system. A Viridian Metal-tail was stealing nectar from the base of the flowers, possibly where a flowerpiercer (a tiny nectar-feeding bird) had already made a hole. The trumpet was by-passed, thus pollination did not occur.

I watched Hooded Siskins in a weedy area close to the hotel. With its sowthistle and dandelions, it was reminiscent of patches of waste ground in England. Nearby the river had attracted a characteristic species. A White-capped Dipper, with white head, mantle and underparts and brown wings, was perfectly camouflaged against brown rock washed by the foaming white water.

After leaving Papallacta we stopped for a brief glimpse of Torrent Ducks racing downstream. Not far away, at a lodge at Guango, the garden was a delight – alive with hummingbirds.

Tourmaline Sunangels and Mountain Velvet-breasts were darting about, feeding on flowers. One Sunangel was highly territorial, continually chasing away the Velvet-breast. She sat on a frond, her long beak pointing skywards, her white throat the only contrast to her brown plumage. Nearby a river reduced to a stream flowed over a boulder-strewn bed, with boulders piled high after a landslide, against a backdrop of steep forested mountain slopes and scattered dwellings.

I sat quietly in the garden, while the others went looking for more "new" species. I never tire of watching hummingbirds; their speed and beauty and extraordinary manoeuvrability seem to endow them with magical qualities. They dart from flower to flower almost faster than the human eye can follow. They spend only a split second at many flowers; some contain no nectar whilst others are dripping with the sweet liquid. The fact that a hummingbird has to visit a number of flowers before obtaining nectar increases the likelihood of pollination.

One of the rarest and most critically endangered birds of Ecuador is a hummingbird, the Black-breasted Puffleg. We were not far from its habitat, near Mindo, 8 miles (12km) west of Quito. Its entire world range consists of an area on the northern slopes of the active volcano Pichincha, and within 10 miles (17km) of the crater. It occurs in one of the few remaining areas of *Polylepis* forest.

Our lunch-time stop was enjoyed on a small bridge over the river, where the sun highlighted the green and yellow plumage of a Green Jay in flight. On the return journey to Quito the oil pipeline snaked along by the main road, a blot on the landscape. We passed a restaurant significantly named *Oro Negro*. Yes, oil is black gold to the Ecuadorian economy and the export of crude oil provides 45% of the country's income.

There were many small settlements with chickens running about and cows and sheep at pasture. A pair of white llamas with an appealing young one caught my eye. Everywhere there was evidence of road-making in the form of huge caterpillars and other machinery. A new road made a brown scar on the landscape. On one side cloud was floating like smoke; on the other was an ugly roadstone quarry.

The weather changed. Next day, departing from Quito at 6am, we found that the heavy overnight rain had turned the roads into a chaos of mud. We took the old Chiriboga road that descends the western slope of the Andes towards Santo Domingo, running alongside the pipeline and flanked by bamboo. We had glimpses into doorways of little shops, some with fruit arranged around the interior, or shabby little stores grandly called *supermercados*. The three-hour drive over the rough roads was uncomfortable. We were shaken violently in our seats as the wheels of our vehicle passed over large stones. Finally, we stopped at a small settlement where a few *Daturas* were growing alongside the road. Very soon a sought-after Sword-billed Hummingbird appeared. He sat quietly in a tree, quite high, and unperturbed by 11 people watching him from less than 6ft (1.8m) away. I was elated!

Through the lens, nothing more than a silhouette could be achieved, so when the rest of the group went in search of other species, I stayed to play a waiting game. This was the Sword-bill's territory – and he would be back. Sure enough, after about 20 minutes he returned. I saw him perched low in a thick hedge and then feeding at *Datura*, his long bill disappearing completely inside the trumpet-flower. It was a satisfying moment.

We continued by coach on the narrow road with spectacular mountain views. When we alighted to walk I pondered on the cloud-covered peaks and ridges, many of which have never been mapped. Passed down over the centuries is the story that the Incas hid their gold here when the Spanish conquistadors invaded. Optimistic treasure-hunters still search the region!

We found feathered treasures: a handsome Grass-Green Tanager, a rarely seen Plush-capped Finch, a gorgeous Powerful Woodpecker, a Black-crested Warbler attired in yellow with a V-shaped black crest, an Azara's Spinetail and then Tyrian Metal-tail and Hoary Puffleg Hummingbirds. Like a picture from a book, a pair of Rufous-naped Brush Finches (the male more colourful than the female) was perched on a moss-covered branch. Superciliaried Hemispingus, Scarlet-bellied Mountain Tanagers and a Plain-tailed Wren gave us good views as we climbed on foot, with low cloud hanging just above us. Down below, huge forest vistas, with the big leaves of *Cecropia* trees dotted silvery and conspicuous through the landscape, were indelibly printed on my mind.

Even looking at the ground was rewarding, to find delicate little flowers whose names will forever remain a mystery. Along the side of the path huge ferns with fronds 4ft (1.2m) long, small palms and shrubby plants, some visited by small butterflies, were of never-ending interest. I lingered where a waterfall splashed down a rock face; to the left was a beautiful and luxuriant growth of a plant with tiny red flowers. Above us the mountain towered, with bare slate-grey or dark brown face visible here and there, but mostly covered by profuse vegetation. Below us, on the left, was always a steep drop or a ravine. I was entranced by the landscape and saddened by evidence of slash and burn agriculture.

The road followed the oil pipeline most of the way and the pipeline followed the river. Sometimes it appeared as a gash, white or black, in the lush green of the forest. The river was burbling away over a stony or rocky floor – but I looked in vain for Torrent Ducks.

We had lunch on the coach, watching a Collared Inca Hummingbird visit some narrow, pendulous red flowers. Our next destination, one hour away, was to view something very, very special in the cloud forest at Guajalito. Leaving the coach we started to descend the mountainside in low scrub, following the oil pipeline at 6,600ft (2,000m). The going became steeper and more difficult. We turned into the forest from which the calls of a male Cock of the Rock had been resounding. It was then a short steep climb down a humus-covered slope to the lek area.

I saw a male immediately. He was only 15ft (4.5m) from me. I sat down to observe him confidently eyeing us, while other males called and danced not far away. Soon a second male appeared. Their beauty was breathtaking! It had a great emotional impact on me: my eyes filled with tears. There were perhaps eight or ten males dancing. I was held spellbound by the occasional flash of red as one flew off, soon to return.

We were permitted to watch them for only ten minutes.

Cameras were taboo. After the allotted time I reluctantly climbed up and away, silent and overflowing with emotion. As I rested by the pipeline I looked back to see a male fly into a *Cecropia* tree on the forest edge. He was eating a fruit. When he flew off two Toucan Barbets appeared! If only I could have lingered there...

The tour company had described Ecuador as "the richest birding experience on earth". It is surely the jewel in South America's ornithological crown – a jewel that even yet has not revealed all its riches!

Update

By 2005 the Black-breasted Puffleg was classified as Critically Endangered and declared the emblematic bird of Quito. In 2007 a small population was discovered in the 250 hectare Alaspungo Community Forest. In 2008, Aves&Conservación (BirdLife partner in Ecuador), with financial assistance from the UK Birdfair, published a Species Action Plan for this hummingbird. A&C started to train community members to provide guides and other services to eco-tourists. It was hoped to declare the forest a protected area, after some members had wanted to convert it to cattle pasture.

Ecuador bird statistics (year 2000). Includes Galapagos.

Critically Endangered 6 (now 7)
Endangered 13
Vulnerable 43
Near-threatened 46

Species not previously mentioned:

Rufous-collared Sparrow (*Zonotrichia capensis*)
Cinereous Conebill (*Conirostrum cinereum*)
Black-tailed Trainbearer (*Lesbia victoriae*)
White-tailed Shrike Tyrant (*Agriornis andicola*) VULNERABLE
Tufted Tit-Tyrant (*Anairetes parulus*)
Ashy-breasted Sierra Finch (*Phrygilus plebejus*)

Plain-coloured Seedeater (*Catamenia inornata*)
Southern Yellow Grosbeak (*Pheucticus chrysogaster*)
Rufous-naped Brush Finch (*Atlapetes rufinucha*)
Plain-breasted Hawk (*Accipiter ventralis*)
Red-headed Barbet (*Eubucco bourcierii*)
Plumbeous Pigeon (*Columba plumbea*)
Andean Emerald Hummingbird (*Amazilia franciae*)
Collared Inca (*Coeligena torquata*)
Booted Racquet-tail (*Ocreatus underwoodii*)
Gorgeted Sunangel (*Heliangelus strophianus*)
Green Violet-ear (*Colibri thalassinus*)
Long-tailed Sylph (*Aglaiocercus kingi*)
Hoary Puffleg (*Haplophaedia lugens*) NEAR THREATENED
Rufous-tailed Hummingbird (*Amazilia tzacatl*)
White-tailed Hillstar (*Urochroa bougueri*)
Buff-tailed Coronet (*Boissoneaua flavescens tinochlora*)
Green-crowned Brilliant (*Heliodoxa jacula*)
White-whiskered Hermit (*Phaethornis yaruqui*)
Mercenary Amazon Parrot (*Amazona mercenaria*)
Lineolated (Barred) Parrakeet (*Bolborhynchus lineola*)
Golden-hooded Tanager (*Tangara larvata*)
Beryl-spangled Tanager (*Tangara nigroviridis*)
Blue-winged Mountain Tanager (*Anisognathus somptuosus*)
Toucan Barbet (*Semnornis ramphastinus*) NEAR THREATENED
Golden-headed Quetzal (*Pharomachrus pavoninus*)
Sunbittern (*Eurypyga helias*)
Lemon-rumped Tanager (*Ramphocelus icteronotus*)
Coral-billed Parrot (*Pionus sordidus corallinus*)
Pale-mandibled Araçari (*Pteroglossus erythropygius*)
Blue-chested Hummingbird (*Amazilia amabilis*)
Maroon-tailed Conure (*Pyrrhura melanura souancei*)
Andean or Scarlet Cock of the Rock (*Rupicola peruviana*)
Tawny Ant-Pitta (*Grallaria quitensis*)
Ecuadorian Hillstar (*Oreotrochilus chimborazo jamesonii*)
Rufous-bellied Seedsnipe (*Attagis gayi*)
Turquoise Jay (*Cyanolyca turcosa*)
Shining Sunbeam (*Aglaeactis cupripennis*)
Sword-billed Hummingbird (*Ensifera ensifera*)
Viridian Metal-tail (*Metallura williami*)
Hooded Siskin (*Carduelis magellanicus*)
White-capped Dipper (*Cinclus leucocephalus*)
Torrent Duck (*Merganetta armata*)

Tourmaline Sunangel (*Heliangelus exortis*)
Black-breasted Puffleg (*Eriocnemis nigrivestis*) CRITICALLY
  ENDANGERED
Green Jay (*Cyanocorax yncas*)
Grass-Green Tanager (*Chlorornis riefferii*)
Plush-capped Finch (*Catamblyrhynchus diadema*)
Powerful Woodpecker (*Campephilus pollens*)
Black-crested Warbler (*Basileuterus nigrocristatus*)
Azara's Spinetail (*Synallaxis azarae*)
Superciliaried Hemispingus (*Hemispingus superciliaris*)
Scarlet-bellied Mountain Tanager (*Anisognathus igniventris*)
Plain-tailed Wren (*Thryothorus euophrys*)

11. Ecuador 2001:

The Amazon Revisited

The picture in front of me was breathtaking. It was a kaleidoscope of colour, an Oxford Street of activity: one of nature's most spectacular shows! My senses were almost overwhelmed, by the brilliant reds, blues and greens and the movement and the flurry of wings, and by the presence of 200 or 300 excited parrots of four species.

Most birdwatchers have experienced a moment of discovery that brought such intense pleasure, everything that followed seemed like an anti-climax. So it was in Ecuador when for the first time I watched the comings and goings of parrots at a clay lick. Parrots are seldom easy birds to observe. You see them one moment and the next they are gone. A clay lick is normally the only site at which you can watch hundreds during an hour or more, saturating your senses with their glorious colours, acrobatic manoevres and the constant chorus of their vocal accomplishments.

The vast Amazon rainforest covers 2.5 million square miles (6.5 million sq km). Two per cent of this forest lies within the borders of Ecuador, including the Yasuní National Park in the eastern Napo region. It was declared an International Biosphere Reserve in 1979 to maintain the forest as intact before oil companies could start prospecting. This was not successful as several companies operated inside, destroying habitat and polluting water supplies.

To reach this green paradise we had flown from Quito in a small plane, the quaintly named Icaro Express, after our exploration of the Andean birdlife. "El Coca" – the popular name for the town of Puerto Francisco de Orellana – is the gateway to Ecuador's Amazonian region which occupies about half of the country. It is an amazing fact that on his first expedition down the Amazon

<u>Neotropical rainforest</u>

One third of all the world's known bird species (nearly 10,000) live in the Amazon region. It contains 60% of the world's rainforests; one quarter has already been destroyed yet it still contains 30% of all the biological material on the planet. Forest captures carbon dioxide (the Amazon holds 60 billion to 90 billion tons, thus helps to reduce global warming) and to stabilise the world's climate. Rainforests generate rain. Without them, much rain would be lost into the sea. Many droughts can be blamed on deforestation.

Black-headed Caique

in 1542, the explorer Orellana wrote about a town on the Rio Negro that "stretched for fifteen miles without any space from house to house, which was a marvellous thing to behold." Within a century the city was gone, its occupants killed by diseases from Europe or fled back into the jungle.

Coca is so-called because of its geographical position at the confluence of the Rio Coca with the upper Napo and Payamino rivers. And the river is, of course, named after the most important plant in this part of the world, the source of cocaine (and of evil worldwide). The plant originated in the Amazon where it was cultivated by indigenous people who chew the leaves as a mild stimulant. So important was it that men were buried with bags of coca leaves to use in the afterlife. Two thousand years later many of us use the word "Coke" every day, not knowing that the popular drink Coca-Cola was originally made using the alkaloid cocaine in the leaves of the plant.

After disembarking from the aircraft, we climbed aboard an ancient, battered vehicle that looked like a cross between a coach and a lorry. The pot-holed streets and the shabby air belied the bustling town's recent affluence. It is no tourist resort but a place

Boarding the Icaro Express

you get out of as soon as possible. What was formerly a forgotten outpost assumed a sudden importance from the oil boom.

We awaited a motorised canoe to take us down the Rio Napo. On a spacious patio outside a restaurant I made friends with a Mealy Amazon. Big and heavy (but not overweight), he stepped on to my hand. His plumage was a light shade of green and his back was a silvery shade of grey. A prominent circle of white skin surrounded the huge, gentle, brown eyes. Looking at him it was not difficult to understand why the local people call the Mealy Amazon *loro real* (royal parrot or king parrot). Nearby three wing-clipped Orange-winged Amazons were sitting on a perch, typically aloof and uninviting but in good feather. Next to them was a cage containing two very young Cobalt-winged Parakeets and a container of rice and papaya.

The Mealy Amazon

Earlier five of these little green parakeets had sped by. They are the most numerous of the parrots of the region.

142

In proportion to its land area Ecuador (twice the size of England) has far more parrot species than any other country worldwide. There are thirty-nine: seven macaws, eight conures, 14 small parrots including parrotlets and caiques, four Pionus and six Amazons. The attraction of this area for birdwatchers was humorously illustrated by a cartoon painted on a riverside building. It showed a toucan examining, through a pair of binoculars, a motorboat full of tourists!

To be whisked away at speed towards the depth of the rainforest was exciting. But this was no pristine Eden. Our otherwise idyllic two-and-a-half hour journey was marred by the heavy presence of the oil industry – a ferry loaded with large vehicles, smaller boats of oil workers and a wire across the considerable width of the Napo from which flaglets were flying. Side by side with this evidence of the 21st century were scenes that have remained unchanged for centuries, the occasional picturesque thatched abodes of Quechua Indians surrounded by fishtail palms and, where the soil was fertile, evidence of cultivation of manioc and plantains.

Few birds were to be seen from the river – Weddell's or Dusky-headed Conure, a large White-throated Toucan perched and a distant Chestnut-eared Araçari in flight. The boatman, Marcello, skilfully navigated the dangerous channels, full of hidden sandbanks. When we reached our destination, we walked along a raised boardwalk above the seasonally flooded forest for half an hour or so. Then we transferred to small canoes (hand-carved from single tree trunks) and glided silently down a narrow creek with a profusion of aquatic vegetation on either side.

As we crossed the ancient ox-bow lake named Pilchicocha, dusk was approaching. Orange-winged Amazons were calling noisily from the *Mauritia* palms along the lake which was edged with reeds, grasses and ferns. Hoatzins, those strange, prehistoric-looking birds that subsist on leaves, were perched there. Caimans, electric eels and piranhas inhabited the brown waters. We had nothing to fear: contrary to popular legend, piranhas are mainly vegetarian and use their sharp teeth for cracking palm nuts! Soon Sacha Lodge came into view. Built of bamboo and thatch and totally surrounded by tall forest, it was reached via a short channel from the lake. Consisting of a reception area and

Sacha Lodge: the entrance

individual cabins just visible through the trees, its thatched roofs looked inviting, neat and well designed. On arrival we were greeted by a tame woolly monkey, holding an apple as big as his head.

Sacha receives about 1,200 visitors every year. The lodge is set within a 5,000-acre (13 square km) private reserve. A recent botanical study there had found 473 species of trees in only one hectare, probably a world record. The reserve is part of the Napo Pleistocene (approximately 20,000 BC) refuge, an area of rainforest believed to have survived the ice age, allowing species to thrive and diversify, generating scores of endemics. Extending over 545,000 hectares, Yasuni is Ecuador's largest national park. Sadly, less than 5% of the world's tropical forests are "protected" within national parks or reserves. This one is just 190 miles (305km) from Quito. The comparatively short distances one travels to experience contrasting ecosystems is part of the appeal of Ecuador.

The most luxurious lodge on the lower Rio Napo, Sacha can boast electricity until 10pm, and each cabin has its own bathroom and verandah, and is connected to the observation deck and dining room by a covered passage. Meals were announced with the calls of a bamboo horn. Excellent food was brought to the buffet table by smiling men in brightly coloured shirts. There was plenty of delicious fare to satisfy even a vegetarian. Amenities included a token library and an aquarium. In a little gift shop visitors could purchase items crafted by the Indians, thus contributing to the local economy, albeit in a small way.

Next morning at 5am we travelled half an hour downstream. As we drew towards the bank Amazon parrots were circling around and calling. We disembarked and our guide Richard, a pleasant young South African, led us to a hide at an angle to a steep bank. This was a clay lick, visited by parrots and other animals. Some researchers believe that that they do this to neutralise the toxins in the seeds and unripe fruits that they consume. The theory is that clay binds the toxins that are then evacuated from the body. However, Donald Brightsmith from Texas A & M University, who has spent more than a decade studying the parrots at the clay lick at the Tambopata Reserve in Peru, and analysing the soils, found that the soils consumed had at least ten times more sodium than the parrots ingested from other food sources. He said: "When we compared toxin adsorption and sodium to bird use, we found that the relationship between bird use and sodium was stronger, supporting my belief that sodium is driving birds to eat soil. However, I cannot rule out the toxin protection theory. More research is needed to tease apart these two theories."

The sodium theory is supported by a report of a flock of about 40 macaws (species not stated) on pasture taking the salt provided for cattle.

There are countless clay licks in the Amazon region, none more photographed than that at Tambopata, famous for its visits from large macaws and film crews. Most licks are inaccessible so relatively few people are privileged to witness what happens at one.

When we arrived at the hide, Dusky-headed Conures were landing on nearby trees. It was a few minutes before they plucked up the courage to descend on the left corner of the embankment. Amazons and Blue-headed Pionus were coming into the trees.

Eventually the Pionus, thirty plus, descended, together with more conures. They sought an area of the brown clay bank that had been "mined" over the years by busy beaks, leaving dips and overhangs in the face. A crescendo of calls was building as more Amazons flew around excitedly. The Pionus kept on coming, now about 60 in all, their scarlet under tail coverts and the Amazons' red wing speculums offering sudden flashes of intense colour among the greens and blues. Once on the bank, they nibbled at the clay. Yellow-fronted Amazons started to come down with the Pionus. One hundred or so Dusky-headed Conures had come in and some were still in the trees.

Mealy Amazons, with the light on their silvery backs, were flying into the trees and surveying the scene. Three or four perched together on an exposed branch just above and to the right of the bank, watching the activity below. Then one flew down. He was joined by more until there were eight or ten together, on the right side of the lick. The smaller parrots were on the left and the Yellow-fronted Amazons in the middle. Some of the conures, subordinate by virtue of their size, took clay by climbing up the left side of the bank. The other parrots favoured the central area. Only a relatively small area of clay seemed to be attractive to them.

Amazons and Blue-headed Pionus at the clay lick

146

By now my senses were saturated. It was a totally different kind of experience to watching, for example, a flock of 200 or 300 cockatoos in Australia, partly because of the intense activity, and because they were concentrated in a small area. At any moment I had expected a bird to take off in alarm, taking the whole lot with him. Suddenly something had frightened them – perhaps the threat of a predator – and most of the parrots flew, leaving only a few Pionus looking startled. Within seconds the others returned and continued to feed. Richard was humorously describing the scene in front of us as "a social gathering where the males are checking out the females. That male might be saying: 'Just look at the length of her tail feathers!'"

There were no big macaws here, unlike Tambopata, but the total newness of the scene (not previously exposed on film footage or in the *National Geographic*), was very appealing. Contentment washed over me like warm waves on a Caribbean beach. If I had come all that way just to visit the lick, it would have been worth it!

After the return canoe trip, I walked slowly through the forest with Bomba, the knowledgeable Quechua Indian guide, enjoying its beauty and diversity. He helped me to interpret what I was seeing. A pygmy marmoset, so small it could fit into an open hand, was climbing around a large tree trunk. Most unexpectedly we came across another small primate, the night monkey or douroucoli. With his huge owl-like eyes, black and white facial markings and brown fur, he made an appealing picture. This is the world's only truly nocturnal monkey.

Bomba showed us how the fish-tailed palm was used to make fibre for roofing. House piers and furniture are constructed from the trunk. We examined the understorey of palms, peppers and figs as he described the medicinal properties of native plants. One of them, called *sangre de drago* (dragon's blood) was used to heal cuts and wounds. Bomba struck the tree until red sap oozed out. I rubbed some of the sap into an infected insect bite on my leg. It worked! Next day the blistered area had gone and the wound had started to heal.

Bright colours, except for the scarlet of the heliconia, are not common in the forest. I came across an amazing flower on the trunk of a lichen- and moss-covered tree. It had a cascade of narrow orange-pinkish, pendulous blooms and, in its centre, sat a minute frog. Not two minutes later I caught a glimpse of a Wire-tailed Manakin, a tiny bird, and vividly coloured with red crown and nape, yellow face and underparts, black upperparts and white eyes. It is unexpected colourful avian sightings that make a walk through the rainforest such a delight.

When we saw Cobalt-winged Parakeets I asked Bomba where they nested. *"Siempre dentro las termitarias"*, he told me. Always in termites' nests. This is a habit shared by a number of small parrot species throughout the neotropics. The widespread and successful Cobalt-winged is a lowland species, found in the canopy and on the borders of humid forest, in partially cleared areas and in secondary woodland. At one clay lick far inside primary forest south of the Rio Napo, thousands of these parakeets have been seen. Their use of these sites varies throughout the year, perhaps according to weather conditions.

Eventually we reached a 5,000-year-old ox-bow lake, where the channel was narrow. Bomba paddled us in the canoe. It was serene and peaceful, gliding along, and hearing only unobtrusive songs, distant calls of wood quail, the buzz of insects and the occasional plop from the river. Minute orchids grew inches from the canoe's wake. There was a brief glimpse of a rufous and brown kingfisher with shining green upperparts.

It was dusk when we walked back through the forest with the aid of a lamp, stepping carefully over tree roots. We found the body of a freshly-killed oropendola in the place where earlier I had seen a bird of prey, probably a Roadside Hawk, glide silently overhead. Apparently his hunting had been successful. The Russet-backed Oropendola, usually found near water and common around settlements, benefits from the trees planted by settlers. I watched one feeding on a papaya tree, clinging to the trunk and gorging on the only orange (ripe) fruit of a large bunch. Oropendolas are large, conspicuous birds. Their woven pendant nests hung from branches like stockings that had been filled at the bottom. Their calls have been described as resembling giant drops of water *glug-glugging* out of a sink.

Two days later I visited another clay lick, smaller and less obvious, deeper inside the forest. We took a small open canoe during a rain shower and ran aground on a sandbank. Eventually landing on a muddy bank, we trekked through thick undergrowth. As soon as we reached the area visited by parrots, torrential rain commenced. Parrots do not descend when it is raining.

There were plenty of Cobalt-winged Parakeets, little more than silhouettes, in the tops of very tall trees. They were making a lot of noise. Suddenly Bomba exclaimed: "Orange-cheeked Parrots". (He did not speak English yet knew the names – no small feat.) I had never seen this beautiful species before. It was frustrating to know that dark shapes high above us were Barraband's Parrots, as they are also known. Not until the heavy rain stopped and the spotting scope was set up could I get a brief look at their smart black heads and orange cheeks, set off by the vivid white eye ring. Bomba said there were ten, all very active and vocal. I was envious that he did not need a scope. He had eyes like a hawk, a supreme example of someone who was finely attuned to the forest. Without his company I would have seen few birds.

Their calls alerted him. He became very attentive on hearing a small parrot that could not be located. It was a Scarlet-shouldered Parrotlet, he said. The *Touit* parrotlets are about 6in (15cm) in length, and this one is manly green with blue on forehead and wings. The male has a striking black-tipped red tail, with the central feathers green. The female's tail is all green. Little is known about this unobtrusive bird that lives in remote areas.

While waiting for the rain to stop, Bomba told me that his father formerly trapped Cobalt-winged Parakeets for the pet trade at this very spot. A brief sighting of four Blue and Yellow Macaws, high overhead, flying two and two in leisurely, majestic flight, prompted me to ask him about their numbers in years gone by. He said they were more numerous fifteen or twenty years ago. Large macaws are nowhere common near human habitation. Sightings had become rare, so unusual that for Richard, this was only his second observation in twelve months. The Blue and Yellow is the most common macaw species in the Ecuadorian Amazon, the Scarlet Macaw is classified as Near-threatened there and the Green-winged continues to decline. Only in pristine areas of forest will the latter two species be found.

We stopped by the landing stage before traversing the boardwalk. I heard a new sound and alerted Bomba who immediately exclaimed "Parrotlet!" A pair of Blue-winged was perched in the top of a tall tree, but soon departed. Bomba was surprised; parrotlets were not common there.

As a contrast to earthbound birdwatching, we were privileged to ascend a tower to observe canopy species. First light was the best time. At 6am we walked through the forest to a hillside where a huge kapok tree emerged above most other forest giants. Around its trunk was a sturdy wooden staircase of 126 steps, with several small balconies on the way up. Soon we were 141ft (43m) above ground. What a view over the surrounding sea of trees! Their canopies formed a mosaic of different shades of green, and different shapes at different heights.

The thicker branches of the taller trees were like miniature gardens, loaded down with fleshy-leaved bromeliads and other epiphytes. They supported many life forms, including tree frogs. A liana dangling from a nearby branch made a convenient vertical perch for a tiny pair of tanagers, Rufous-bellied Euphonias. The black and orange male and the brown female, like a little wren, were nest-building and carrying material. The handsome Many-banded Araçaris with boldly marked yellow and black toucan bill and underparts, seemed as curious about us as we were about them, approaching within a few feet. Tanagers, such as the Masked Crimson and Paradise, provided sudden and brilliant flashes of colour. In a single morning as many as 80 bird species had been seen from the canopy platform.

The vocalisations of a pair of Yellow-fronted Amazons were a joy to hear. They sounded so happy! I saw one land in the canopy, its wings momentarily displaying the red speculum. There was a brief glimpse of a pair of Blue-headed Pionus. A group of four Black-headed Caiques were feeding and flying around, their white breasts distinguishing them from other parrots. My camera caught one bird with wings spread like the mythical Phoenix. Often they sat at the top of a tree, exposed against the skyline, their shrill yapping calls echoing through the forest.

Thomas Marent, the renowned wildlife photographer, wrote: "Every rainforest is different, yet all have the power to overwhelm your senses with life's sheer intensity and raw beauty."

The phrase "overwhelm your senses" was, for me, never more true than here. My eyes feasted on the view and my ears were continually alert for bird sounds, such as the spluttering, bubbling vocalisations that accompanied the energetic display of the Yellow-rumped Cacique. Like oropendolas, they build their pendulous nests in colonies, often near vespiaries of aggressive bees or wasps. The insects defend their territories against intruders but accept their feathered neighbours. Oropendolas and caciques are conspicuous birds of character that cannot fail to be noticed by visitors to the Amazon rainforest.

The panoramic view from the platform was impressive, especially after the downpour. Then the sun came out, lighting up a hundred shades of green, from forest giants to miniature canopy gardens, with the Rio Napo glinting in the far distance. The pleasure of this observation was spoiled by the myriad small biting flies aiming at my eyes; my hair felt full of them. After a couple of hours the abundant insect life that followed the rain drove us down. The richness of insect species in the Amazon region is extraordinary. The chances are that eight out of ten of those you set eyes on in the canopy are unknown to science and have yet to be formally described. Earthbound species are better known.

Although this is one of the most species-rich environments on earth, one can walk through it and see very little that moves. It is not the dangerous place of travellers' tales, with snakes waiting to leap out at passers by or jaguars waiting to pounce. You would be very lucky indeed to see one of these big cats and snakes avoid humans. Much more dangerous are the trunks of trees covered in conical pointed spikes or army ants travelling along the forest floor. Finding birds is difficult, especially in areas where bird trapping has been heavy, and on a brief trip there is seldom time to sit and watch which, for me, is the most rewarding way to find birds.

Nevertheless, it is a fascinating experience to share their habitat. Listening to their calls, watching them flying, feeding and interacting with each other, offers an insight into the very essence of parrots and other birds. The lure of parrots in the wild draws me back to the tropics over and over again. It provides me with a satisfaction that is unlike any other and strengthens my desire to aid their conservation. Hopefully, other ecotourists will share that emotion and, in so doing, will visit this unique region, making it an economic resource valued above oil.

Update 2007
August 9 2007 report from Amazon Watch

Two months after the Government of Ecuador launched a pioneer proposal to save its most treasured national park from oil extraction, the international community is stepping up to support what could be a precedent setting victory for the environment and indigenous rights worldwide. **Yasuni National Park is the most biodiverse rainforest on the planet, boasting the most plant and animal species per acre found anywhere.** *Below the ground sits an estimated 1 billion barrels of oil whose revenue is seen as critical to Ecuador's export-led economy, but would only last 12 days according to current global consumption levels. The groundbreaking initiative seeks to keep the oil in the ground and still meet the country's fiscal responsibilities by obtaining financial compensation from the international community. Several hundred million dollars are needed over the next decade. Now governments, public and private sector donors, and international aid organizations are joining the cause.*

President Rafael Correa obtained a commitment from the United Nations and the Government of Spain last week for $4 million dollars. Norway has also committed support and funds, as has Italy and other countries within the EU. Even private companies, most looking to green their image, have approached the government with offers of significant financial contributions. On a trip this July to Ecuador, Trudie Styler, environmental advocate and wife of singer Sting, pronounced her support for the Yasuni proposal after an in person meeting with Vice President Lenin Moreno. She pledged financial *support from her foundation and made a commitment to promote the proposal and raise funds. Styler has made several trips to Ecuador to witness the impacts of oil extraction in the Ecuadorian Amazon at the hands of Texaco, now Chevron. Chevron is currently on trial for environmental damages caused during its two plus decades of operation in what was once pristine rainforest and indigenous homeland.*

In Ecuador, a national grassroots movement is emerging to support the government's innovative plan. Tens of thousands of signatures supporting the proposal from all of the country's provinces are creating a national mandate to save the park and keep the oil in the ground. Although the country's average monthly income only totals roughly $250 dollars, citizens are lining up to 'Buy a Barrel' of oil to preserve the crown jewel of Ecuador's Amazon.

In exchange for keeping its oil in the ground in Yasuni (there are proven reserves of 920 million barrels of petroleum), the Ecuadorian government has requested compensation of $350 million a year for ten years. Resource conservation and alternative energy could be the future sustainable source of Ecuador's national wealth. Yasuni and its rich biological diversity could be saved. This would be a giant step forward for Ecuador and perhaps for other areas of the tropics where similar plans might unfold.

Species not previously mentioned:

Cobalt-winged Parakeet (*Brotogeris cyanoptera*)
Chestnut-eared Araçari (*Pteroglossus castanotis*)
Wire-tailed Manakin (*Teleonema filicauda*)
Roadside Hawk (*Buteo magnirostris*)
Russet-backed Oropendola (*Psarocolius angustifrons*)
Orange-cheeked or Barraband's Parrot (*Pionopsitta barrabandi*)
Scarlet-shouldered Parrotlet (*Touit huetii*)
Blue-winged Parrotlet (*Forpus xanthopterygius crassirostris*)
Rufous-bellied Euphonia (*Euphonia rufiventris*)
Many-banded Araçari (*Pteroglossus pluricinctus*)
Masked Crimson Tanager (*Ramphocelus nigrogularis*)

Paradise Tanager (*Tangara chilensis*)
Black-headed Caique (*Pionites melanocephala*)

Woolly monkey (*Lagothrix lagothricha*)
Night monkey or douracouli (*Aotes vociferans*)
Pygmy marmoset (*Cebuella pygmaea*)

12. Costa Rica 2002:

The Great Green Macaw

George Powell was the key force behind the renowned Monteverde, one of the earliest and most important reserves in the neotropics. An American, he went to Monteverde in 1972 to study mixed flock behaviour in birds as part of his thesis. He realised the importance of conserving this unique cloud forest and raised the money to buy 300 acres. Today the reserve covers 26,000 acres.

In 1993 this forward-thinking man started a project to safeguard the Great Green or Buffon's Macaw. He believed passionately in the importance of the venture and invested a great deal of his own money in trying to save this majestic and neglected macaw. Olivier Chassot and Guisselle Monge Arias carried on his work. Funding from the international conservation organisations had been difficult to acquire, despite the fact that the project had built up the best database on individual wild macaws in existence. It had the information to save the species – but not the finance. This is what Guisselle and Olivier had told me when I met them briefly at the Selva Verde Lodge in November 2000. This young couple were such genuine, dedicated people and their whole lives revolved around the macaw and its future. I vowed to do something to help.

Found only in Central America and small areas of Colombia and Ecuador, only two other macaw species, both Critically Endangered, have a smaller range. Compared with the range of the Scarlet Macaw, that of the Great Green covers about 1/20th in area. Much had been made of the decline of the red species but the plight of the green one was virtually unknown. Its range had contracted with alarming speed; by 2002 the northern part of Costa Rica was the only area of that country that held breeding pairs, and the population was in the region of only 200 individuals. Satellite images revealed that about 35% of the forest in the breeding area was destroyed between 1986 and 1992. The macaw was in desperate trouble and there were no funds with which to save it.

On January 16 2001 I received the following message from George Powell: "We could not face giving up the project and felt certain that one of our dozen or so proposals sent out would bring in the desperately needed funds. But so far this has not happened and we have been forced to set January 31 as the date we will have to shut down the project if no funding is forthcoming."

My reaction to this was: "Over my dead body!" This magnificent macaw, the second largest, was edging towards extinction. Basically, no one cared because the bird was green! If it had been blue (like the iconic Hyacinthine Macaw), the whole conservation community would have been lining up with aid. I was determined to raise enough money to keep the project – and the Great Green Macaw – alive. I felt I could rely on the power of my pen to raise funds. I wrote articles that were published in avicultural magazines throughout the UK, Europe and the USA. The response from parrot keepers was overwhelming. More than $25,000 was raised in Europe and the USA. Further afield, in Australia, at Adelaide Zoo, two young Blue and Yellow Macaws raised more than £2000 in their first seven months of flying displays. The project was saved and the macaw's plight had gained world-wide attention.

In 2002 Guisselle and Olivier invited me to Costa Rica. By way of thanks, they would show me these imposing macaws in their natural environment. I arrived in San José on May 8. The following day I went with them to *El Centro Scientifico Tropical*. Olivier introduced me to the Director, Mario Buza. The father of the national parks system in Costa Rica, Mario told me how he was motivated to initiate such areas. "When I was a student", he said, "I won a scholarship to the USA, and while I was there I visited the Smokey Mountain National Park. I realised that if similar protected areas could be established in my own country the survival of many species would be safeguarded." This was in the 1970s when many countries in the neotropics had no protected areas. Olivier explained that the aim now was to found a new reserve in ithe Great Green Macaw's breeding

Left to right, Mario Buza, Guisselle Monge Arias and Olivier Chassot

range in northern Costa Rica, the Maquenque National Park, to cover 30,000 hectares.

My friend Marti Everett, working with a project to reintroduce to the wild captive-bred Scarlet Macaws, joined me when we set off with Guisselle and Olivier to Puerto Viejo, north of San José. In torrential rain we found a little back-packer's hotel; a double room cost $16. It was a scruffy building with a cavernous wooden canopy at the side where the restaurant was located, encircled by huge stands of bamboo. It had rained incessantly for four days and we were going to travel in an open boat...

Next morning, by some miracle, the rain had abated. We boarded our boat on the Sarapiqui River. It had a roof! At first we travelled slowly, looking for wildlife. Kingfishers were common and my eyes searched along the river margins for reptiles and other wildlife. The branches of a dead tree, now partly submerged, were bleached a ghostly white by the sun. A Rufescent Tiger Heron was using it as a perch. This distinctive species is intricately barred with brown and black.

I noticed the serious erosion of the riverbank. Cattle grazed at the water's edge, and pasture and plantations were close by.

There were a few small settlements, including one with a school and a clinic. The polluted river (with soapy bubbles) and despoiled habitat were depressing. We navigated first the Rio San Carlos and then after a couple of hours we reached the Rio San Juan which formed the border with Nicaragua. What a contrast – pristine forest! Untouched! Beautiful!

Feeling as though we had just turned back the clock several decades, we disembarked at a small wooden building on stilts to have our passports stamped. The border official needed to list our names and professions but being unable to understand the concept of someone who looked after animals for a living, he was totally confused by Marti's occupation! But he was pleasant. It cost $9 per person to enter Nicaragua. There was a bargain rate of $7 on weekdays! Nicaragua is Costa Rica's poor neighbour with a gross national income of only US$2,500 per person compared with US$8,500 for Costa Rica and a literacy rate of only 68% (95% for Costa Rica).

A local man arrived with a small boat and a plank was found to form a seat. We navigated a narrow channel, ducking to avoid the vegetation in this swampy area, with low palm trees and a large expanse of waterweed. A scene of untouched beauty was revealed. The channel opened into a beautiful lagoon inhabited by kingfishers and jacanas and a strange and endangered large prehistoric fish, the gaspar. We sat quietly in the boat and ate our lunch. It was so peaceful there. The lagoon seemed to have an ethereal quality and I wondered if Marti and I were the first

Great Green Macaw

NICARAGUA

The largest, also the least populated, republic of Central America, its population density is only 101 people per square mile, compared with Costa Rica's 195. Major export crops are coffee and cotton but this is a poor country. Politically, it is as volatile as its volcanoes. An earthquake destroyed the capital, Managua, in 1972.

tourists ever to visit it. This remote area would form part of the proposed national park. Olivier was enthusiastic about the future. "If we can start an ecotourism project here, it might eventually raise enough revenue to protect this pristine and important place", he said.

At 1pm we started on the return journey, huddled into our ponchos as the rain came down. We peered out at howler monkeys high above. Spectacled caiman, distinguished from crocodiles by their long, pointed snouts and by the large tooth that projects from each side of the jaw, abounded. This is the most common crocodilian species, able to live in fresh and saltwater.

We transferred back to the bigger boat and made a brief walk into the forest. A few Amazon parrots were chortling in the treetops or flying in distant pairs. Tiny strawberry poison-dart frogs with brilliant orange-scarlet bodies were hopping along the forest floor. Their blue feet give them their Spanish name: *rana con blue jeans*! Adults measure about 2in (5cm) long and we saw babies no bigger than a pea. These beautiful creatures belie their looks. They can produce a deadly poison in their skin glands, enough to paralyse a cat or a dog.

It was nearly 6pm when we arrived back at Puerto Viejo. It had stopped raining and during our absence the river level had fallen an amazing 6ft (2m). We collected our belongings from the hotel and set off for Boca Tapada, only stopping for a delicious meal of rice and prawns. At 10pm we reached La Laguna del Lagarto Lodge.

Set in 1,250 hectares (500 acres) of virgin tropical forest, this would have been an ideal place to linger, to enjoy the birdlife. Three hundred and fifty species have been identified there. Next morning I hurried outside and saw a Channel-billed Toucan close by in a bare-branched tree. Chestnut-mandibled Toucans came to the feeders. One took a piece of fruit and fed it to his mate. A pair of White-crowned Pionus Parrots was high above and Red-lored Amazons shrieked and chortled all around. The forest was close by and we had no time to explore, but the birding from the lodge was exciting enough!

Chestnut-mandibled Toucan

I had just sat down to breakfast when I glimpsed a Brown-hooded Parrot near the deck. I ran over with my camera and photographed a pair in poor light, excited because this was my first sustained look at the species. They were not in a hurry to leave and I watched them for a few minutes. When they took off, four were revealed. They came back later and one fed on a hand of bananas. This secretive parrot is normally hard to observe but here, encouraged by the "fast food", they were used to people. Found throughout Central America, mainly on the Caribbean side, they are just over 8in (21cm) long, and stocky in build with short tails. A palette of contrasting colours, the head is various shades of brown, the bend of the wing is violet-blue and the undersides of the wings are scarlet.

It was raining heavily at 8.30am when Olivier and Guisselle arrived with two Great Green Macaw project members. I was introduced to Ulysses Aleman as the man who knows more about *La Lapa Verde* (the green macaw) than anyone else. Cheerful, with laughing eyes, you could not help liking him. I asked him how long he had been studying the macaw. Eight years, he said. And how long had he known the species? Since 1989, was his reply. He and his colleague departed on quad bikes and we followed in a four-wheel-drive vehicle. A red dirt track took us out of the hotel grounds – and we were soon in trouble. The road was steep and rough and waterlogged. Out came the wheel chains to rescue us from the mire and assist us over the slippery mud in the torrential rain. We drove or slithered over bad sections of the track through secondary forest, inhabited by tapirs and peccaries, and past plantations of melina trees – grown for paper production.

Soon we were on cattle pasture. Huge felled trees, left where they had fallen, lay in paddocks. I asked Olivier why they had been cut down. "Because the people feel it is necessary to tame nature", he said. The wood had not even been used. It was an appalling sight for the trees included the endangered and "protected" *almendro* (almond) on which the Great Green Macaw relied for food and for nest sites.

We came to a stop several times to re-negotiate bad sections of the track. The rain was torrential. Eventually Olivier pointed out a large *almendro* tree; it contained the much-studied nest of a pair of Great Green Macaws. From a distance, I saw the pair fly in! Formerly used by Barn Owls, the nest was so small it was impossible for the young ones to exercise their wings inside. It was unusual for macaws to choose such a small hole, and in an isolated tree in the middle of pasture, with the forest not far away. Perhaps they could not find a more suitable nest.

Olivier knew what time the macaws would come. They are creatures of habit. We parked under a nearby tree and walked over to the nest. A young macaw was looking out of the nest spout! It was a thrilling moment! The feeling of satisfaction and camaraderie among the four members of the project was stimulating. A look of pure joy and elation had infused Guisselle's face when she saw the young macaw. Slender, dark and normally rather reserved, the anticipation that the Great Green Macaw population was about to increase by two, was a reward for the long hours and little financial return that she and Olivier endured. After a while the parent macaws entered the nest to feed the two young. When they emerged, they sat high in the huge tree, gently preening each other with their enormous black beaks. Through my binoculars I could see the band of bushy scarlet feathers covering the forehead and the almost bare pink skin of the cheeks decorated with lines of tiny black feathers.

Torrents of rain came down again and after an hour it drove us away. But I was elated, declaring it to be *"Un dia estupendo!"* I had felt deeply privileged to be there. The first youngster fledged the next day and the second soon after.

On the day following the nest tree experience I met Olivier and Guisselle at the British Embassy in San José, where they had an appointment with the Ambassador, Georgina Butler. Tall, blonde and oozing confidence, she had a keen mind and, fortunately, a great interest in conservation. They explained to her their proposal to establish a national park along the Nicaraguan border between the San Carlos and the Sarapiqui rivers. The park would be designed on the basis of the research findings, with a wildlife corridor that would connect it with 29 other protected areas in Costa Rica and Nicaragua, allowing macaws to migrate between protected breeding and non-breeding areas, within and outside Costa Rica. It would also preserve important species of fauna or flora, including the jaguar and the *almendro* tree. Miss Butler was clearly impressed. She gave us one hour and twenty minutes of her time and made some valuable suggestions.

The official meeting over, Marti and I decided to visit the Gold Museum. It was closed. Nearby I saw parakeets flying around the highest building near La Plaza de la Cultura. There were seven – landing on the top of six storeys of car parking, apartments and offices, or on the second highest balcony. The red under wing coverts indicated that they were Red-fronted or Finsch's Conures, probably escaped or unwanted "pets". I watched these parakeets with interest while Marti went to McDonalds for her longed-for burger and chips.

Next day we took the bus to Puntarenas on the Gulf of Nicoya, a two-hour journey. We were heading for the privately-owned Curú National Wildlife Refuge, on the Nicoya Peninsula. Marti worked for Amigo de las Aves, an organisation founded by a dedicated American couple, Richard and Margot Friseus. They started to breed Scarlet Macaws in the early 1980s and dreamed of releasing them back into the wild. Despite the many difficulties, they succeeded. Due to illegal trapping and habitat loss, the Scarlet Macaw had become extinct throughout much of its former range in Costa Rica. The first release, of 13 macaws, took place at Curú in 1999. Since then many more have flown free with the support of local and national conservation officials, at Curú and at other sites.

At Puntarenas we walked through the hot little town and boarded a boat. The sea crossing takes little more than sixty minutes and saves many hours on bad roads on the peninsula. When we disembarked a bus for Paquera took us near the

Scarlet Macaw at Curu

reserve. The guard let us in. The reserve has a small research centre and is known for its reintroduction of spider monkeys. There was dry forest here, hot and arid and inhabited by Orange-chinned Parakeets and white-faced capuchins. There were also cattle, for this was a working ranch.

Three years after the first release, Marti wanted to check on the macaws' condition. Two volunteers greeted us at the camp. With Tommy (from Sweden) I went to feed the macaws at 3pm. Some still came in for an afternoon feed of sunflower seeds! Eight swooped down from the palm trees, the afternoon sun lighting up their intense red and gold plumage. In flight the vivid skyblue of the rump and upper tail coverts and the bright blue wing feathers are visible. This truly is one of the world's most colourful and impressive birds, resulting in it being illegally trapped throughout its range. It is also killed for its gorgeous plumage. Each spectacular scarlet tail feather measures about 18in (45cm). They were in demand by some tribes, including Indians of the south-western states of the USA, for ceremonial costumes. One tribe in Panama would use as many as 65 Scarlet Macaw tail feathers in one headdress. Moulted feathers from captive macaws in the USA have, perhaps, reduced the demand.

Today many tourists in Costa Rica aim to locate these birds in the wild, whether or not they are birdwatchers. So here it was exciting to see the founding members of a new population of these magnificent birds.

We stayed in a hut. There were beds but no sheets, a shower but no towel, light bulbs but no electricity and, next day, taps but no water! I arose at first light and wandered down to the beach. The ocean-frontage of clean sand led to coconut palms, sea grape and flowering flamboyant trees with gorgeous orange blossoms. The little bay was rocky in parts and surrounded by dry forest. Many of the trees resembled greyish skeletons, without leaves in this season. A hummingbird was feeding high up on scarlet blossoms and White-tipped Doves were calling their mournful tunes.

Enticing odours from the kitchen of the research area called me to breakfast for the tasty beans and rice, lightly spiced with herbs. Marti and Tommy declared that they were "starving to death" and snacked on biscuits! No one expected them to eat *chivo* (goat) but they rejected the beans and rice that are usually on the menu in Central America.

That morning we visited a large kapok tree where a pair of the released macaws were nesting. This was good news indeed, proof that former captive birds could breed successfully. The nest entrance was located at a height of about 60ft (18m). One scarlet beauty was hanging downwards out of the entrance and took its time climbing back in.

Later I walked on a trail, on a bridge over the mangroves and through the tall trees of the dry forest – which has less biodiversity than rainforest. Nevertheless, despite the reserve's small size of 87 hectares, more than 200 bird species, about 80 species of mammals and 87 of reptiles have been recorded there. Handsome ctenosaurs, the large boldly striped lizards, abounded. I avoided eye contact with a tame released capuchin in the trees above. Such monkeys can be dangerous. A tame coati, friendly but untrustworthy, was also a menace. Now I understood why meals were taken inside a cage of welded mesh!

We were lucky to get a lift to the boat leaving for Puntarenas at midday, where we disembarked and walked through the dusty little town. The bus was just pulling out as we jumped on. I still had my purse in my hand and foolishly put it into my bag. A "kind" fellow helped me to put my bag on the rack. The jolting of the bus caused it to move towards the back of the bus – perhaps assisted by a human hand. When I got off I found that he had emptied my purse of about £60 and removed a 300mm lens and my binoculars. Both the latter were worn-out and needed replacing so I was not too bothered. That was the only occasion in my entire travels that I was ever robbed and I had only myself to blame!

Update

On April 26 2003 Environment Minister Carlos Rodriguez signed an Executive Decree that would lay the groundwork for the Maquenque National Park. Approximately $10 million had been raised towards its estimated $25 million price tag. To date, 2009, the park does not yet exist. It is worth noting that 26% of national territory was by then protected in parks and reserves but the northern lowland tropical forests, so important to the Great Green Macaw, were not included.

In 2008, and again in 2009, released Scarlet Macaws, hand-reared at Amigo de las Aves, fledged young of their own into the wild – hopefully the first of many generations. Sadly, Margot Friseus died at the age of 88.

Species not previously mentioned:

Great Green or Buffon's Macaw (*Ara ambigua*)
  VULNERABLE
Rufescent Tiger Heron (*Tigrisoma lineatum*)
Channel-billed Toucan (*Ramphastos vitellinus*)
Barn Owl (*Tyto alba*)
White-tipped Dove (*Leptotila verreauxi*)

Gaspar (*Atractosteus tropicus*)
Spectacled caiman (*Caiman crocodilus*)
Strawberry poison-dart frog (*Dendrobates pumilio*)

Almendro tree (*Dipteryx panamensis*)

13. Panama 2003:

Marvellous Manakins

Panama has been described as a land bridge where the fauna of North and South America meet and intermingle. Due to this position its avifauna is large: approximately 900 species. For millions of years the two areas were divided by hundreds of miles of ocean and their fauna took different evolutionary paths. Then twenty million years ago geological upheaval brought the two together; volcanoes were thrust up and mountains appeared. Central America was formed: a turbulent region where volcanoes are never far away, except in the eastern part of Panama where the isthmus is at its most narrow. This is where the canal was built.

In 1524 King Carlos of Spain came up with the idea of joining the Caribbean and Pacific oceans – but the technology did not exist. It was not until 1903 that the USA purchased the rights to build the 40-mile (64km) long canal. Completed in 1914, this masterpiece of engineering technology might never be surpassed. I defy anyone not to watch with fascination the process by which a ship, guided by two steam engines on the banks, passes through the locks. In the 17-hour process 200 million litres of water flow out to sea and the ship is saved the three weeks it would take to circumnavigate South America.

The forest of the Soberiana National Park surrounding the canal acts as a giant sponge, soaking up rainwater and releasing it at a steady rate throughout the year. A drastic drop in water level occurred for the first time in the late 1970s due to illegal destruction of the forest at the rate of about 11 to 19 square miles (30 to 50 sq km) per annum.

There was no money to implement the 1987 law that forbids the felling of trees. The economic impact of this was enormous. By 1994 the drop in the water level meant that the largest ships

PANAMA

The easternmost country in the isthmus of Central America, with the highest standard of living, Panama was part of Colombia until 1903. The canal was built at the narrowest point of the isthmus where only 36 miles (58km) separates the Caribbean Sea from the Pacific Ocean. Panama extends over 20,000 sq miles (77,000 sq km). The major export trade is in bananas. Within the neotropics, it shares with Belize and the Guianas the distinction of having only one endangered bird species.   Harpy Eagle

were being turned away, losing US$350 million per annum in canal tolls.

In January 2003 I had been invited to speak at a bird meeting in Florida. It was interesting – but the glossiness of Miami Beach was not for me. The renowned American ornithologist Roger Tory Petersen once said that if immersing oneself in birds is an escape, it is an escape *to* reality – not from it! I needed that escape. Panama is only 600miles (960km) due south of Miami, so I decided to make a brief visit after the convention. My hotel was right by the canal and 15 minutes from Panama City. Just before dusk I ventured out with my binoculars. The canal bank was lined with stately palm trees and the elegant form of a suspension bridge curved over the water. Joggers were running along the wide promenade and families were testing the evening air. Two mockingbirds were drinking from a tiny puddle in a drain cover.

Within three or four minutes I had located a pine tree in which a flock of Dark-backed or Lesser Goldfinches were settling down for the night. The males are glossy black above, bright yellow below, delineated with a precise line through the head. The females are much duller in colour. Twenty or so flitted about within the tree, before they took up their roosting position. The sunset that evening was unforgettable, a subtle symphony of colour and art, tingeing pink the white sails of the many small boats on the canal.

Next morning I hurried outside just before 6.30am to watch the goldfinches awaken. It was barely light yet some were already moving among the branches, then gradually departing in groups of four or five. I could hear a flock of Orange-chinned (Tovi) Parakeets in a large tropical almond tree not too far away. I approached slowly to watch them from 7ft (2.1m) away. From a distance their chattering sounded like that of Budgerigars – and I was surprised to see a blue Budgie with them – so much more elegant in flight than they. The parakeets were clambering about, feeding and squabbling, dwarfed by the leaves of the tree. Sometimes one or two would come to the edge and their green plumage, with golden-brown scapulars, glowed in the morning sun.

Yellow-fronted (Panama) Parrots, the rarest of Panama's three Amazons, were in the area. I found a nest tree and guessed that it belonged to this species, because a hole had been cut out where the chicks had been stolen. The species is prized for its

Orange-chinned or Tovi Parakeets

talking ability thus illegal theft of young takes place at most accessible nests. To my delight, after hearing a couple of Amazons in the distance, the pair landed in the almond tree where the parakeets were feeding. Obviously they had come to partake of the fruits but were so wary of humans that, on seeing me, they changed their minds. One was perched on the edge of the tree against the skyline, allowing me to take a couple of photos before the dreaded whirring of my camera indicated that the film was at an end. It was guaranteed (in the days before I went digital) that just as you bagged the longed-for species in the viewfinder, the film would run out!

As I was changing the film, the pair took off to a distant palm tree. I saw one land on a frond and swing there playfully. I followed but they were soon lost from view. I returned to the parakeets' tree where a few handsome Fork-tailed Flycatchers

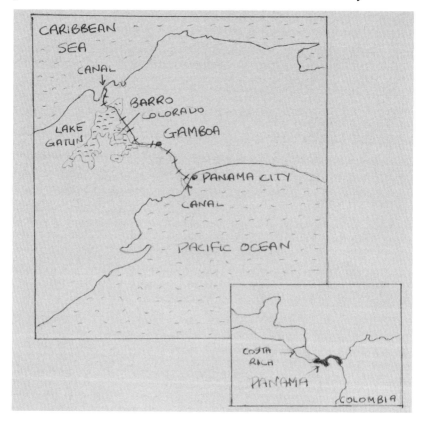

alighted briefly. Flycatchers are the bane of birders – there are hundreds of them to identify! But this is one of the most distinctive and handsome with its enormously long black tail and sooty black head.

Perhaps the most famous birding spots in the neotropics is Panama's Pipeline Road. This winds through 10 miles (17km) of forest and wetland and is recognised as Panama's most outstanding and easily accessible (only 20 minutes from Panama City) forested area. The former world record of 450 species in 24 hours was achieved here in 1985. Nearby is the well-known Canopy Tower hotel, originally an American radar military station and now known to birders worldwide. But accommodation there is limited, so not far away I checked into the Gamboa Rainforest Resort, with its spacious gardens and views of endless forest stretching into the Soberiana National Park. This has been described as the best preserved lowland rainforest in Central America.

An early morning visit to the Pipeline Road, laid on by the hotel, was not early enough but nevertheless produced striking Keel-billed Toucans with their bizarre multicoloured beaks and dazzling green skin around the eye. More soberly attired were the black White-shouldered Tanager and the grey and brown Common Tody-Flycatcher. My old friends the Fasciated Antshrikes were also here. A flock of little Blue-black Grassquits were feeding near the swampy area where capybara can be seen on a good day. Three-toed sloths were easier to find once you knew their shaggy somnolent forms were likely to be hanging from *Cecropia* trees. If you see one bat an eyelid in its mask-like face you are lucky! What you *can* see are the three strong curved grasping claws on each foot. The coat of these strange animals has a greenish tinge due to the algae (microscopic organisms) living within. This is apparently a symbiotic relationship. The sloth is able to lick its coat to acquire extra nutrients and the algae can reach the sunny treetops via their host, where they can manufacture food through photosynthesis.

Without the guide and his powerful scope, I would never have located the Blue Cotinga. The male is brilliant shining turquoise, which contrasts with the intense purple of the throat and abdomen. There are about 90 species of cotingas, identified by

Three-toed sloth

certain anatomical features, such as the peculiar structure of their vocal organs. These fruit-eaters live high in the forest canopy, plucking fruits in flight and eating them on the move, or perched on a hand of palm fruits.

The beauty of the Blue Cotinga and four other related species has attracted an unfortunate trade. Their feathers are prized by anglers for fly-tying. I was shocked to read a commercial description of the feathers of the Blue Cotinga, that they differ in shade and have oval tips, whereas those of the Spangled Cotinga have "nice pointed tips". How sad that these beautiful birds are killed so that anglers can lure fish to their death…

For a mere human, cotingas are difficult to observe. Few people have an opportunity to meet this species high in its own world. One who did so was photographer Carl Hansen. On Barro Colorado Island, not far distant from the Pipeline Road, he was hoisted 100ft (30m) into the air on a crane with a 115ft (34m) boom. There he photographed the "gorgeous shining blue male".

The crane belonged to the Smithsonian Tropical Research Institute (STRI). Barro Colorado became an island when the

Chagres river basin was flooded to create Lake Gatun during the construction of the Panama Canal. It was declared a reserve in 1923 and has been administered by STRI since 1946. The island's flora and fauna is among the best studied in the world and probably over a longer period than anywhere in the tropics.

For years I had read about the Smithsonian Institution's work on Barro Colorado, a 1,600-hectare island. I was keen to visit. Six other people in my group, plus several researchers, were on board the boat that departed at 7.15am. After landing we walked up to the research building where we taped the tops of our trousers into our socks as protection against the ticks. By then it was 8.30am. As far as bird watching was concerned, the morning was already over. I saw only one bird but it was a beauty – a Violaceous Trogon, with purple-blue head and throat, metallic greenish back and yellow underparts. One member of the group saw a White-whiskered Puffbird. This species is rufous-coloured with the abdomen streaked brown and white. Puffbirds (I love the name!) look very appealing, something like puffed-up kingfishers.

Our guide was a young girl doing her Master's degree on ants. For four and a half hours she talked about ants and leaves. I know that ants are fascinating creatures but there are also many other intriguing residents of that forest! Our progress through the trees was slow as we had to wait for an American lady with a physique like a snowman to catch up. We learned nothing about the research at the centre where agoutis, ocelots, antbirds and others are tagged with radio transmitters. Every other day their whereabouts are checked using seven giant radio antennae above the island. Extensive research has been carried out on trees and seed dispersal and the behaviour of bats. If we had been told about these achievements the day would not have been such a disappointment.

The same could not be said of my visit to Summit Zoo and Gardens where the wild birds are unafraid and easy to observe. First I visited the Harpy Museum. It depicts the eagle in art and in nature. Observing the Harpy Eagles who live in an enormous aviary built over the tops of large trees was an awe-inspiring experience. The eagles can be viewed on two levels – ground and treetops. One bird was down low and the other was perched high. I have seen Harpies in zoos before but never in such a good setting. I feasted my eyes on them, surely the most magnificent of all birds! I took in the width of the tarsus – as thick as my arm – the claws as big as a bear's and the wonderful long feathers of the crest and the ruff which, when erected, frames the entire head. Such strength and perfection… And beauty!

My most memorable sighting in Panama came when I was close to the canal and the Gatun lock. It was about 3.30pm and I was walking in a park-like area not far from a former military camp. Suddenly I exclaimed "Manakins!" as I heard a snapping sound. I could hear them but I could not see them, so I pushed my way through undergrowth to get nearer to the loud clicks. I did not know which species I would find.

When at last I saw a male I was spellbound. His plumage was stunningly beautiful in bright yellow and black. A Golden-collared Manakin, he displayed only a few inches from the ground and when I first saw him he was shooting up and down, in and out of sight. Then he came nearer, using two vertical saplings, whizzing down them with great speed.

At the approach of a little olive-green female, he became very excited. I was amazed when I saw what he did then. The brilliant yellow feathers of his throat (lengthened and stiffened) shot out horizontally. Imagine a bird with a flowering dandelion under his bill, and you get the picture! I was mesmerised by this performance – one of the most amazing avian displays I have seen. It was really too fast for the eye to follow and my view was interrupted by the dense vegetation but it seems that the female does join in the jumping dance.

Heightened by the vivid golden plumage, my observation was made even more exciting because I had not known of the existence of this lovely bird. It is usual for small groups of males to dance in the undergrowth, within hearing, if not within sight, of each other. Each male clears an area of leaves and other debris, up to 2ft (60cm) wide, to make the "court" at which he performs.

The morning after observing the Golden-collared Manakins, an interesting and friendly black girl called Zaida took me on the trail, down into the rainforest of the Sierra Llorona. Before we reached the trail I saw coming towards us two young men holding each end of a curving branch from which a cage was hanging. My curiosity was aroused. As they drew close we stopped to talk to them on seeing the occupant of the cage was a mature Salvin's Amazon. Where were they taking it? I wanted to know. They explained that they had moved house and they were taking the parrot, obviously a cherished pet, to their new home. I asked how long he had been part of the family: "About 16 years", they told me.

Then we ventured into the mountain forest. A stream meandered over a rocky bed. Ferns grew among the rocks and a small brown frog was half concealed among roots. After about half an hour Zaida pointed upwards. There sat a tiny manakin who would have been invisible in the poor light but for his glowing red head, the plumage colour separated in a straight line from the velvety black body. His neat little beak and intense white eyes completed his portrait. He was a Red-capped Manakin.

His display perch was as high as the Golden-collared's was low, and as exposed as the other manakin's was private. A horizontal

Moving house with the parrot

twig 20ft (6m) above ground, devoid of foliage, was where he held court. Suddenly there was a snapping sound and he was joined by an olive-brown female – and the show got under way. He whizzed backwards and forwards, like a mechanical toy, covering about 8in (20cm) of the perch and showing his brilliant yellow thigh feathers (normally hidden). Every now and then he would fly high over my head to a perch about 30ft (9m) away. Almost before I could turn to try to locate him, he was back on his display perch.

Then he would repeat the performance, vibrating his wings and making a cracking sound. This is apparently achieved by striking together the shafts of the enlarged, stiffened secondary wing feathers. When he zoomed high above me again, I could hear the *chu, chu, chu* of each wing beat. From such a tiny creature, less than 4in (10cm) long, it was amazing. Deep in the forest behind him two males shared the same perch, also 20ft (6m) above ground, but they did not dance. As in the Golden-collared Manakin, males gather to display in small groups, and each one has his own special "patch".

Manakins are so extraordinary, so endearing, so beautiful! My memories of their courtship dances contribute greatly to the essence of what makes the neotropics so special to me.

My short stay in Panama was nothing more than a taster of this extremely interesting country. I had experienced perfect weather, excellent food and friendly people. The roads are good and this area is outside the hurricane belt. Further afield than the canal area, it has so much more to offer. Perhaps one day I will go to its eastern limits, the Darien, remote and even more rewarding.

Panama bird statistics (year 2000)
Endangered 1
Vulnerable 15
Near-threatened 16

Species not previously mentioned:

Lesser Goldfinch (*Spinus psaltria*)
Panama Yellow-fronted Amazon Parrot (*Amazona ochrocephala panamensis*)
Fork-tailed Flycatcher (*Muscivora tyrannus*)
White-shouldered Tanager (*Tachyphonus luctuosus*)
Common Tody-Flycatcher (*Todirostrum cinereum*)
Blue-black Grassquit (*Volatinia jacarinia*)
Blue Cotinga (*Cotinga nattererii*)
Violaceous Trogon (*Trogon violacea*)
White-whiskered Puffbird (*Malacoptila panamensis*)
Harpy Eagle (*Harpia harpyya*) NEAR THREATENED
Golden-collared Manakin (*Manacus vitellinus*)

Tropical almond tree (*Terminalia catappa*)

14. Bolivia 2003:

Wings of flame on the wind

There were nine of us, four from the UK and five from the USA, and our rendezvous was Santa Cruz airport on August 19. The four Brits consisted of a couple, Krystyna and Karel, and a single traveller, Colin, and, of course, myself. It was a lucky accident that the chemistry between the four of us, based on a slightly wry sense of humour, was electric, and sparked off a lot of hilarity. We enjoyed each other's company hugely from the moment we met.

Jean-Paul Ayala of Green Bolivia was waiting to guide us for the first part of this trip (arranged by the World Parrot Trust). Founded in 1560, Santa Cruz is the economic heart of Bolivia, situated at 1,380ft (416m). The modern district is distinguished by its absence of high-rise buildings, due to the unsuitable terrain. Colin and I ventured out to experience a *surazo*, the fierce wind that blows all the way from the Argentine pampas. After half an hour in the dusty streets, with dust blowing into our eyes and mouth, we returned, defeated, to the hotel.

BOLIVIA

A republic of the western central part of South America, land-locked Bolivia covers 424,000 square miles (678,000 sq km) – more than 4½ times larger than the UK , with a population of about 8.5million.

Blue-throated Macaw

This is the poorest country in South America, with a high rate of unemployment.

Quechua and Aymara Indians form 55% of the population which numbers nearly 9 million.

Crested Screamer

Next morning two thirty-minute flights took us west to Cochabamba, with good views of the Andes and their stark grandeur. Then we flew north to the town of Trinidad, which dates back to 1686, the capital of the department of Beni. My fleeting recollection of it relates to the dark little store in an unpaved main road where we stopped to buy Wellington boots. We travelled through the seasonally flooded lowland savannah, in the Bolivian part of the Pantanal. Scattered palm trees and numerous termite mounds decorated the landscape that was covered in low sedges. Giant Jabiru Storks searched a field near the roadside for frogs and snails, ungainly on the ground but spectacular in flight. Quite extraordinary birds, with long neck and head bare black with bright red skin where the white plumage meets the shoulders and standing 5ft (1.5m) high, they have a huge wingspan of 8ft (2.4m).

Wattled Jacanas stepped on the water lilies in little pools, yellow under wing coverts gleaming in the sun, and the occasional Crested Screamer, big as a turkey and with a loud honking call, took to the wing. Stately Cocoi Herons were common and flapped away gracefully at the approach of our vehicles.

179

From the dirt road (that even the previous week had threatened to be impassable after rain) various parrots were seen in flight: the common Weddell's or Dusky-headed Conure, and two small macaw species, the Severe and the Yellow-collared. Blue-headed Parrots were feeding on the orange flowers of a *Cosorio* tree, making a pretty picture with their pink and black bills and scarlet under tail coverts.

Our destination was the Llanos de Moxos, a vast mosaic of forest and seasonally flooded lowland savannah, where we were to search for one of the world's rarest parrots. The Blue-throated Macaw Lodge was located near the Rio Mamore and 42 miles (68km) from Trinidad, the nearest town. The lodge, very basic, had been set up recently to cater for the rare tourists visiting this remote ranch that spans more than 100,000 acres. I was surprised to see a Toco Toucan quite close to the ranch house as I had incorrectly associated this species with more heavily forested areas.

We were hoping to glimpse what is almost certainly the rarest macaw in the world, after Spix's. Only four species of macaw are endemic to single countries: two (both Critically Endangered) to Brazil, and the Blue-throated and the Red-fronted (Critically Endangered and Endangered) to Bolivia. The fifteen macaw species occur in South and Central America. All those with small ranges have threat categories ranging from extinct in the wild (Spix's) to Endangered. Nearly all have declined very seriously in the past half-century. The two species most difficult to locate are the Bolivian ones. Without knowledgeable guides the chances of seeing them would be almost nil.

Fewer than one hundred Blue-throated Macaws were known, at that time, to exist in their habitat of palm islands among natural savannah used as cattle pasture. This macaw faces a precarious predicament. It survives only on privately-owned land; the wealthy landowners are many miles away in the cities, perhaps completely out of touch with nature. The cowboys and their families have thus become the most important players in its future.

The macaw's precipitous decline was due to the large numbers caught in the early 1980s, soon after its location was discovered by trappers. Ironically, this remained unknown to scientists until 1992. In 1983 it had been placed on Appendix I of CITES and the legal export parrot trade from Bolivia ceased. The illegal trade continued until this macaw became too difficult to find.

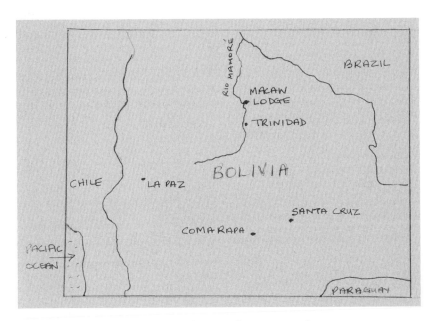

The picture in my mind of those who trap such rare species was one of lean, hard-faced men who cared nothing for the birds they trapped. This mental picture was shattered when I met Pocho, a former trapper, who was our guide. Solidly built and of medium height, he seemed very pleasant. Next morning, we left the lodge long before first light to travel over two hours by road to reach a palm "island". When the sun came up small Yellow-collared Macaws were flying by the roadside across the savannah. On reaching our destination we crossed a swampy area (hence the Wellington boots) to reach the island. As we did so Blue and Yellow, and Green-winged Macaws flew overhead in exuberant early morning flight.

Blue-throated Macaws are strongly associated with dry groves of *motacú* palms elevated above the surrounding seasonally flooded grasslands. On reaching one such "island" a pair of Yellow-fronted (Yellow-crowned) Amazons took to the wing. We sat quietly on fallen logs under the low shady trees dominated by *Scheelea* and other palms. Giant dead fronds, 10ft (3m) long, hung from them like shabby skirts. It was tinder-dry underfoot and the palms were interspersed with much low, shrubby growth and numerous rotten logs. With a machete the men opened the *Scheelea* palm nuts on which the macaws feed, so that we could photograph the interiors.

Blue-throated Macaws are shy; we needed to be quiet. Sitting next to Pocho I was curious to know about his involvement with the trade in these macaws. He was very knowledgeable about the local birds and, later, his love for them was apparent. When I plucked up the courage to ask him how many *barba azul* (blue beards) he had trapped he gave me what I believed to be an honest answer: "Ocho" (eight). It was, he said, "muy dificil" (very difficult) to trap this wary species. These days men still come from afar asking for information on where the macaws can be caught. He tells them they are too late. Now he only wants to protect them.

We sat for hours, waiting. A pair of Severe Macaws flew over. The cooing of doves and the liquid calls of oropendolas were the only sounds. We were entertained by a gorgeous pair of Rufous-tailed Jacamars; they resembled giant hummingbirds with

Blue-throated Macaw

glittering iridescent green plumage. At 10.45am a pair of macaws flew above us. I jumped to my feet on hearing them call – higher pitched, more scared-sounding and less throaty than that of the Blue and Yellow. They were Blue-throated Macaws! They looked magnificent in flight, the sun lighting their brilliant shades of turquoise blue and rich yellow. More slender and slightly smaller than their well-known relatives, they are supremely elegant with enormously long blue tails and a majestic bearing. This was a special moment for me. I had an intense interest in this species that stretched back more than 15 years. I had never, ever, expected to see it in its natural habitat.

I followed on foot the direction of their flight to find one of the pair perched in a large deciduous tree. I gazed at its face, watching me so warily, through my binoculars and gave a sigh of contentment, guessing that this was to be the only chance to observe it. All too soon the pair had gone. They did not return. Possibly they were preparing a nest site in a hollow palm tree somewhere. These macaws start to breed during the second half of the dry season – usually September to November.

We stayed quietly on the palm island. Soon we were visited by a loquacious family of Green-winged Macaws. Imposing and stunningly coloured in deep red and green, this species has a huge beak and a shorter tail in proportion to its body, thus lacks the elegance of its neighbour species. On several occasions the adults arrived in total silence, then gave a call when they observed us. Their youngster was "parked" in a large tree a little way off. They did not seem to be alarmed by us – just curious. At 5pm the sun was setting, an orange globe in the sky, as we made our way back across the swamp. Blue and Yellow Macaws were flying in the distance.

Not far along the road we stopped to distribute pencils, crayons and drawing pads to a teacher with a group of excited children with big sparkling brown eyes. We offered these items as a small contribution to the community. We also wanted to reinforce the idea that tourists who come to see the macaws are beneficial to the local people, therefore the macaws are worth protecting.

Next morning when we left at 7am to return along the road to Trinidad, a mist was hanging just above the ground over the wide vista of the palm savannah. Every excuse to stop brought a feast of birds, including the tiny Blue-winged Parrotlets. It was only when the White-eyed Conures, so called for the area of bare white skin surrounding the eyes, took to the wing that their hidden colours were revealed – red and yellow under wing coverts. A flock of 13 small and uncommon Bare-faced Ibis perched close to the road.

The winter-flowering *Tabebuia* trees added unexpected touches of colour to the landscape, especially those with glorious deep pink flowers. Some of the low, fire-resistant palms were scorched from the annual burn of the savannah that brings dozens of birds of prey to feed on the fleeing creatures. The early morning landscape was filled with bird song and the harsh cries of conures. Giant Jabiru Storks and pink-plumaged Roseate Spoonbills were gathered around a waterhole. A group of blunt-faced capybara left the water in descending order of size, from hulking adults to tiny "rodentlets". On the road in front of us six Weddell's Conures were drinking from a puddle. Gleaming iridescent green, a kingfisher was perched by a roadside pool poised to strike, but flew away, startled by our vehicle. A pair of Black-capped Mockingthrushes was foraging on the ground for insects. We wanted to linger – but we had a flight to catch!

Our group flew to Cochabamba, and then back to Santa Cruz. Next morning, August 23, we drove through the outskirts and on through small towns, stopping to buy tiny bananas and tasty tangerines from two little girls. Two Maximilian's Parrots, green with bronze wings, were perched on a roadside bush and a number of Blue-crowned Conures were flying around. The landscape changed with the hours, the small towns giving way to lush countryside, then desert with huge cacti. At 5,900ft (1,800m) we reached Comarapa, an agricultural community where most of the dry forest had been destroyed. Our base for the next two nights was the optimistically named Hotel Paraiso in the main street. Located between typical small one-storey dwellings with tiled roofs, its backdrop of brooding mountains was partly obscured by low cloud.

Our destination was a very special area. On the dirt road in the arid mountains we passed a dam, then came to a very steep incline that our vehicle was unable to negotiate at the first

Red-fronted Macaws

attempt. Feeling cautious, we decided to disembark and leave the driver to it. On subsequent trips we had more confidence in him and had no such qualms!

Sixteen miles (25km) west of Comarapa there were spectacular views over the green, irrigated Mizque valley floor far below us. Small adobe houses dotted the fields bordered by trees and giant cacti. Peanut farmers were working in the sun. Peanuts (groundnuts) – not nuts at all but legumes – were the clue to our next species. We were looking for Bolivia's second endemic macaw: the Red-fronted. Confined to an area that is a dot on the map of central Bolivia, this endangered species occupies a strange habitat for a macaw: arid montane scrub at 3,600 to 8,200ft (1,100 to 2,500m). Its range is very small, apparently only approximately 112 miles (180km) from north to south and 93 miles (150km) from east to west. The total population is difficult to assess but seems unlikely to exceed 1,000 birds. Between 1973 and 1983 when it was placed on Appendix I of CITES, hundreds were trapped and exported. It is uncertain what impact this had on its population in view of the fact that it was or is persecuted as a crop pest by the maize and peanut farmers. Its main problem now is that its entire known habitat has been converted for agricultural use.

The people here are so poor that the success of their crops is crucial to their survival. They sow *mani* (groundnuts) and wait for the first green shoots to push through the stony ground – but the macaws often find them first and their crop is ruined. So why would they protect the macaws? There is only one reason: eco-tourism potential. I saw what this meant on the following day when we all gave money to the old, wrinkled peanut farmer over whose land we had been walking. With a hand as hard as cured leather, he pressed these notes to his lips, then shook us by the hand. We had probably given him more money than he would reap from the potato crop he would plant next week to follow the corn and peanuts.

This was the best way to impress on this community that Red-fronted Macaws are valuable as an occasional cash bonus, despite any damage they might cause to the crops. For hundreds of years peanuts have been bred for taste and to produce high yields. They are vulnerable to disease because the original plant has been lost and its genes are needed. There is a theory that it originated in south-eastern Bolivia.

That first afternoon in the Mizque valley was disappointing. The wind was so strong that Jean-Paul's spotting scope was in danger of blowing away. After a while we heard macaws calling and had glimpses of distant birds as they flew down the mountain. But

The peanut farmer's house

the wind was so strong they did not stay. The sun lit up their orange under wing coverts for a brief second as eight birds flew high above us to roost somewhere in the mountains. We headed back to Comarapa, stopping to watch a truly magnificent pair of large, scarlet-headed Cream-backed Woodpeckers.

Early next morning we were back in the valley, anticipation running high. At once our spirits lifted: in the field far below we could see a flock of macaws. More and more were flying in. Excitedly I counted 45 – but there were more than that! Jean-Paul was elated. "This is the largest flock I've seen in years!", he said.

I leaned happily against the Landcruiser, an alpaca shawl around my shoulders. It was cold up there! Far below I could see the macaws playing, feeding, squabbling and walking around or hanging upside down from small, leafless trees. They were showing off their fiery and lemon-coloured under wings and blue flight feathers and tail. Through the scope I tried to count juveniles on the ground. In one group of fifteen macaws there were three, possibly four. The flock members strutted around the earth for all the world like rooks back home searching a field of cereals, or even cockatoos in Australia, but so unlike most parrots in South America!

The Mizque Valley

The macaws spend several hours a day walking on the ground, searching for food that is often scarce in this arid landscape. Their bright colours were a stark contrast to the greyish-brown soil, the scattered grey trees with light green leaves and the tall cacti, spiny or fluted. There was amusing interaction between a young macaw perched in a tree and two Plush-crested Jays. At this early age and with the close support of an adult, it was determined to assert its authority. Even when the adult flew, the young macaw would not give way. The jays were left bouncing on the end of the bough until they gave in to the superior weight of their psittacine neighbour and flew away defeated.

We climbed down the slope to the field where the macaws were feeding on remnants of corn from the recent harvest. The peanuts that they relish had gone. Jumping across two little streams and climbing a couple of stiles, we crept closer and closer, disturbing a family of Blue-fronted Amazons that had been feeding in the top of a flowering tree. I was sorry that they flew. The Bolivian birds are surely the most beautiful Blue-fronts throughout the whole huge range, with their big yellow shoulder patches and blue-tinged underparts.

The young macaws, identified by their red-brown (not orange-red) foreheads and lack of orange on wings and thighs, were incautious, the last to move away from the onlookers. Two sat in the field, oblivious to danger. The adults moved further off but stayed for another hour or more. Gradually they drifted away and we left at 11am.

Returning to Comarapa we enjoyed the colourful, bustling Sunday market. A popular event, it attracted visitors from as far away as Cochabamba – a twelve-hour return journey by bus. The people were so friendly and smiling when we spoke with them. The children were beautiful with their dark eyes and sleek dark hair. You could buy anything from dried coca leaves to live turkeys. Indian women with plaits, none taller than 5ft (1.5m), were wearing brightly coloured ponchos or shawls and knitted hats. They sat behind vegetables laid in mounds on sacks on the ground or boxes full of tomatoes. Melons, oranges, pineapples and potatoes were in profusion. Some vendors had rigged white tarpaulins for shade over their produce. A woman with a baby, its head appearing out of the poncho on her back, was laden with heavy plastic bags. (Even here there was plastic...) Two white ducks were tied to a post with string. Absorbed young men were enjoying themselves at the "gaming tables" – some kind of football game where the ball or the players were manipulated by means of steel rods on the miniature football pitch.

We returned to Hotel Paraiso for lunch of peanut soup, chicken, rice, beans and green beans. Outside in the courtyard two beautiful, big Blue-fronted Amazons were preening each other's heads. One belonged to the hotel, the other to a local man. When he came to eat there he brought his parrot so that the two birds could socialise for several hours. They looked so happy together!

At 3pm we set off again, back to the Misque valley. We stopped to watch five Andean Condors circling high above us, and a group of Blue-crowned Conures, resting and preening in a roadside tree.

"Our" macaws were there, in the same field, and we climbed down to watch them. This time we were lucky: the sun came out, turning them into kaleidoscopes of blue, pale green and orange as they floated down to the field in their typically fluttering

The busy market at Comarapa

189

flight, so different from the leisurely flaps of the larger macaws. Shutters clicked as they grew bolder and flew above us, possibly as curious about this strange group of humans who did not work the land as we were mesmerised by their beauty. When a flock landed in a treetop, it was as if the tree had suddenly burst into orange flower! Sometimes the macaws hung on the wind, apparently with the sole purpose of displaying those flame-coloured under wing coverts!

This medium-sized macaw, substantially smaller than the Blue-throated, is one of three macaws that have evolved to survive in arid regions. As previously mentioned, Spix's is already extinct in the wild and Lear's came perilously close to extinction. Open habitats made these three extremely vulnerable to trapping.

The large macaws are among the most spectacular and the most endangered of all birds. They are charismatic, flagship species whose appreciation through tourism can result in the protection of large areas and countless species. The sightings we had of Bolivia's two endemic macaws would cause envy in many people, bird lovers and twitchers.

We all came away with abiding memories of their beauty. Indeed, so replete were we with our views that day, that next morning we opted to visit a totally contrasting habitat, the lush cloud forest of Sierra Siberia 12 miles (19km) north of Comarapa. Cloud forest, when it is not raining, is a magical place to be. The trees are loaded with epiphytes, mosses and ferns, their ghostly outlines appealing in the dull light. Plants with blossoms of a dozen shades of mauve and yellow completed the canvas. Birds were few on that day. The Chiguanco Thrush, like a European Blackbird but slightly larger, and the handsome Rufous-naped Brush-finch, with black mask and orange head, were seen. Small reddish-brown finches were flitting about near the ground.

It was cool but dry, with lush montane vistas as the mist cleared away. From a nearby habitation three children appeared. One tiny girl carried off (almost staggering) the hand of bananas we gave her. At 9am we left with reluctance the quiet of the forest and drove for more than five hours back to Santa Cruz.

Updates

The few Blue-throated Macaw nests studied indicated that breeding success rate was low. In 2005, for example, five of the six nests monitored failed in the late stages of incubation, some flooded, some predated by toucans. The 2006 season was the most successful of the five seasons, with six chicks fledging from four nests out of a total of seven active nests, in the population of about 80 macaws. Researchers had by then made drainage holes in all known nests, to prevent them flooding. By then it was revealed that two common species were causing deaths among the population of this critically endangered macaw, Toco Toucans were eating the chicks and Great Horned Owls were attacking adults and fledged young. Nest-boxes that precluded entrance by toucans and the larger Blue and Yellow Macaws were erected and one box was used in 2007.

The estimate of the Blue-throated Macaw population was revised substantially to about 350 individuals in 2007 as a result of intensive fieldwork and protection. A miraculous find was a hitherto unknown population of about 70 birds on a large ranch in Yacuma province. Even better was the news that this 8,785-acre ranch was purchased by Armonia with funding from the American Bird Conservancy and the World Land Trust, now known as the Barba Azul Nature Reserve. The long-term goal is to increase the protected area to at least 30,000-acres. At last this macaw's future is beginning to look brighter!

Alas, the same was not true for the Red-throated Macaw. Trade and increased habitat destruction had caused further population decline. In 2008 the population was estimated at possibly below 1,000 individuals and the status of the species was on the threshold of being upgraded to Critically Endangered. The Genetics Center in Cochabamba was working to create a protected area in the Mizque and Rio Grande areas. Only 10% to 15% of the macaw's range was protected. Other conservation initiatives were continuing, including field work to identify the most important nesting cliffs.

Bolivian bird statistics (year 2000)
Critically Endangered 2
Endangered 7
Vulnerable 18
Conservation dependent 36
Near-threatened 1

Species not previously mentioned:

Jabiru Stork (*Jabiru mycteria*)
Crested Screamer (*Chauna torquata*)
Cocoi Heron (*Ardea cocoi*)
Severe Macaw (*Ara severa*)
Yellow-collared Macaw (*Propyrrhura auricollis*)
Toco Toucan (*Ramphastos toco*)
**Blue-throated Macaw (*Ara glaucogularis*) CRITICALLY
ENDANGERED**
Green-winged Macaw (*Ara chloroptera*)
**Yellow-fronted (Yellow-crowned) Amazon (*Amazona
ochrocephala nattereri*)**
Rufous-tailed Jacamar (*Galbula ruficauda*)
Blue-winged Parrotlet (*Forpus xanthopterygius flavescens*)
White-eyed Conure (*Aratinga leucophthalmus*)
Bare-faced Ibis (*Phimosus infuscatus*)
Maximilian's Parrot (*Pionus maximiliani siy*)
Blue-crowned Conure (*Aratinga a. acuticaudata*)
Red-fronted Macaw (*Ara rubrogenys*) ENDANGERED
Cream-backed Woodpecker (*Phloeoceastes leucopogon*)
Plush-crested Jay (*Cyanocorax chrysops*)
Blue-fronted Amazon (*Amazona aestiva xanthopteryx*)
Andean Condor (*Vultur gryphus*) NEAR THREATENED
Chiguanco Thrush (*Turdus chiguanco*)
Great Horned Owl (*Bubo virginianus*)

Motacú palm (*Attalea phalerata*)

15. Peru and Bolivian border 2003:

Inca Culture and Rainforest Revelations

A very contented group of World Parrot Trust members flew from Santa Cruz to Cuzco (Cusco) in Peru, via La Paz, flying over the sea-like expanse of Lake Titicaca. Our hotel, Los Andes de America, one and a half blocks from the main square, was old and quite charming. Situated at 11,700ft (3,500m), this city is the most important cultural centre in Peru – perhaps even in South America. A fascinating afternoon was spent exploring the nearby extensive Inca ruins of Sacsayhuaman (Saqsaywaman), including the monumental structure known as the House of the Sun in the Inca era. Some of the enormous stones from which it was constructed weigh 50 tons each. How the Incas could move them into position defies the imagination but legend has it that they were assisted by devil spirits. Close by is an impressive semi-circular amphitheatre.

This site, and those of Puca Pucara and Tambomachay of equal antiquity, clearly displayed the degree of sophistication of their architects and engineers. The precision with which the giant blocks of stone were cut, probably in the 15th century, was awe-inspiring. Our wonderful Quechua guide Luis Diaz was, without doubt, the best tour guide I ever encountered, imaginative and informative – also very good looking as are so many descendants of the Inca race who today make up about half of Peru's population. These people flourished throughout the Andes from the 12th to the 16th century.

Near the cathedral we encountered a Quechua lady in native costume – a yellow woollen jacket beautifully embroidered on cuffs and front with colourful designs, and a green shawl and black skirt similarly decorated. She was accompanied by two young llamas – appealing animals with thick fawn and white woolly coats. They looked around haughtily with their big, brown doe-like eyes. From tourists looking for photogenic subjects she earned a few pesos.

PERU

Immediately north and west of Bolivia, Peru is an exciting destination for birdwatchers with a wealth of different habitats within its three distinct regions: coastal, Andean and rainforest. It extends over 496,000 square miles (1.29 million sq km) and has a population of 27 million people, 45% indigenous. At 12,000ft (3,600m), its capital La Paz is the highest in the world.

Green-winged Macaw

Some of us instantly fell in love with Cuzco while others had problems coping with the altitude. The doctor was called to my room-mate Lin, a young Japanese American. He administered oxygen to her and instructed me to do the same at midnight and again three hours later. The patient slept soundly while I, worried about the responsibility, had the only sleepless night of my life! Next morning, to my amazement, she arose and departed at 6am for a train trip to the Inca city of Machu Picchu!

That day was unforgettable. At 7am I ventured out to explore the local produce market, bustling and colourful. I could have purchased whole pigs, frogs and enormous round loaves. Children on their way to school were buying their breakfast at the market stalls that stood in the shadow of a cathedral with twin bell towers. Women in modern dress mingled with those in traditional costumes wearing full skirts and tall hats with narrow brims.

Again with Luis, our friendly guide, four of us, the Brits, climbed into the mini-bus and set off for the Sacred Valley (*el Valle Sagrado*). The scenery *en route* was dramatic. The sides of the snow-capped mountains were terraced centuries ago to a great height by the Incas for crop-growing. A woman shepherdess and her sheep were dwarfed by the imperious

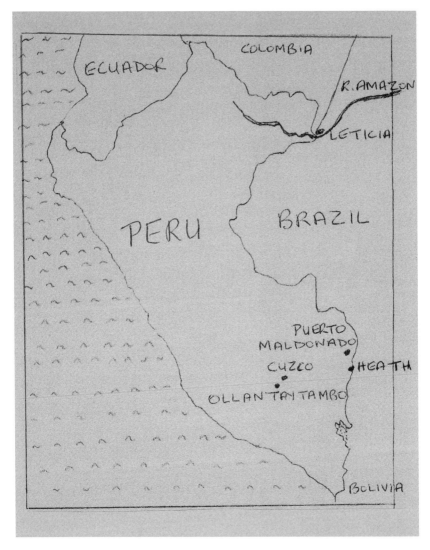

landscape. The fertile valley plains produce exceptional fruits and vegetables, including the largest corn cobs in the world that grow only in one area of the valley. We stopped to look down on the plains, dotted with adobe houses, built around tiny courtyards, next to more modern dwellings with tiled roofs, also walled in but containing plots of green trees or crops. The Inca trail led steeply upwards through the bare jagged mountains towards the Amazon region.

195

The ruins of an Inca village at Pisac (Pisaq), precariously positioned on a crag, are eclipsed only by those at Machu Picchu. The site, one hour's climb from the town, contains some of the finest surviving Inca stonework. A round mound of a mountain looms over the town. We spent a happy hour in the near-deserted market in between little houses with carved wooden doors set in cobbled streets. I was unable to resist the purchase of a sensuously soft rug made from llama wool, depicting a white llama against a black mountain. The domesticated llamas and alpacas were often seen, their coats varying combinations of black, white and brown. They bore wonderful wool with which to produce the softest knitwear and the market stalls sold high quality examples. The alpaca provides the finest, longest and silkiest wool produced by any animal.

In a courtyard near the market I bought *empanadas* filled with cheese and onion that were truly delicious. After much persuasion, Colin sampled one and had to agree with me that it was very good. Later I discovered that another member of our group had been very ill after eating an *empanada* from another vendor. I didn't tell Colin and I thought twice about buying them in future!

Thirty-eight miles (60km) from Pisac, we visited Ollantaytambo, the only town in Peru to retain its original Inca layout. It was a remarkable experience to walk through the narrow streets flanked by very high stone walls and to realise that they had been in use for more than 450 years. Our visit to an inhabited Inca house at the end of a cobbled street, constructed about 1550, will never leave my memory. Four families occupied this dwelling and several families shared the courtyard. Its one room sufficed for cooking, eating and sleeping. Sprays of millet were hanging up to dry next to the skulls of ancestors displayed in an alcove. About 20 guinea pigs ran around the floor. How did the occupants decide which one to eat next? I wondered. But, of course, to the indigenous people, these little animals are not pets.

We climbed up to the ruins of the Holy Temple of the Sun, above the town, and here Luiz was at his best. His knowledge and his delivery were superb, lacking the pedantic manner of some

The courtyard of an Inca dwelling

guides, offered like an informative friend. Again we marvelled at how the huge blocks of stone of the temple ruins could have been manoeuvred into position so many centuries ago – and at an altitude of 9,300ft (2,800m). The temple had been built at a defensive point, where two valleys meet, the mountains towering above it on every side.

A perfect day ended at the Tunupa Restaurant, listening to musicians, one of whom we had made friends with on the previous day. With his unkempt hair and beard and gentle voice, he had demonstrated to Krystyna, Karel and I about 20 different local instruments. We had been fascinated. Here we were entertained by his group and by local dancers with their exquisitely colourful costumes. The men wore glittering waistcoats, intricately decorated with floral designs, over their white shirts. The women's red petticoats, in a similar style, were revealed as they danced, under their black tiered skirts.

On leaving the restaurant, we took a walk around the main square. The floodlit cathedral and the lights from the other ancient buildings and lamps gave it a romantic air. There was hardly a bird in sight yet I had enjoyed Cuzco so much…

197

Four Brits at the Temple of the Sun

Next day, August 28, we flew to Puerto Maldonado on our way to experience the contrast of forests and rivers. At the airport we met Charles Munn, an American and formerly a senior research Zoologist for the Wildlife Conservation Society in New York. His pioneering (and often controversial!) initiatives in the Peruvian rainforest are widely known. The three hours spent in the motorised canoe (briefly on the Tambopata River and then on the Madre de Dios), provided a good opportunity to learn more about his work. He did not need any prompting. He is passionate about macaws. "I have used macaws as the flagship species to protect and preserve thousands of acres of habitat. Manu National Park covers 1.5 million hectares and the research centre at Tambopata, 10 hours up-river, is now famous", he said.

In 1990 the Tambopata-Candamo Reserved Zone was created, bounded by the Bolivian border. It surrounds the Rio Heath sanctuary to which we were headed. Charlie had spoken about his work at a number of symposiums for parrot breeders in the USA, where he was always received like a celebrity. He told me: "Parrot lovers do not do enough for wild parrots. If each one donated just $10 a year so much could be achieved." He echoed my own years-old opinion.

Conservation is expensive. Charlie described a canyon in Peru where the declining Military Macaw is breeding. "It costs

$10,000 per year to protect the macaws there", he told us. This is why he was so keen on developing "macaw tourism" and had been instrumental in the creation of several lodges. To him it was of crucial importance to involve the indigenous people and to make sure that they received a good part of the profits from these operations. The next lodge we visited at Sandoval was jointly owned by a non-profit conservation society, of which Charlie was chairman, and five indigenous families of Brazil nut collectors. "When all the profits from tourists go to large companies, there is no incentive for them to protect the wildlife", he said. Eco-tourism and finding uses for more tree species will help to maintain the biodiversity. Protection of the clay licks will be vitally important for the future of the macaws and of the region.

The combined Tambopata-Madidi Protected areas are about 20% the size of the UK, and reach from lowland rainforest up to 19,000ft (6,300m) glaciers. The forest is the stronghold of Green-winged, Scarlet, and Blue and Yellow Macaws. Few areas in the world have such a rich biodiversity. However, threats to the protection of south-eastern Peru include gold-mining and the associated use of mercury. Lost mercury poisons the rivers; miners strip off the finest topsoils and destroy mature forest to get to the gold dust in the sands of former river bottoms.

Our canoe headed upstream (south) along the Rio Heath. This river forms the boundary between Bolivia and Peru. The Heath River Wildlife Centre and its comfortable thatched cabins are situated in the forest close to the river. The lodge had been built in the previous year. We did not see it in daylight as we had a 3.30am call next morning. The night had been surprisingly cool and blankets were necessary on our mosquito-netted beds.

Setting off at 4am (with four or more layers of clothes, plus lifejackets!) for what promised to be the most exciting day of the trip, almost immediately we ran aground on a sandbank. Imagine the scene: three of our men with trousers rolled up to their knees jumping into the Rio Heath in the dark and pushing the canoe! This caused a good deal of hilarity but resulted in us taking more than one and a half hours to travel six miles (10km). This problem was due to be solved with the introduction of shallow-draft boats that would take only 45 minutes. The journey is slow and difficult only during the low-water months of July to September. At least we could not drown if we fell overboard!

We were on our way to a very special place, one of the best *collpas* in Peru. This is the name for a clay lick (cliff) visited by hundreds of parrots. When we arrived it was light and already bustling with parrot activity. A few macaws had overtaken the canoe and, as we came near to the lick, the cries of Mealy Amazons filled the air. They were circling around above a large tree. In the top I could see a recently fledged young one and hear its loud *uh-uh-uh* demands for food, characteristic of young of this genus. We disembarked on to the floating hide in front of the lick. Inside, seats were positioned around the sides, with a ledge for our cameras and binoculars and, just above it, observation slits in the palm thatch. As I sat down excitement surged through me! About to unfold in front of us was one of the most colourful and exhilarating spectacles of the tropics! This is as good as it gets where bird watching is concerned – *and* we had the privilege of viewing in comfort! This was clay lick heaven!

The lick consisted of an exposed bank of yellowish clay about 18ft (5.4m) high, topped with tall straggly white-barked trees and more stunted vegetation. The branches of some trees were bare, no doubt stripped over the years by visiting macaws. The macaws are the most wary visitors and always the last to come in. First came the small ones, the little Weddell's Conures, inconspicuous and grouped closely together on the lower face. The Blue-headed Pionus were also early arrivals, unmistakable with their brilliant head coloration and red under tail coverts. They, too, kept together on the lick face, more flighty than the big Mealy Amazons that soon come down, after perching for a while in the trees to survey the scene. How beautiful are these Amazons in their natural habitat! The sun lit up their silvery backs as they dropped down to the lick face with a confidence lacking in the little Pionus. They are indeed the kings of the mainland Amazons, big, bold and boisterous. I watched two swinging on a palm frond close to the clay face. Another was holding a piece of clay, then striking out at a companion trying to steal it, both actions achieved with his foot. Finally, he flew off still holding the clay lump clenched between his toes.

Four Green-winged Macaws flew over. More macaws were landing above. Green-wings and more Green-wings, shrieking and dropping into the trees, playing on the wind a little, giving us the opportunity to photograph them with open wings. They looked spectacular! Very cautious at first, they took their time to assess that it was safe, then dropped down directly on to the clay, or hung on the branch in front of the bank, swinging there playfully. The volume of their calls filled the air and their sensuous redness caused me to draw in my breath with happiness. In front of us was a constantly changing scene: macaws dropping down, feasting on the clay, taking off, circling around in pairs emitting their deep, throaty calls, then coming back for another feed of clay.

Fifty or sixty Green-wings were present. Where were the Scarlet Macaws? Only one pair had arrived. They came early and did not stay long. Does that mean, I wondered, that most pairs of Green-wings don't linger, that there are so many they are soon replaced by others? I suspected not, rather that they were not in a hurry to leave. On that first morning we had incredible luck for the Green-wings stayed for one hour and 25 minutes, which is two to three times the average length of the "macaw show".

Among the Pionus were two little parrots, gleaming emerald in the sun, their red under wing coverts briefly visible in flight. Through binoculars I studied their beautiful faces with striking contrasting markings of orange and black. These were the Barraband's or Orange-cheeked Parrots. One of four species present in small numbers that morning, the others were a family of Yellow-fronted (Yellow-crowned) Amazons that did not stay long and a small number of Severe (Chestnut-fronted) Macaws. My first ever sighting of the little Golden-crowned or Peach-fronted Conures, half a dozen or so, was enjoyable. But neither name is accurate. The forehead (not the crown) is orange (not peach-coloured)! There is something very pleasing about these neat, gentle-looking parakeets, with their black beak and bluish crown.

Clay-eating, known as geophagy, has been studied at the University of California, combining Charlie Munn's fieldwork with analysis carried out by laboratory scientists. "In the Amazon," he said, "nearly all animals that eat leaves and seeds have been observed eating clay, including monkeys, tapirs, deer and guans. Their food is rich in toxic compounds. Even the highland Indians in Peru eat it! They mix clay with toxic wild potatoes to make them edible!"

He believed that the clay protects the mucus film of the gastro-intestinal tract, preventing chemical irritation but not everyone is convinced that this is why birds eat clay (see Chapter 10). Some clay seams are of particular interest and are mined with enthusiasm by macaws, while other clay faces are ignored by all animals. They definitely know what they are looking for!

Charlie told us that Green-winged Macaws mainly inhabit the *terra firme* forest where there is an abundance of trees with toxic and armoured seeds, whereas the Scarlet Macaws also live in the flood plain. "It is great to climb big trees!" he said enthusiastically. At one clay lick he had scaled a 150ft (45m) tall tree and used it as an observation tower to record the direction from which the macaws came. In one hour he watched 54 Green-wings arrive – 52 from the *terra firme* forest. Charlie looked thoughtful as he explained: "I calculated that each wild parrot at these sites annually generates at least several thousand dollars of foreign exchange."

Green-winged Macaws at the clay lick

The predominance of Green-wings at the lick, when there were plenty of Blue and Yellow Macaws in the area, interested me. Charlie said there are about one hundred clay licks in Peru but Blue and Yellow Macaws are present at only five or six – and in the hundreds at two of these. Thus far, only seven clay licks are accessible to tourists.

The large macaws are among the most charismatic birds on the planet, normally glimpsed only fleetingly as they fly overhead. On mornings with good weather conditions, clay licks provide almost guaranteed and unparalleled sightings of macaws and other parrots. Currently the licks at Manu, Tambopata and other sites in Peru, draw more than 6,000 tourists annually, providing an incentive to preserve huge tracts of rainforest to the local people who might otherwise hunt or trap parrots. Since 1984 the licks have generated approximately one thousand jobs at rainforest lodges.

Our enthusiasm for the Heath River lick was still high when we crawled out from under our mosquito nets at 3.30am next morning. This time the canoe travelled only a few feet before it ran aground! Again, Karel, Colin and Charlie removed their shoes and jumped into the river to push us off the sandbank. So again it was 6am before we arrived. Four Severe Macaws were flying by the riverbank and countless Mealy Amazons were congregating. Ten minutes later seven Blue-headed Pionus flew into the trees above the lick (12 more were perched higher) and five minutes later the first Pionus went down, quickly followed by a Severe Macaw and three Yellow-fronted Amazons.

The moving picture that unfolded this morning was quite different. The birds were nervous: there was a predator in the vicinity, perhaps an eagle. Several times all the parrots took off in alarm with a huge *whoosh* of wings. Then the lick might be empty for as long as 20 minutes, in contrast to the continuous activity of the previous morning. When the birds returned the sub-plots were absorbing. Two Severe Macaws were perched in a tree, the lower one, probably a youngster, was bobbing its head in food-soliciting mode. A group of eight or more Golden-crowned Conures kept close together and, at 6.35am, two Barraband's Parrots flew on to the lick with a sudden flash of scarlet.

All this time a Horned Screamer had been perched in the top of a tree. At 7.45am its mate flew in honking and landed a foot away. At 7.50am the first Green-wings put in an appearance. Soon 50 or more were perched warily in the treetops, squabbling, swinging, preening and peering. It was half an hour or so before they overcame their fear and flew onto the lick. What a dazzling sight they made as they gnawed at the clay or, in one case, lunged at an innocent little Golden-crowned Conure! At 8.53am the macaws sounded the alarm as their fifty pairs of wings took to the air. This became the signal for our reluctant departure. I wished I could have stayed forever.

But we had to move on, travelling for several hours on the Madre de Dios River to reach Sandoval Lodge. Now in the Tambopata National Reserve, we walked for half an hour through moist tropical forest until we reached a small landing stage and a narrow canal. We were paddled by canoe through a flooded forest, disturbing a heron from his patient fishing. A Black-tailed Trogon, with a gleaming bronzy head and breast and red abdomen, sat quietly among foliage.

Next we embarked on a double-hulled canoe and suddenly entered an oxbow lake of extraordinary beauty. The clarity of the water was magical, with myriad reflections of the tall *Mauritia* palms, rows and rows of them, that fringed the lake, standing in the water. In the fading light a nightjar, the Pauraque, ventured out for a nocturnal hunting session, his white outer tail feathers contradicting his otherwise cryptic coloration. Then we were served with potato crisps and banana chips and a delicious guacamole dip. Memories are made of such unique and unexpected moments!

Built close to the edge of Sandoval Lake, the lodge has been described as the most scenic and wildlife-rich of the fifteen rainforest lodges in the Tambopata region. The rooms in which we stayed were located along a corridor leading off the main building. They had hot showers in the *en-suite* bathrooms and mosquito-netted beds with blankets – but insects had not been a problem at any time.

After breakfast at 5.30am (it felt like a luxurious lay-in!) we took a canoe-trip across the lake to explore the forest with Enrique

Castillo, an outstanding guide. For me, a tropical rainforest is the most awe-inspiring habitat on earth. In some people it engenders claustrophobia; in me, a feeling of being protected by the ancient trees. And some are truly ancient. Some of the Brazil nut trees alive today were not even young when the conquistadors arrived 500 years ago. Soaring above the canopy, it is said they live for 800 years, perhaps more.

The Brazil nut tree is arguably the most useful and one of the most magnificent in the forests of the Amazon region. It grows in Peru and Brazil, also in Colombia, Ecuador and Bolivia. Unlike other nuts, it cannot be grown successfully in plantations. Attempts were made, but production was so low that it was not economically viable. This is because its flowers are pollinated by female orchid bees whose long tongues are adapted for the purpose. The male bees search out orchids and scrape off the waxy, scented secretions to attract the females. These bees live only in undisturbed forest which, obviously, is becoming increasingly rare. But the most important player in this story which demonstrates how all life is interwoven and dependent on other forms, is the agouti. This rodent, with its sharp little teeth, is the only creature able to open the pods and release the seeds. Like a squirrel, it buries many of the nuts, never retrieves most of them, and a young tree grows.

I was fascinated to meet a *castañero* – a nut collector. With his machete, he opened a "pod". The nuts grow in pods the size of a large grapefruit and take about 15 months to mature. Each pod weighs up to 5lb (2.3 kilos) and contains about 20 nuts. Incidentally, when walking in the forest, it is highly unlikely that you will be pounced upon by a jaguar or bitten by a venomous snake. Death from a falling pod is far more likely!

A small lick inside the forest was sometimes frequented by a group of Orange-cheeked Parrots, said Enrique. He asked us to remain still and went off to silently approach the lick. It was unoccupied. We moved on, as quietly as we could, along the narrow trail. I was at the back of the line. I glanced upwards to see a pair of White-bellied Caiques near the top of a bare white tree. These little parrots were sitting in the sun, their heads a glorious vibrant orange. I had never seen this species in the wild before, so this was the high spot of my day. When they flew, I moved on to find the rest of the group watching them further into the forest. An exciting moment came when we crept up on five Blue and Yellow Macaws feeding on palm fruits. As they flew off the strong light lit the golden hues of their plumage.

Back at the lodge a Chestnut-eared Aracari delighted me. This colourful small toucan, with yellow underparts crossed by a red band, was perched on a palm trunk only a few feet away. The four of us went down to the stream and sat close to the hummingbird feeders in the forest. Soon two species of Hermits, Reddish and Needle-billed, put in an appearance and were joined by a pair of Fork-tailed Woodnymphs – as beautiful as their name. It was so peaceful there, with only the soothing sounds of the water and the occasional whirr of hummingbird wings, until the explosive calls of the Screaming Piha rang forth: *Pee-pe-yo*. These plain grey birds are actually members of the usually colourful cotinga family. Males display at leks – perhaps a bit like pop stars as visiting females are said to be more interested in their voices than their looks!

In the late afternoon we went out on the lake to glimpse two rare giant otters, gambolling near the shoreline. This was a privilege as only about 300 survive in Peru. Thousands were killed up until the 1980s and they are now listed as endangered and occur only on the more remote rivers and lagoons. They really are giants, attaining a length of up to 5ft (1.5m).

A pair of Yellow-fronted Amazons took this intrusion into their territory quite personally and, as dusk fell, they flew around screaming insults at us. It was so typical of the feisty nature of this species! As we were rowed back, the setting sun cast an orange glow over the now tranquil lake; the Amazons had gone to roost.

We all regretted when our last day at Sandoval dawned and we started our journey back to the realities of life. I, for one, did not want to think about it – and the magic qualities of the lake in the early morning light soon dispelled such thoughts. At first the mist was hanging over the water and the *Mauritia* palms took on a ghostly appearance. The only sound was that of the dipping oars and water lapping against the palms on which huge philodendrons were climbing. Red-bellied Macaws flew in pairs and trios above us. We stopped in the still dim light to watch a pair feeding on the palm fruits, the big hands of ripe orange fruits making a splash of colour. Enrique told us that these fruits are used to make juice and ice cream. I would like to have sampled both!

As daylight crept up, the mysterious Hoatzins called their harsh cry from low down in lakeside vegetation. High above, Severe, and Blue and Yellow Macaws flew in the distance, over the palm forest. Tiny black and white Fork-tailed Palm Swifts swooped and dived above the lake surface.

Then the sun came up and the light had an ethereal quality that was a photographer's dream. The trunks of the palms that lined the lakeshore took on a golden hue. These palms provide nest sites for the Red-bellied Macaws, now more numerous on the wing. Nearby a Limpkin and a heron skulked at the water's edge. A turtle was sunning itself on a log. Glimpses of noisy little *Brotogeris* parakeets, probably Cobalt-winged, and Blue-headed Pionus and Amazons flying above, reminded us of the parrot riches we were leaving all too soon...

We started our journeys home with so many memories and thoughts. What an unforgettable two weeks it had been! There was so much variety in the places we visited, the habitats and the bird life. There was so much colour in the markets, so much character in the weather-beaten faces of the Bolivian and Peruvian people we encountered: so much poverty yet laughter too. The guides had been wonderful and we had been so well looked after.

When I asked my room-mate Lin for her impression she told me: "I was overwhelmed to learn, by seeing the whole system, how hard Dr Munn had been working for years and years to save the macaws. That was the strongest message I got from the trip. I want people to know that one serious, dedicated and hard-working person can make such a big difference in conservation. His presence was as strong as those Green-winged Macaws. I want my friends to experience this!"

Update
Many people believed that Munn was a committed

conservationist and that he worked in the best interests of the local people. By 2006 opinions had changed. The community reported that the company called Tropical Nature, that he ran with another man, reputedly used strong-arm tactics to take managerial control of the Napo Lodge for a few months and kept all the lodge's income during that time. By May 2006 Charlie and his partner were expelled from the community and from the lodge management.

Lin was as good as her word. She went back to the USA and organised macaw-watching holidays for people from Japan!

Peruvian bird statistics (year 2000)
Critically Endangered 4
Endangered 23
Vulnerable 46
Near-threatened 55

Species not previously mentioned:

Golden-crowned (Peach-fronted) Conure (*Aratinga aurea*)
Black-tailed Trogon (*Trogon melanurus*)
White-bellied Caique (*Pionites leucogaster*)
Reddish Hermit Hummingbird (*Phaethornis ruber*)
Needle-billed Hermit (*Phaethornis philippi*)
Fork-tailed Woodnymph (*Thalurania furcata*)
Screaming Piha (*Lipaugus vociferans*)
Fork-tailed Palm Swift (*Reinarda squamata*)

Alpaca (*Lama pacos*)
Giant otter (*Pteronura brasiliensis*)

16. Argentina 2003:

The Burrowing Parrots of El Cóndor

Krystyna and I landed at Ezeiza airport early in the morning. We made our way to the bustling Terminal del Omnibus del Retiro, a huge coach station with 40 *plataformes*. It was the evening before a bank holiday and the place was one huge hive of activity, people rushing about carrying a strange assortment of items – one man had his bed with him – and big coaches coming and going with efficient regularity. We boarded the bus that departed at 9.30pm and journeyed south 13 hours to Viedma. A cheap and comfortable method of travel, the coach had luxurious seats that opened out into beds. I awoke just before 5am when the sun was breaking through and the full moon was

---

ARGENTINA

A republic of more than one million square miles

(2.6 million square kilometres), and about 2,300

miles (3,680km) from north to south, this is

the world's largest Spanish-speaking country.

The population is mainly middle-class of

European descent, mostly Spanish and Italian,

with a Welsh community in Patagonia. The climate

is predominantly temperate, also subtropical in the

north and very cold in the south. Within the Andes

chain is Aconcagua, the highest mountain

outside the Himalayas.   **Burrowing Parrot**

---

still hanging in the sky. The scenery was flat, horizon to horizon, interspersed with trees and cattle and crops. We could almost have been in England except for the large, American-style tractors and the wide vistas.

But we were in Patagonia. After the enjoyable trip to Bolivia and Peru, Krystyna and I decided to join forces to visit southern Argentina. We were heading for a place that you will not find on most maps. On reaching Viedma, we took a taxi to El Cóndor. As we neared the small town I spotted Burrowing Parrots perched on the telegraph wires. My heart leapt! Also known as Patagonian Conures, it was these large, elegant parakeets that had lured us to this remote region.

Comparatively few parrots are true colony nesters, although it is not uncommon for a number of pairs of the same species to nest in close proximity. Today, unfortunately, it is rare for sociable nesting parrots to be found in large numbers yet there still exists one colony so large that it is reputedly not exceeded in size anywhere in the world. The prospect of observing this colony was, for me, so exciting, that I had to go there – to El Cóndor!

It lies in the north of Patagonia; the south is famous for the world's most southerly town and the third largest ice field. Located 19 miles (30km) south-east of Viedma, Balneario El Cóndor was growing quickly; in five years the number of houses had increased from 1,000 to 1,500, yet only 300 were permanently occupied. During the short summer season, beach-lovers flock there. I could hardly wait to visit the shore. It was not the sea and the sand that attracted me, but the sandstone cliffs that span approximately five and a half miles (9km) of the beachfront.

Soon I was watching one of the world's most graceful and sociable psittacine species. Worldwide, few parrots have a more southerly distribution – and most of these are in New Zealand. Patagonian Conures are so beautiful! I was to discover that their true beauty can be savoured only when they are in the air.

Leaving the village with the coast on our left, we walked for 20 minutes until the cliffs came into view at a right angle to the road where bungalows gave way to low dunes. Above us parrots were flying. A path led up to a white lighthouse conspicuously perched on the flat-topped cliffs but we headed for the beach where the sea had left little rivers in the sand. Then came a sensational feeling, like nothing I had ever experienced before – or since. The craggy cliffs, containing hundreds of fissures, burrows and caves, were alive with parrots. Due to our arrival, dozens and dozens took to the air, hovering above us, against the deep blue of the sky. Others remained perched on the cliff ledges. The noise and numbers were deliciously overwhelming. It was such a contrast to the general rule of parrot-watching in the neotropics where, with the exception of clay licks, parrots are seen fleetingly as they pass overhead or seek shelter in the crown of a tree. Here I could take my fill of their glorious colours and joyful aerodynamics. With swept-back wings, revealing the glowing yellow rump, pairs swerved

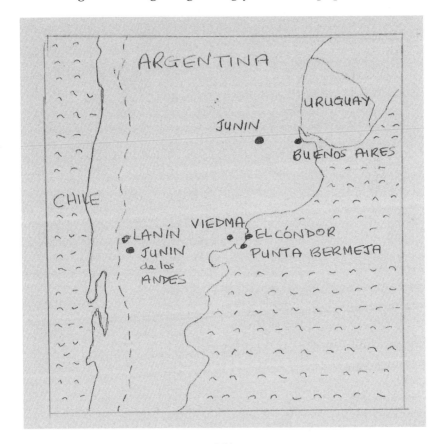

out to sea, then turned and headed towards the cliffs. Inside their burrows, their chicks were waiting to be fed.

The beach was deserted but for our small group. The holiday season had not yet begun and the windy weather was a deterrent. I was with Juan Masello, an Argentine biologist, and Petra Quillfeldt, his German wife. They had been studying this colony since 1998 and, when funds allowed, spent October to January or February working here every day. A contrasting couple, dark and fair, Latin and Nordic, they were remarkable for their enthusiasm and endurance. As research scientists they had little money but were utterly dedicated to the project.

I asked Juan about the attitude of the local people to the *loros barranqueros*, as they are known. He recalled the very first visit that he and Petra had made. At the petrol station he was asked: "Why do you want to study those squawking creatures. They are useless. They don't even talk!"

Juan told me that the tradition of persecuting these handsome birds was a long one. The parrots are not protected – quite the reverse in 1963 when they were declared agricultural pests under an Argentine National Law. Until the 1980s the El Cóndor colony was sprayed with DDT to kill the birds – a painful death, resulting in the young also dying in the nests. These parrots were still shot and poisoned. Juan's face darkened. He grew angry when he told me what happened during the 1990s. "They dynamited a section of cliff between the first and second kilometre of the colony – just for pedestrian and car access from the cliff top to the beach." I was horrified, imagining the birds that were killed and maimed. "Hundreds of nests were destroyed", he said. "Many chicks would have died."

We stayed on the beach until 8.30pm, watching Juan and Petra working, with their field assistant, Lu. Juan went to the top of the cliff and secured a rope to a metal post. He was then able to climb down the cliff and to remove young from certain nests. The chicks, with their grey down and intelligent eyes, were very appealing. They looked around with interest, usually with no hint of panic. Each chick was weighed and measured and, when it reached 100g, ringed with a numbered stainless steel ring, then quickly returned to the nest burrow. Handling ceased when the

Juan and Petra working by the cliff with their assistant Lu

young were near to fledging. In one season, ninety one percent of young in the nests that were monitored survived to fly. This highly successful rate is partly due to the fact that predators cannot reach the nests. It is what happens to them after they leave the nest that causes concern. One of the chicks Juan had ringed ended up in a pet shop in Spain.

Early next morning, Krystyna and I went out at 6am. Sitting in the brush on the cliff-top, we seemed to catch the full fury of the violent wind. The only sounds I could hear were those of the sea and the wind and the strident calls of the long-tailed parrots. They were seldom silent in flight when humans were present. Every couple of minutes a group of ten or so would rise on the wind above the cliff top, then sink down again to where the multitude of nest entrances decorate the cliff face. The flight of these parrots is exquisitely graceful; they move through the air like gulls, hanging on the thermals, being carried backwards, then hanging motionless. In a tight little group, their wings almost touching, they were watching us.

To my right was a small sandy bank, with the occasional low shrub. A Long-tailed Meadowlark perched briefly on its top, swaying in the wind. The female of this common species is marked with brown, buff and black while the male is almost black with scarlet throat and underparts.

The wind was gusting, violent; it was cold: all the way from New Zealand (two-thirds of the globe away) without meeting land. The sea was grey-blue that morning, with foaming breakers. A few small clouds dotted the sky. It felt so strange to be watching parrots in a beach environment on an Atlantic coast, to see them swooping around in small flocks. I was mesmerised by the grace of their flight. We walked down to the beach and selected a spot protected by the cliff to eat our breakfast. Suddenly there was a rockfall and we realised the foolishness of sitting there.

December is, of course, the start of the Austral summer. The beach stretches for 19 miles (30km). Holidaymakers could avoid the colony yet, at the height of the season (Christmas to the end of February), cars are parked four deep along the sand below the nesting cliffs. One afternoon I was horrified to see a paraglider. He was gliding in front of the colony a few feet from the nests. Juan seemed resigned. "I have already asked him to glide elsewhere, but he just ignores me."

An attempt to prevent public access to this section of the beach, to protect the nesting colony, had failed. A judge in Viedma first ruled that the parrots should not be disturbed but his decision caused such an outcry that he was forced to reverse it. When the beach was crowded, at the height of the breeding season, the parrots were too nervous to enter their nests to feed their young. Worse still, people from the town threw stones at the parrots and were known to shoot them "for fun".

The western end of the cliffs was the most highly populated. It was marked with hundreds of holes that formed entrances to nest burrows from about 10ft (3m) up from the beach to near the top of the cliff, the height of which varied from 36ft to 90ft (11m to 27m). The parrots can with ease excavate their nests in the greyish sandstone. Some burrows have a shared entrance, branching off into separate chambers. The species is very tolerant: aggression has no place in a closely-packed colony. The parrots arrive from hundreds of miles distant to nest there. The first birds turn up in September. Eggs are laid during October

In joyful flight over the cliffs

and November and hatch after 25 days. Fledging starts at the end of December and continues until the end of January.

Sweeping across the beach and in front of the cliff face, the parrots turned first one way and then the other. They would sweep back, low overhead, and the glorious orange and yellow markings on the abdomen caused me to draw in my breath with delight. I never tired of trying to photograph them in flight against the blue of the sky. Little groups perched on the cliffs, watching our every movement. The birds that were not brooding or feeding young, or out foraging, would gather at the top, in ever increasing numbers, to peer down at us, silently observing our movements.

They were used to Juan and Petra whose studies have resulted in the publication of papers in such important journals as *Emu*, *Journal of Avian Biology* and *The Condor*. (Juan was not pleased though when on submitting a paper to one important ornithological journal, it was returned by the editor with the scrawled remark: "We have published enough on Burrowing Owls." He had not even bothered to read the title.) Part of their work involved monitoring the growth of the young in about 30 nests each season. Juan had used tiny cameras placed in a few burrows. Hundreds of hours of video footage had given a new insight into the parrots' behaviour.

Young are reared mainly on small seeds, such as those of a large thistle, smaller thistle species and other seeds, including dock so familiar to us in Britain. In the El Cóndor area the Burrowing Parrots feed on the flood plain of the Rio Negro, on the ground or in bushes, on berries and buds, in an environment of Patagonian steppe. (Steppe is the name given to large areas of dry grassland.) There are few trees. In the cliff-top region the parrots could be seen sweeping low over these grasslands. They were attracted to recently burnt ground. On examining it after they had flown I found no evidence of the food source – perhaps tiny particles of charcoal. We saw two ground dwelling species up there – little Burrowing Owls, with their long legs and startled eyes – and viscachas, attractive burrowing rodents not unlike chinchillas, but larger.

In the cliff-top habitat where trees are scarce or stunted, the parrots perch on telephone lines, one hundred or more together, sometimes dropping down to the scrubby ground to walk about in search of food. In the evening the non-breeding birds gathered in their hundreds against a backdrop of the oldest lighthouse in Patagonia and the evening sun turning the sky orange. Then they flew to the little town to roost. Here again telephone lines were favoured sites. One roosting area was near the house in which we were staying. I could hear their strident calls throughout the night!

In the village there was a weed-covered area that had yet to be built on. Saffron Finches and Hooded Siskins fed there. An intriguing species could often be seen in small active groups, its baggy, shaggy plumage setting it apart from nearly all other birds. This was the distinctive Guira Cuckoo, the only member of its genus. Black and brown and white-streaked above, its plumage below is whitish. I was always delighted to see them because they are so full of character and curiosity. Their breeding habits are unusual: several females lay their turquoise eggs in one nest – an open platform of sticks.

Life could be very good for the Patagonian Conures here – except for the activities of the earth's most destructive animal – man. This is a declining species, already extinct north of Buenos Aires and in the province of Córdoba. Much of its steppe habitat has been converted for agricultural use. It is regarded as a pest, shot and poisoned because it is said to damage crops. There is very little evidence of serious damage.

In recent years Birdlife International from the UK and its partners in other countries worldwide have designated "Important Bird Areas" for many countries. This is the most effective way of protecting a number of endangered and threatened species in one region. When I arrived in El Cóndor Juan and Petra had given me some very encouraging hot news. Eighty-seven IBAs had been designated for the region and El Condor was assessed as the *fourth most important.*

One afternoon we took a trip south to Punta Bermeja, about an hour away, to see a protected colony of fur seals. From a high vantage point and battered by the icy wind, we watched the dozens or hundreds of animals. They were lying motionless on the beach in front of the cliffs or on little rocky outcrops. One seal stood out. It was almost white – a southern elephant seal, so called for the male's enormous size and huge proboscis which, in exaggerated fancy, resembles an elephant's trunk. Males can reach a length of 18ft (5.4m) and weigh up to two tons (2,000 kilos). These remarkable seals were hunted almost to extinction by the end of the 19th Century. Now their numbers have increased to a safe level.

Fur seals at Punta Bermeja – with an elephant seal top left

217

The small colony of Burrowing Parrots in the coastal cliffs attracted my attention, protected, to a degree, by the presence of the seals. It was a strange, almost unreal sensation, to watch these parrots with their bright colours that seem to epitomise the tropics, in this bleak, wind-swept temperate Atlantic setting. They flew against a backdrop of steely-grey ocean and flat-topped black rocks. When the sky brightened after icy raindrops had fallen, their golden rumps lit up the sky like some precious jewels glinting in the sun. No matter how strong the wind (at times we had to cling to the railing), these parrots rode it. With their long pointed wings and rudder-like tails, they are masters of the air. We stood on a headland and the parrots swooped around us with a *joie de vivre* that will forever stay in my mind. How anyone can catch these birds and cage them, just to make a few pesos, is beyond my comprehension.

Young Burrowing Parrots

Unfortunately they do – and in large numbers. A very important step for the conservation of the Patagonian Conure would be to prohibit its export. In the year 2000 the appalling total of 10,275 was exported from Argentina. In that year it was one of only six parrot species worldwide with an export total in excess of 10,000 birds.

In the previous year, when Juan was not able to work at the colony during the breeding season, many young were collected from nests there. Juan told me sadly that dead and dying chicks were left scattered about the beach. The species will not be able to withstand collection at this rate for much longer. And for the individual parrots, export is a tragedy. They belong in a colony of hundreds. They evolved as highly social beings. When they are isolated from their own kind, when they are not tame (particularly when caught as adults) they suffer unimaginable stress. You have to see them in their normal environment, in flocks, to understand just how cruel it is to keep one bird on its own. Stress will cause a single bird to pluck itself and/or to call continually for its own kind.

Their nesting cliffs must be protected and regarded not as

human playgrounds but as valuable natural habitats. The colony here is a unique wildlife resource that must be conserved forever.

Several factors make El Cóndor arguably the best place in the world to watch parrots at the right time of year. You see them flying over when you walk down the main street, you see and hear them at night when they roost on the power lines and above all you could watch, all day and every day for nearly five months, the fascinating activities of the breeding colony. Unlike most parrot-watching locations, there are no doubts: the parrots will be there! They have the potential to bring prosperity to this little-known corner of Patagonia. Only in this way can their conservation be guaranteed, like macaws at clay licks.

Updates
After my visit I encouraged Juan, and helped to raise funds, for a local education programme. This started well in schools, with lectures to children and adults, and guided visits to the colony. Unfortunately, due to some problems – more political than practical – this programme could not continue, so Juan and his colleagues designed a leaflet describing the importance of the colony and the need for its protection, and distributed 10,000 in nearby towns and ecotourism destinations. In December 2004 they presented a proposed Act to declare the colony a nature reserve. This act has yet to be passed. An additional one thousand leaflets were used as posters and displayed in shops, hotels and internet cafés. Local TV and newspaper coverage created interest. During the 2006-2007 field season, 8,000 more leaflets and 3,000 posters were distributed further afield.

Burrowing Parrots are still officially and inaccurately described as agricultural pests. In January 2005 Juan and his team followed flocks using a Cessna aircraft. Sixty-four feeding flocks were located in patches of natural vegetation, six in pasture and two close to crops.

The threats to the colony continue. The surrounding habitat is rapidly being transformed to agricultural land. Clearance of native vegetation has been estimated at 3.7% per annum. Burning large sections of the steppe are carried out every year to protect private property and power lines from natural fires. This causes erosion and threatens the stability of the cliff supporting the colony. The future of this most important breeding site in the entire range of the species is far from secure. However, education in the form of continuing school visits to the colony is starting to pay off and killing the parrots has stopped.

In 2009 a new and horrible threat to the species came to light. Illegal traffickers were catching Burrowing Parrots and dying them with hydrogen peroxide in an attempt to pass them off as Blue and Yellow Macaws – a much more valuable and, of course, a much larger species. The poor birds – those that survived – were then sold at fairs in Buenos Aires – fairs that operate despite protection laws that are not enforced. The dying process can cause the liver to malfunction, thus the unfortunate parrots might survive for a very short time. The young are acquired by stealing them from nests, putting additional pressure on the declining breeding populations.

Argentine bird statistics (year 2000)
Critically Endangered 4
Endangered 4
Vulnerable 31
Near-threatened 53

Species not previously mentioned:

Burrowing Parrot or Patagonian Conure (*Cyanoliseus patagonus patagonus*)
Long-tailed Meadowlark (*Sturnella loyca*)
Burrowing Owl (*Athene cunicularia*)
Hooded Siskin (*Carduelis magellanicus*)
Guira Cuckoo (*Guira guira*)

Viscacha (*Lagostomus maximus*)
Southern elephant seal (*Mirounga leonina*)

Thistle (*Carduus mariana*)
Dock (*Rumex crispus*)

17. Argentina 2003:

Lanín – Land of Lakes and Volcanoes

It seems unlikely, I know, but there are parrots that live alongside glaciers and snow-capped volcanoes. This scenario is in total defiance of the image of these colourful birds eating Brazil nuts in tropical forests or resting in coconut palms on the fringe of a reef.

In 1982 BBC television showed a film series entitled *The Flight of the Condor* about the wildlife of the Andes. For me the most memorable sequence was that which showed Austral Conures in the southern beech forests of Patagonia. These parakeets live by ancient glacial lakes whose chilly blue waters are sometimes lashed by bitter winds that turn them frothy white. I never forgot this film sequence. I wanted to go there and see the parrot with the most southerly distribution on the planet.

It took me twenty-one years to achieve this wish. As I recounted in the previous chapter, the primary purpose of my visit to Argentina was to see the world's largest parrot colony. If I travelled about 400 miles (650km) westwards, towards the border with Chile, I could see this species too. The *Cachaña*, as it is known locally, occurs only in the southern parts of Chile and Argentina.

I had a good contact who could tell me precisely where to go, pin-pointing to within a few metres the location he had seen them! This was the huge Lanín National Park, extending over 379,000 hectares, created in 1937 to preserve a representative section of the Andean-Patagonian region absent from other national parks.

Sometimes travelling in a foreign country can go disastrously wrong. This happened to me in my search for the *Cachaña* – but in hindsight it became a memorable experience. After leaving El

Cachaña or Austral Conure

Cóndor, Krystyna and I took a taxi to Viedma and then a bus to Bahia Blanca. At the bustling transport station we waited until 8pm for our bus which we duly boarded. We were bound for Junin de los Andes, close to Lanín National Park.

We disembarked at the awful hour of 4am. As I looked around a growing fear assailed the pit of my stomach. This was a large town. Panic set in. We must have come to the wrong place! This was confirmed by a group of taxi drivers waiting hopefully for a fare who assured me that there was no hotel here called San Jorge. We were in Junin, yes! But not Junin de los Andes! That was almost one thousand miles (1,600km) away! The men were very concerned. We could not wander the streets at that hour and one drove us to a hotel not far away. It was 6am when we fell into bed.

We breakfasted at 9.30am and I told the waiter our story of woe! It was overheard by a sympathetic man called Mario, a baseball coach. He suggested that we went to a travel agent not far away to book a flight to San Martin which was close to our destination. The lady in the travel agent was extremely kind and helpful. Apparently we were not the first to make this geographical error! However, the only plane to San Martin had already departed. We returned to the hotel where Mario insisted on accompanying us to the bus station to find out if we could continue our journey by road. There were no seats left for today, we were told. This statement had been made without the man in the ticket office making a phone call and I guessed that each bus station had a certain allocation of seats. I suggested that we should return just before the San Martin coach was due to depart on the chance that seats would be available.

Meanwhile we went in search of a bank in the main plaza. Most banks would not change foreign currency, even US dollars. Finally we found one that would and the queuing and the transaction took more than one hour. It was then time for lunch – and we struck lucky. The chef, another Mario, made us the most delicious pasta with two kinds of cheese and a sauce of cream and walnuts. I ignored the calories and enjoyed the uniqueness of the dish!

The kindness of these people knew no bounds. We went back to the bus terminal, accompanied by Mario and the hotel owner. Mario said it was essential that he should buy the tickets. What he told the clerk at the office I do not know – but it must have been convincing. Not only did we get on the bus but we had the best views in the vehicle – the front seats upstairs! It was a long journey – a little adventure in itself. The ticket price included a free meal during a midnight stop at San Rosario. The food was the antithesis of that served by chef Mario – but who wants to eat at midnight, anyway? Next morning, at 8am, we arrived at Neuquén. From there we took the 9am bus to Junin de los Andes. Three hours later there were distant views of the snow-capped Andes. We had arrived! Remarkably, considering the distance and the journey by road, we were only a little over one day late. It was 3pm and the sun was brilliant in a clear blue sky.

Our hotel, one of only two in the little town, was a disappointment. Although it was mid-December, the Austral summer, it was not busy as most people prefer to stay in nearby San Martin. We took a quick shower and called a taxi. We could not waste any more time and wanted to visit Lanín National Park at once.

It is strange how fate steps in and takes a hand. If we had arrived on the previous day (which had been cold and windy) we would probably never have met Carlos. It was one of those chance meetings that can transform a short stay and provide memories that never fade. Carlos was the taxi driver, slim, dark and intelligent. He proved to be a treasure. We quickly discovered that he understood some English when Krystyna said: "I like him – he's nice!" – and he grinned. He instantly became a friend who could not do enough for us. It was a delight to see how quickly he adopted the spirit of birdwatching, borrowing our binoculars and looking up species in *Las Aves de Argentina y Uruguay* (Birds of Argentina and Uruguay).

From San Martin it took about 90 minutes to reach Lanín National Park. The road led through a swampy plain, with grasslands and little pools inhabited by various ducks. Twenty or more Ashy-headed Geese were grazing, lifting their heads warily now and then to keep an eye on us. These geese are an exquisite study in shades of cinnamon, brown and grey with black and white striped flanks and orange legs. In flight their predominantly white wing markings form conspicuous flags against the green and brown landscape. They are *so* handsome!

We encountered a flock of about sixty Buff-necked Ibis feeding in a field, busily probing the earth. I found them very beautiful, their muted colours appealing to me more than those of the Scarlet Ibis of the northern part of the continent. Feeding in a little roadside pool, close to the car, was a Snipe and, with a bill half the length of its body, it was searching the mud for its next meal.

The scenery, of no particular merit, changed with extraordinary rapidity as we reached the national park. Lanín is in the centre

Ashy-headed Geese

224

Lanin volcano, flanked by Araucaria *trees*

of an area of lakes that stretches for 200 miles (322km) from north to south, on either side of the Argentina/Chile border. An area of outstanding natural beauty, its lakes and mountains are often likened to Switzerland.

At once I fell under the spell of the *Araucaria* trees (sometimes known as the Chilean pine), exquisitely formed and glossy dark green against the backdrop of the almost perfect conical shape of Lanín volcano. This area of great natural beauty is dominated by the volcano which rises to 12,380ft (3,775m). The national park is one of the few places in which this tree still survives. Known locally as *pehuén*, it is seen in the UK as an ornamental tree, under the name of monkey-puzzle. Unfortunately, its wood was heavily exploited at the beginning of the last century and this tree is now a threatened species. According to a book published in 2003, in Argentina it is listed on Appendix II of CITES yet it is on Appendix I (endangered) in Chile. In Argentina it has a restricted distribution, being limited to the province of Neuquén. I was shocked to find how few *Araucarias* remained in this protected area, usually in very small groups (rather than stands) called *bosquecillos* – little woods. This tree is an important food source for the *Cachaña*, the parakeet that had brought us here.

My first sighting, near the Tromen lake entrance to the park, was of a flock of eight birds in the air. It was a thrilling moment! Then a pair flew into the top of an *Araucaria* a few feet away. I moved slowly towards them until I was on the same side of the tree. One bird fed on a cone at the top, its olive green plumage blending in with the spiky branches, and the sun highlighting its dull red abdomen and tail. The other bird stood guard, not feeding. I watched them for several minutes. That afternoon we were treated to several more sightings, usually of pairs in flight over the forest.

What a beautiful place they live in! This ancient forest (not unlike those in New Zealand), where the trees are draped in mosses and the trunks covered in lichen, is made up of evergreen beech, pellin oak and the rich green many-forked branches of the *Araucaria*. Photographed against the glistening snow-covered volcano and the brilliant cloudless blue of the sky, and laden with rounded green cones, the *pehuén* was surely the most beautiful tree I had ever seen. And when on its branches the *Cachañas* were perched, the day became perfect.

The *Araucaria* trees are of interest to the local people. The nuts are considered to be a delicacy, an expensive one. I picked up a few that had been opened by the conures beneath the trees . Each nut case is nearly 2in (about 4cm) long and is split open leaving one side undamaged. This tree must reach the age of about 40 years before it bears its first seeds. Slow-growing in the extreme, the cones take two to three years to mature. Each one contains between 120 and 200 nuts. Bearing in mind the relatively small number of surviving trees, it is easy to see how collection of the nuts could have a detrimental effect on the future of the tree and of the parakeet. Although the latter apparently has no shortage of food sources, it might be that these nuts play a special role in its diet.

It has been said that there are more "monkey-puzzle" trees in British gardens than there are in their natural habitat. Certainly in the 20th century it was a popular ornamental tree. The story of its introduction to England (according to Kew Gardens) is a curious one. In the late 19th century Archibald Menzies was visiting Chile when he was invited to dinner by the Governor. While seated at the dinner table he pocketed some seeds (served

One of many tranquil lakes

as a delicacy). Five of these seeds were propagated and one of the resulting trees grew at Kew for many decades.

The next morning we set off well before daybreak to reach one of the most scenic routes in the world, the Seven Lakes road. The cold start to the day added to its appeal with mist hanging just above the surface of the lake. The chill gave way to a blue cloudless sky, warmth and beauty. The roadsides were glorious in blue and yellow – lupins and broom – and the mountains were reflected with extraordinary clarity in the still waters of the lakes. Notro trees, with their flaming red flowers, made a spectacular display. I marvelled at the beauty all around me. The air was so pure and the light so brilliant. I had never experienced anything quite like it before.

Carlos was also enjoying himself. He lived comparatively close yet only once had he previously visited the national park. He, too, was beguiled by its landscape. His working day was spent driving along the streets of the small towns – only a few kilometres away – yet they were a different world. And the people who inhabited or visited them apparently never strayed from their artificial environment to the natural one. Such riches lay almost on their doorstep yet they had never seen them. It was inconceivable. I felt as though I had discovered a secret world – a place of peace and perfection.

The area was almost devoid of human life but the lakes were alive with geese, Black-necked Swans, ducks and coots. A group of Coscoroba Swans flew above us. At Lake Villarino, where a family of grebes was gliding gracefully, four *Cachañas* crossed overhead. At Lake Traful, I stopped to ask the warden about them. They were present 12 months of the year, he said. The previous week he had seen a flock of 13 near the lake.

When I told Carlos that we wanted to depart even earlier next day, at 5.30pm, he was reluctant to believe me. But at the appointed hour his white taxi, bearing the *Remise* sign on its roof, drew up and Carlos got out with a welcoming smile. Soon after a colourful sunrise turned the sky pink-orange, but it was over in seconds. We returned to Lanín National Park. Just before the entrance six parakeets were perched on a low tree close to the road in an open area. We stopped. Another five flew in, unconcerned by our presence. We studied them in the half-light, thinking wistfully of the photos we might have taken had the sun been up! Later, pairs and small groups were flying, searching for seeding cones. They could land in the top of a tree and instantly disappear, completely hidden from view, only to reappear when they flew.

Their early morning feeding session over, we decided to venture into Chile. After answering questions at the Customs point while the under-worked officials filled in a few forms, we crossed the border into Villarrica National Park. At once we came across a lake where the handsome blue-billed Andean Ruddy Duck could be found. Verdant forests stretched away into the distance, some bisected by little moss-covered waterfalls, foaming down the steep side of craggy mountains. At Lago Quillehue, Great Grebes, coots (with five young) and Ruddy Ducks lived in the shadow of Vulcan Hermoso. So tranquil and unspoilt, I could have lingered here for days. About 37 miles (60km) to the west we would have encountered the active volcano of Villarrica. Another time, perhaps…

This scenery left a deep impression on my mind, as it did on poet Pablo Neruda, whose lines are translated here:

Under the volcanoes, beneath the glaciers,
Among the huge lakes, the silent, the tangled, the Chilean
   forest…
Anyone who has not been in the Chilean forest does not
   know this planet.

There were *Cachañas* here too, flying swiftly above the beech trees in a direct flight path. They nest in December, so perhaps even now they were returning to a hole in an oak tree or even a deserted woodpeckers' nest.

No direct threats to the existence of this conure were apparent and it was not recognised as having pet potential. Indeed, most people do not know of its existence. An encounter near Lake Tromen with a couple from Buenos Aires demonstrated this. He was a veterinary surgeon and they were both interested in wildlife. When they asked me which birds I had seen I told them about the *Cachaña*. She was, quite frankly, disbelieving and I was not surprised. "Parakeets are tropical birds", she said, inferring they could not be found in this setting. Fortunately I could get out *Las Aves de Argentina y Uruguay* and point to the bird and its distribution map! She was not inclined to argue with the book and went away a little wiser!

In San Martin I went to the national parks office and asked if anyone knew about *Cachañas* and on what they fed. A helpful employee said that they eat the berries of elder and of all species of *Berberis*, including *B.linearifolia,* also the berries of a species of *Sorbus* – the same genus as the mountain ash which is so familiar as an ornamental tree in the UK. They also eat emergent leaf buds of poplars and other trees.

My brief stay had not been a disappointment as so often happens with longed-for destinations. It was a glorious success and the snapshots in my mind of snow-covered volcanoes reflected in crystal clear lakes will always live on.

Update 2008

Little was known about the Austral Conure, considered a common species, until Dr Ana Trejo, Soledad Díaz and Valeria Ojeda from the Universidad Nacional del Comahue commenced to study its foraging and reproductive biology in 1998. They described its conservation status as "uncertain". Their studies revealed a growing interest in it as a pet – not only at a local scale. Trapped birds were sold at a very low price, equivalent to US$3 (£2). The conures were being persecuted and hunted during winter, when large flocks were found around villages. They witnessed people (mostly children) hunting the conures with slings; many were injured or killed. They contacted the authorities on discovering this and found a "total lack of enforcement" of protection laws. Their conclusion was that, without a conservation and education programme, the parakeet could become endangered within ten years.

Species not previously mentioned:

Austral Parakeet or Conure *(Cachaña)* **(*Enicognathus ferrugineus*)**
Ashy-headed Goose *(Chloephaga poliocephala)*
Buff-necked Ibis *(Theristicus caudatus)*
Black-necked Swan *(Cygnus melancoryphus)*
Coscoroba Swan *(Coscoroba coscoroba)*
Snipe *(Gallinago gallinago)*
Andean Ruddy Duck *(Oxyura ferruginea)*
Great Grebe *(Podiceps major)*
Ruddy Duck *(Oxyura jamaicensis)*

Notro tree *(Embothrium coccineum)*
Chilean pine or monkey puzzle tree *(Araucaria araucana)*

18. Argentina, 1988 and 2004:

Mountains of the North

Argentina is a country of quite extraordinary and thrilling diversity. From the subtropical forests of the north to the glaciers of the south, it has an amazing array of bird life to match the different habitats.

Within its northern borders, it can claim part of one of the world's most famous natural landmarks, the Iguazú Falls. After flowing for 600 miles (1,000km), the Iguazú River created the waterfall as it turned from a south-western to a north-western course. Here it cut into a deep layer of basalt, the remains of a lava flow which is 120 million years old. Described as the most overwhelming and spectacular falls in South America, they are without doubt a natural feature unequalled by anything I have seen anywhere in the world (so far!). My brief visit in October 1988 will forever remain in my memory.

The volume of water was not at its greatest but the sight of these falls, and the rapids extending for two miles (3.5km) above and along them, was overwhelming. In effect a 180ft (60m) high precipice, the falls are surrounded by a national park extending over 850 square mile (2,200 square km). Three-quarters lies within Brazil and the rest in Argentina. The tourist is unlikely to see the jaguars, anteaters, capuchin monkeys and anteaters that dwell there and few people explore beyond the main attraction. In the limited time available we could explore only the vicinity of the falls, but even here there were parrots and toucans. Maximilian's or Scaly-headed Parrots, apparently two males, were courting a female. White-eyed Conures went shrieking overhead.

A small group of Red-bellied (Maroon-bellied) Conures flew over the thundering waters to land in trees at the water's edge. They bathed in a small rock pool and flew back, wet, to preen their plumage dry in the sun. One bird entered a hole in the rock face and I wondered if it was nesting there. Others fed in the trees on small seeds.

I clambered on a rock overhanging a cliff and a waterfall to photograph a rainbow that had formed in the mists of spray. Below me the water resembled a white cloud as it thundered over the shrub-covered crags. At the parking area, a colony of Red-rumped Caciques were flying backwards and forwards to their pendulous nests – built from plant material and hanging beneath the branch. They were so beautiful with their glossy black plumage, brilliant scarlet rump, yellow beak and blue eyes. Furthermore, they tolerated a close approach.

My group, including a number of distinguished ornithologists, then took a coach to the part of the falls that one can reach across a long walkway. There butterflies were attracted to the salt in the mud – ten species swirling about like snow in an artificial snowstorm globe! We walked out to the falls, cooled by a gentle breeze. To reach almost to the centre was breathtaking. The pounding waters and their prehistoric power were mesmerising.

This area boasts 448 bird species, the most famous of which are

The spectacular Iguazu falls

232

the Great Dusky Swifts. They breed *under* the falling torrents of water, flying into the spray to land on the rock face behind it. With a choice of 275 cascades, they prefer the most magnificent of all, the *Garganta del Diablo* (the Devil's Throat). In sunny weather, hundreds of swifts are flying in their quest for insect prey, dwarfed by the majesty of their surroundings.

The falls are among nature's greatest miracles, and designated a World Heritage Site in 1984. Some years later I was to be dismayed and saddened at what had happened to Argentina's forests in other regions – and thankful that at least these natural riches had survived.

Brazil and Paraguay – briefly!

I had visited the falls with participants of an ornithological meeting in Curitiba, Brazil. From the falls we crossed over into Paraguay to see the engineering feat of the great dam, constructed from massive steel girders. Men and tractors were at work, dwarfed by an enormous crane. The renowned Brazilian ornithologist, Pedro Scherer Neto, told me that twenty years previously Green-winged Macaws were nesting in the riverbank.

It was the same story when I stayed with my friend Carlos Keller in his one-hundred-year-old hacienda in Pirassunanga in Brazil, on the Rio Mogi-Guassu. All around, except on his property, the forest had been cut. He told me sadly: "Until 1935 Hyacinthine and Green-winged Macaws were nesting here. Even the pretty golden Saffron Finches, which up until seven years ago fed in flocks on the seed I scattered on the terrace, have been trapped out of existence." Sightings of the once common Maximilian's Parrot had also become rare. It was so peaceful there, amid acres of farmland and trees that were remnants of the once great forests of Pirassununga destroyed between 1823 and 1973.

Kingfishers, handsome Muscovy Ducks, bearing little resemblance to the domesticated form, various species of tanager and Violaceous Euphonias abounded. The male euphonia, blue-black above and yellow below, is a wonderful songster and mimic, with the ability to imitate many other bird species. A pair of cotinga-like Swallow Tanagers, the male gleaming turquoise with a black mask, the female dull green, was feeding on mistletoe berries. Pretty little Rusty-collared Seedeaters were hopping about on the grass. They are members of a large genus of about 30 species attractively garbed in shades of brown, black and white. At 6pm we walked down to the farm to watch the sun set, streaking the sky with orange. At this hour Blue-winged Parrotlets were usually in evidence, said Carlos, but that day they were missing. His lifelong passion for birds had resulted in an immense reserve of knowledge on the subject.

It was here that I witnessed for the first time one of the most amazing spectacles in the bird world – the dance of the manakin. Carlos had an aviary in which he kept and studied the fabulous Blue or Swallow-tailed Manakin. The little blue male (5in long) with glowing scarlet crown, has an intense beauty which contrasts with that of his green female. Early one morning I watched two males displaying to a female who sat quietly nearby. It was a breathtaking performance. The males changed places on the perch at breakneck speed, whirring one over the other, up and down, up and down, their wings moving too fast for the eye to see. After two or three minutes the performance changed, the males flying differently, less rapidly, and making a clacking sound with the wings for a few seconds. They rested for four or five seconds and then started all over again. I crept nearer and nearer, mesmerised, but they took no notice of me during a performance that must have lasted for ten minutes.*

Exploring the farm gave me an insight into what life was like in southern Brazil. The hacienda was built in a quadrangle, with a covered terrace in the middle, and surrounded by a verandah. Hummingbirds fed from the feeders there. Inside, all was plain and serviceable and old. The cook produced tasty meals from basic foods – delicious beans and rice, little fritters of heart of palm, Swiss-style fried potatoes and salad, followed by tinned peaches with coconut that had apparently been boiled with sugar until it was jam-like. I appreciated this as in restaurants in Brazil at that time I had found no vegetarian options.

---

*Sixteen years after this performance I received an e-mail from Carlos. Attached was a recent photograph of one of the males I had seen dancing! Yes, he was still alive!

Argentina, April 2004

While in Patagonia the previous year I had bought a pair of salad servers carved with an Andean Condor's head. The vendor told me about the region from which they originated, in the north-west. It was an area of great natural beauty, she said. I wanted to know more about it. On returning I found a ten-day bird-watching trip to northern Argentina in the brochure of a company that specialises in wildlife tourism. When I read the itinerary and saw that the Andean sub-species of the Burrowing Parrot was listed, my mind was made up. I could see this parrot in a mountainous environment! I departed from Gatwick in mid-April and met the other nine members of the group in Madrid, where we took an overnight flight to Buenos Aires.

Day 1
From there it was a two-hour flight to Salta. This was the first region of Argentina to be colonised by the Spanish. When Buenos Aires was no more than a village, Salta was a thriving and important city. Founded in 1582, it has some fine colonial buildings of which we had only fleeting glimpses. We transferred to a small motel near the beautiful San Lorenzo canyon, about half an hour from the airport in a residential area for the better off, with attractive houses and gardens.

We met the guide who was to accompany us, who I will call Santiago. In late afternoon we birded the main road, stopping to watch Burrowing Owls. Maximilian's (Scaly-headed) was the most frequently observed short-tailed parrot and several family groups were passing overhead. Flocks of Mitred Conures – 50, 30, 40 and 15 – sped overhead on their way to roost. This 15in (38cm) long parakeet, with scarlet markings on the head, was the parrot most commonly seen.

I surreptitiously studied Santiago who was not like any guide I had met before. A man of rather few words, these mainly related to the names of the species we encountered. Most guides are so passionate about their job! Being paid to go birding is their idea of heaven, despite having to cope with such difficult creatures as humans. The enthusiasm and excitement with which they infuse their work was lacking. However, this was amply compensated by the superior birding skills of one member of our group. Alan

235

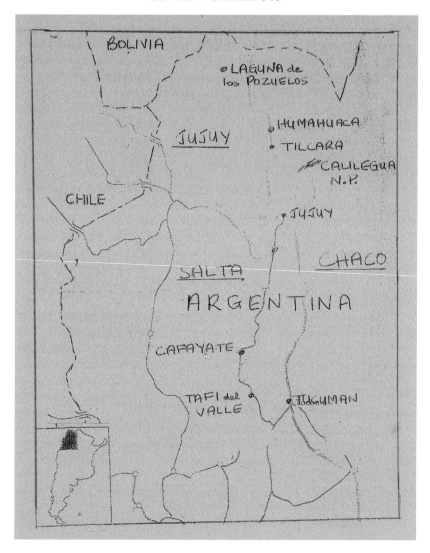

Davies, from Wales, managed the Conwy RSPB bird reserve and had travelled widely. He had a talent for finding birds with enviable speed. We were all glad of his company. (Alan became famous in 2008 as the man who set off around the world, with Ruth Miller, to beat the record of the number of species seen in one year.)

Santiago's scope was of such poor quality it was like looking into fog. Then a generous member of our group gave him a better lens. Four members had excellent spotting telescopes and were very kind in sharing sightings with those without them. They were a good crowd and we all got on well.

The charismatic Red-legged Seriema with its long, curvy eyelashes.

Day 2

Next morning the gloomy weather was still with us. Our group visited the nearby Huayco reserve, newly established from the donation of 1,200 acres. Two men were busy cutting down exotic trees. Formerly hunters, they had once been active there, killing birds and brocket deer. The guans had survived! A Dusky-legged Guan swooped across the path in front of me with a heavy *whoosh* of its wings. Later another flew behind me. Guans have always been persecuted. Good eating, they are more slender and elegant than turkeys, with small heads.

Leaving the reserve for a main road, two large ground-dwellers of the region were encountered. The flightless Greater Rheas, South America's equivalent of the Ostrich, in small groups, and a pair of Red-legged (or Crested) Seriemas were observed hurrying away. With their long necks and elongated bodies, these birds are allied to cranes but their legs are not quite as long and their plumage includes a feathery crest. Three seen on cultivated land might have been searching for small snakes, a favourite item of their diet. These birds prefer walking to flying – and some say that Seriemas recall a remote ancestor, the gigantic *Phororhacos*, a flightless bird standing more than 6ft (2m) high. It roamed the vast plains of Patagonia during the Miocene period (23 million to five million years ago).

The sun shone on our afternoon visit to Lago Lagunilla. In the swampy area surrounding the lake I was delighted to encounter stately Southern Screamers. The three species of screamer form an interesting family the size and shape of small turkeys. Each wing is armed with two sharp spurs and their long toes enable them to walk on floating vegetation. Nearly all their bones are hollow, even those of the wings and toes. White-faced Ibis were also on the lagoon and the pretty little White Monjitas made one wonder why a flycatcher would be white (except for the flight feathers).

Day 3
Early next morning we set off for Tilcara in Jujuy (pronounced Hoo-hooey), the most northerly province that borders Bolivia in the north and Chile in the west. It is one of Argentina's smallest and poorest areas. Several flocks of Mitred Conures, numbering between 30 and 50 individuals, were leaving their roosting sites and flying high overhead. About 150ft (45m) from the roadside, not far out of Salta, was a reddish cliff face. A few conures had settled in the trees above the bank and were flying down to partake of the clay.

That day we lunched in the sunshine by a rocky river, soothed by the sound of water rushing over rocks. We walked upstream to find two species associated only with fast-flowing waters. I can still recall the Rufous-throated Dipper standing on a rock in brilliant sunlight dipping into the white rushing water. Only a few feet away, was a pair of striking Torrent Ducks, the female with red-brown body and the male with black and white facial markings. I was captivated by the way they dived off a rock, disappeared into the fast-flowing water, and suddenly reappeared downstream. Sightings of this species never fail to thrill me. Some observers have been privileged to see the moment when ducklings, in an apparently suicidal leap, leave the nest and hurl themselves into the foaming waters. They weigh so little that, like a cork bobbing on a pond, they

238

invariably surface unharmed. I marvel at the instinct that propels them.

That afternoon, as we came closer to the green oasis of Tilcara, we took a mountain track behind a petrol station. There was a large dry lake on our left, and human habitation in the distance. After 20 minutes or so Santiago called "Parakeets!" I was half expecting Mitred Conures, as they seemed to be everywhere! Instead, a pair of Aymara or Grey-hooded Parakeets flashed by. They were gone in a split second. I was disappointed and did not feel that I could claim to have seen the species. A few minutes further down the track a hawk-eyed member of our group spotted one ahead. We crept up and looked. I was instantly captivated! Here was a bird that was unobtrusive yet elegant, tiny yet stream-lined.

The one I was watching, the female, was biting off small daisy-like heads from the plant on which she was perched, holding the stem in her foot and extracting the tiny seeds. I was quite enthralled at this unexpected close sighting. So absorbed was I that it was some while before I spotted the well-camouflaged male (distinguished by the larger head and slightly darker head markings) behind the track, to her left. Had I been alone, I would have missed these Budgie-sized birds, clothed in soft shades of green and grey. Watching this pair for ten minutes or so made the whole journey worthwhile.

Day 4
Next morning we left the hotel at 5.30am for a long drive. Sunrise was at 7.15am. It was bitterly cold when we stopped by a small lake, inhabited by three flamingos, for breakfast of dry pastry-cum-biscuits and fruit. (It *was* a budget tour!) Despite my thermal gloves, my fingers felt frost-bitten for two hours afterwards.

When any little brown bird was spotted our mini-bus was stopped for half an hour to investigate. Managing time was not Santiago's strong point. We paid for this later! Alan spotted a pair of Grey-breasted Seedsnipe, not unlike small partridges. This was the highlight of the journey. As the mountains receded into big open plains, dotted with tufts of grass, we came across groups of llamas. More exciting were the distant, wary vicuñas

– so beautiful and elegant that I yearned for a closer view, but long ago they learned not to let humans anywhere near them. The *puna*, stony windswept, treeless plains are, geologically, a remnant of the Brazilian massif of ancient crystalline rocks. Rivers are absent. Rainfall collects in lakes and forms saltflats.

The projected lunchtime came and went and Laguna de los Pozuelos (the lagoon of little wells), to which we were heading, seemed to be no more than a mirage. At one of the frequent stops, a condor flying overhead came lower to look at us. I could see the white of its wings gleaming in the sunlight. A young tinamou ran across the road and the Puna Yellow Finches added brief splashes of colour to the flat landscape. A few isolated and poor houses, roughly constructed from mud bricks, perhaps belonged to the llama herdsmen.

At 1.45pm the lagoon came into view, in the heart of the *altiplano*. We were now at an altitude of 12,000ft (3,650m). This is a harsh climate where the temperature can drop to minus 25 degrees C in winter. Santiago declared that we would now have lunch. We each consumed a tired cheese roll and the packet of crisps was shared between 12 people! It was a 30-minute walk to the lagoon across the parched earth. It was hot yet the wind bore a chill.

Eleven Puna Flamingos came into view. Distinguished by the broader, mainly yellow beak and black primary wing feathers, they are unique among flamingos in lacking a hind toe. Also known as James's Flamingo, they were believed to be extinct until a remote population was discovered in 1956. Hunting and egg-collecting had taken their toll. Fortunately, now their numbers have increased; they are protected in all four Andean countries in which they occur. The new threat is climate change affecting the levels of the saline lakes where they feed. In fact, in recent years the flamingos have been deserting this huge reserve due to falling water levels.

Much further out, their reflections shimmering in the heat haze, were two thousand or so Chilean Flamingos. Many small waders, Andean Geese and Andean Lapwings completed the picture. Behind the lagoon bare, rolling hills rose steeply from the salt-bush covered ground.

Due to the frequent stops during the nine hours *en route* on the bumpy roads, we could stay only 45 minutes in this strange landscape. It was disappointing, to say the least. There were little known high-altitude coots and ducks up here, such as the Andean Crested Duck, a very unusual bird, considered to be a link between shelducks and dabbling ducks. Rarer than the duck is the Horned Coot, known only from a few Andean lakes with dense submerged aquatic plants.

To avoid altitude sickness at 12,000ft (3,600m) Santiago had told us all to drink plenty of water. This was difficult considering that there was nothing in sight higher than a blade of grass – and certainly not a Port-a-loo!

To make up for lost time we were now to drive the five hours back without stopping, however, a "new" species for the group resulted in a three-minute stop. Three Mountain Parakeets flew near the coach, then around it several times as though putting on an air show for us. One perched briefly on a nearby rock. I was absolutely enchanted by these gorgeous little parakeets, the male's face flashing golden in the sun. Their flight was amazing in its speed and grace. They lit up my day and the brief glimpses were treasured. We moved off after three minutes. This seemed totally unfair as every LBJ ("little brown job" in twitcher parlance) was accorded at least ten minutes! When we whizzed by a field full of Buff-necked Ibis I was not happy! Ibis are fascinating birds.

We passed extraordinary humbug-striped mountains of pink, green and grey. This was the renowned gorge, *Quebrada de Humahuaca*. The rocks were layered in unreal hues, like nothing I had ever seen before. These mountains were extraordinary, the tall fluted columns, worn down by hundreds of years of wind and rain, stood starkly against the azure-blue sky. At their bases were scattered tiny rectangular adobe (mud-brick) houses of a colour that matched the nearby mountain. But stopping for scenery never entered the equation! It was after 9pm when we reached the hotel at Tilcara. I went straight to bed: my eyes were aching from the strength of the sun at such a high altitude. But my heart was still fluttering with the wingbeats of the unforgettable Mountain Parakeet.

Day 5
Next morning breakfast was as late as 7.15am, followed by a short drive to look for the Red-tailed Comet Hummingbird. After a fleeting glimpse of a single bird a little girl approached and told Santiago to go to the ruins at Pucera. Local knowledge, even from one so young, is invaluable. There we spent an hour watching these gorgeous hummingbirds. The male is spectacular with his long ruby-coloured iridescent tail that accounts for nearly half his length of 9in (22cm). Two other hummingbirds, the White-sided Hillstar and the Sparkling Violet-ear, were eclipsed by the beauty of the comet.

We drove back to Salta via the Santa Laura forest where several small groups of Maximilian's Parrots flew overhead in the failing light of late afternoon. One group landed in the dense foliage not far away. We were at 7,900ft (2,400m). Large flocks of Mitred Conures sped overhead, hurrying to roost. This must be the most numerous parrot of the region.

Day 6
We set off south before sunrise for Los Cardones National Park, an area of spectacular scenery. Varied habitats entranced us, from pampas grass and yellow daisies falling down lush slopes, with wide stony river beds only trickling with water, to arid cactus scrub and bare rocks of delicate pinks and browns, softly shaded, occasionally with striking contrasts of deep pink rock. One stretch of mountains was rumpled into shapes resembling organ-pipes. At 10,500ft (3,200m) there were brief and distant glimpses of little Aymara Parakeets, a speeding flock twittering overhead and a pair perched high up in a shady bush against a backdrop of far-away snow-capped mountains. The highest was one of Argentina's six peaks that exceed 19,700ft (6,000m).

Los Cardones National Park is named after the cardon cactus found only above 6,560ft (2,000m). When the cactus reach nearly 20ft (6m) in height, they are believed to be between 100 and 200 years old. The wood, marked with narrow holes, has been used for centuries to build houses and furniture. It is said that during the War of Independence, troops would clothe these cactus in ponchos and hats to hide their numerical inferiority from the opposing Spanish! There were signs of former human habitation

Los Cardones National Park

in the form of isolated cemeteries, with some monuments built like flat-topped miniature houses.

We passed forest-covered slopes, where little streams trickled across the narrow road, dangerously curving, with sheer drops. Countless crosses remembered those who had not been careful. We passed a shack sporting a Coco-cola sign where an old lady tried unsuccessfully to attract the driver's attention, for us to spend some pesos. Rarely, a few green crops were etched into the mountains, and scattered roadside cows and chickens completed the pastoral scene.

At higher altitudes Andean Condors were ever-present, even flying *below* us. We were so high! Then there were a pair and four together, their huge wings silhouetted against the blue of the sky or nearly lost against the bare mountain slopes, as they rode the thermals. The sun lit up the white feathers on their wings like snow glistening on the far peaks. The landscape was one of impressive grandeur, with range after range of mountains, each one receding more fuzzily into the distance. I sat on a rock, enjoying the solitude while the others searched for an elusive species, and a condor circled lazily above.

243

Andean Flicker

A group of Andean Flickers entertained me. These woodpeckers are strikingly barred above with black and brownish white. One keen photographer, intent on capturing their image as they foraged on the ground, stalked half a dozen birds. He was not getting any nearer; they always kept the same distance away! After he took his photos, I stood quite still and the flickers gradually returned. One of them hopped up on to a rock and posed for me, first front, then back, his bill pointing upwards! After fleeting glimpses of various little brown birds, such as canasteros and cinclodes, the flickers were a joy! They had so much personality!

We stayed too long in Los Cardones. We then had a non-stop four-hour drive south to Cafayate – well, almost non-stop. As we approached Cafayate I scanned the power lines from the vehicle. Yes! I saw a single Burrowing Parrot. This was the *andinus* sub-species, "new" for the group so we pulled up sharp. Another four parrots were sitting on the wire. A flock of 12 swept into view, swerving over the road calling, and swung back round again, before disappearing. Through my binoculars I could see their dark abdomens; the lack of orange defined this sub-species. The light was fading fast. All around I could hear their familiar calls. I walked down the road a little way to see six silhouetted on the tops of tall cactus plants. My glimpse of *andinus* had been frustratingly brief but Santiago assured me that we would see more next morning.

That night the stars were amazing – like the roof of the Planetarium. The moon was a silver sliver lying on its side just above the trees.

Day 7

I knew that Cafayate, a popular summer holiday centre, was the best place to see the Burrowing Parrots. We saw nothing of the town but next morning we did see, just as the sun was coming up, evidence of what the area is most famous for: white wine produced from the special Torrontes grapes. To my surprise a flock of Burrowing Parrots, probably one hundred strong, was hovering over the vineyards – "like a swarm of locusts", said one of our group. It was an amazing sight – but also a worrying one. Did it mean that the parrots were persecuted as crop pests?

What were they doing there? Through my binoculars I watched them on the ground. They were probably feeding on small seeds or on grit. Part of the flock would rise, and then settle again on the earth. Within minutes our group moved off in our mini-bus, much to my disappointment. We drove on, then stopped to look for another species. By now the light was excellent. Burrowing Parrots flew by and settled in a field. I could not reach it but a few stragglers landed on a power line, close enough for me to study their coloration against a clear blue sky. I walked up the road and four birds detached themselves from a group and came right over my head. So I got my shot! The four were perfectly positioned, none with tail or wing-tips overlapping. And the lack of orange or yellow on the abdomen, typical of *andinus*, was clear in one bird. It was the last frame on the film and I returned to the mini-bus elated.

It irked me that we passed them again, or another flock, without stopping, then spent two hours searching, in dry, sandy thorn bush scrub and rocky cliffs, for the White-throated Cacholote, much sought by birders. I couldn't help thinking that only mad dogs and Englishman would be traipsing over the sandy semi-desert in the searing heat of midday. The cacholote was lying low!

245

This was the Chaco Serrano (dry Chaco) of the Calchaqui Valley, dotted with small gnarled trees and cacti and low thorny bushes amid the sandy ground. Burrowing Parrots were flying by the side of the road. Could they exist here or were they flying to a different area? Part of the fascination of this part of Argentina is the rapidity with which the scenery and the environment change. It is also steeped in history. The area was once densely populated until the indigenous people were defeated by the Spanish.

A couple of hours after leaving the Chaco Serrano we were at 9,800ft (3,000m) on the slopes of Mount Aconquija. The gullies were lined with low green vegetation where Bar-winged Cinclodes hopped about. There were otherwise vast expanses of grassy slopes, with boulders and little rocks covered in pale green, yellow and soft orange lichens. Many of the stones and small boulders sparkled as though sprinkled with ground-up diamonds – muscovite, said Santiago. Occasional flowers were tiny, and pink.

It was very windy on the slopes, but not too cold. The combination of wind and altitude took my breath away, and I sat down on a rock, savouring the sight of the colourful lichens and the tiny flowers beneath my feet, and surveying the great expanse of sky of the deepest, purest azure. Down below, not far below, cloud was obscuring all but the gloomy peak of a distant mountain. It drifted towards me. Suddenly, four horses came galloping out of the cloud, their manes flying; it was a surreal experience.

After leaving the wide-open spaces of Aconquija's slopes, we drove to Tafí del Valle at 6,500ft (2,000m) in the province of Tucumán. Before reaching our hotel, only ten minutes away, we visited the alder forest above the town. It was swathed in cloud, cold and with an unfriendly feel. The path was rocky and the ground was carpeted in wild strawberries. I tasted one – all pips and no pulp. There were dandelions and other temperate plants. The spindly alder trunks were covered in what looked like small parasitic plants. It was silent except for the stream trickling over the rocks and the calls of the Yellow-striped Brush-finch.

The valley of Tafí was sacred to the pre-Columbian Indian people who lived in underground dwellings and grew crops on the terraced hillsides. Today an artificial lake is richly populated with ducks, coots and geese. We stayed in Tafi, famous for its archaeological sites, for one night. That was enough.

Day 8
I didn't like the area. Perhaps I was biased against it by having to return to that miserable alder forest again the following morning! The aim was to see the Tucumán Mountain Finch, a little brown bird with rufous head and throat. It remained elusive – but I sat in the vehicle. I had no intention of *freezing* to death! The others had left the hotel at an early hour for another attempt to see the mountain finch. They returned cold and dejected. I had the luxury of lying in bed until 6.30am followed by a breakfast of excellent bread and the apple jam I had bought from "the jam lady" on the previous night.

My companions were off to Buenos Aires airport and home. *En route* the coach climbed higher into lush, green-clothed mountains. A lunch-time stop provided distant sightings of two species of kingfisher and brief glimpses of a Blue-capped Puffleg Hummingbird with glittering blue forehead and golden-green underparts. All the Pufflegs look as though they are wearing white furry muffs! Everyone was desperate to see one of the large, red-headed woodpeckers, the Cream-backed. We hung around for an hour. After we had eaten, four woodpeckers appeared, giving brief and difficult glimpses. My memory of the pair near Comarapa in Bolivia was more satisfying!

We had seen a host of interesting species that I had not previously encountered – but there was no doubt in my mind what the highlights were. Three species of parakeets (two of them tiny) had provided brief and tantalising views but, more importantly, an understanding of the kind of habitat in which they survived.

Argentine bird statistics (year 2000)
Critically endangered 4
Endangered 4
Vulnerable 31
Near-threatened 53

Species not previously mentioned:

Red-rumped Caciques (*Cacicus haemorrhous*)
Great Dusky Swift (*Cyseloides senex*)
Muscovy Duck (*Cairina moschata*)
Violaceous Euphonia (*Euphonia violacea*)
Swallow Tanager (*Tersina viridis*)
Rusty-collared Seedeater (*Sporophila collaris*)
Blue or Swallowed-tailed Manakin (*Chiroxiphia caudata*)
Mitred Conure (*Aratinga mitrata*)
Dusky-legged Guan (*Penelope obscura*)
Greater Rhea (*Rhea americana*)
Red-legged or Crested Seriema (*Cariama cristata*)
Southern Screamer (*Chauna torquata*)
White-faced Ibis (*Plegadis chihi*)
White Monjita (*Xolmis irupero*)
Rufous-throated Dipper (*Cinclus schulzi*) VULNERABLE
Aymara or Grey-hooded Parakeet (*Bolborhynchus aymara*)
Grey-breasted Seedsnipe (*Thinocorus rumicivorus*)
Puna Yellow Finch (*Sicalis lutea*)
Puna or James's Flamingo (*Phoenicoparrus jamesi*) NEAR
    THREATENED
Chilean Flamingo (*Phoenicopterus chilensis*) NEAR
    THREATENED
Andean Goose (*Chloephaga melanoptera*)
Andean Lapwing (*Vanellus resplendens*)
Andean Crested Duck (*Lophonetta specularioides alticola*)
Horned Coot (*Fulica cornuta*) NEAR THREATENED
Mountain Parakeet (*Bolborhynchus aurifrons*)
Red-tailed Comet Hummingbird (*Sappho sparganura*)
White-sided Hillstar Hummingbird (*Oreotrochilus leucopleurus*)
Sparkling Violet-ear Hummingbird (*Colibri coruscans*)
Andean Flicker (*Colaptes rupicola*)
Andean Burrowing Parrot or Patagonian Conure (*Cyanoliseus
    patagonus andinus*)
White-throated Cacholote (*Pseudoseisura gutturalis*)
Yellow-striped Brush-finch (*Atlapetes citrinellus*)
Tucumán Mountain Finch (*Poospiza baeri*) VULNERABLE
Blue-capped Puffleg Hummingbird (*Eriocnemis glaucopoides*)

19. Northern Argentina 2004:

More Soya, less Forest

I waved goodbye to the group at Tucumán airport. I would miss them. It was a four-hour drive on the main highway back to San Lorenzo where I said goodbye to Daniel, our driver, an extremely kind man, polite and friendly. He gave me a small piece of rock containing muscovite that looks like little pieces of mirror. Now I had only Santiago for company – and I was not totally happy about that. I had extended my visit in the hope of a glimpse of Alder Parrots, or Tucumán Amazons, as they are also known. It would have been foolish to travel this far and not go a little further to achieve this goal.

After a very comfortable night at a good hotel, I set off with Santiago at 8am. We drove for a couple of hours north on highway 34 in the eastern part of Jujuy province. I chatted to him about his life and discovered that his heart was in engineering. He admitted that driving around looking at birds was not what he really wanted to do. This explained, I thought, why he wore a red and black jacket in forested environments! (A subtle clue that he was not in tune with nature.)

We made a brief and sudden stop to watch a group of Maximilian's Parrots feeding on the seeds of the red quebracha. There were ten or so, their green and grey plumage inconspicuous against a cloudy sky. Then we made a detour along an unpaved road to look for Blue-fronted Amazons. But there were none. Where once there was forest, now there was field after field of soya, a monoculture that could support very little wildlife. It made me sad when I thought of the rich birdlife that enjoyed the forests here not long ago. In 1996 the company Monsanto introduced genetically engineered soya beans to Argentina, and even reserves were stripped of their protected status and auctioned off to agribusiness. All this to grow soya, mainly for cattle feed…

After lunch of *lasagne verdura* at a roadside restaurant – quite the best meal of the trip – we set off again. My spirits lifted when we encountered a group of six Toco Toucans, feeding on both sides of the road. Through my binoculars I watched one eating flowers. To see these iconic birds in their natural habitat is tremendously rewarding. I could have observed them for hours: I was enjoying a species that is big, bold and colourful.

We turned west off the main highway towards Calilegua National Park. The weather was not good. Our 4WD vehicle crossed a small stream into the reserve. Created in 1979, it covers more than 76,000 hectares, protecting cloud forest, peaks and sub-tropical valleys. Tapirs, pumas, otters and more than 300 bird species live here. We were in the *yungas*, a distinctive habitat found in a narrow strip between 5,660ft (1,700m) and 7,333ft (2,200m) from southern Bolivia to north-western Argentina.

By 2004 sixty per cent of the *yungas* had already been lost to timber extraction, pine plantations, livestock production, gas pipeline construction and soya monoculture. A tragedy: it was considered to be an international hotspot for biodiversity. With the adjoining Great Chaco American forest, it was until recently a haven for jaguars and giant armadillos. Now thousands of hectares per year are lost to soya in the lower *yungas* forest alone. When these two forest systems are destroyed – and the destruction is proceeding at one of the fastest rates in the world – any wildlife in the bulldozer's path is shot and smaller animals are often burned among the groups of fallen trees, stacked in the newly deforested fields.

Seeing the situation only from the human economic perspective, Santiago told me that conservation of the forest was essential to protect the watershed. Without water the surrounding 200,000 hectares of sugar cane, citrus and tobacco could not exist. As we entered the *yungas*, cloud was obscuring everything. In the distance we heard then saw a pair of Yellow-collared Macaws in flight. We ascended 3,000ft (1,000m) in two hours, on a narrow road right up to the top. There was silence except for the dripping of water from the trees. You couldn't feel the rain – you could only see it. The cloud gave an atmospheric feel, a mysterious touch to the sopping, moss-laden trees. I was glad to be there, just to see the habitat of the Alder Parrot and to revel in the cloud-shrouded beauty of the *jungas*.

Conservemos al Loro Alisero y las Yungas

PROYECTO LORO ALISERO

A plea to conserve the Alder Parrot and the Yungas

Suddenly Santiago stopped the vehicle. Five Alder Parrots were flying. They soon disappeared into the trees – but I had seen them! This was a special moment for me, to catch a glimpse of what were probably a pair and their three young. It was my sole reason for coming here. These parrots are green with red forehead and wing speculum and a small bill for an Amazon parrot. Now as endangered as their habitat, in the mid- and late 1980s, 19,000 were exported, even although the demand for them overseas was practically nil, and many more were captured and died. Today they are rare in captivity and not popular as pets. Export had achieved nothing except lining the pockets of bird dealers. Twenty years ago exporters in Argentina acquired any parrots they could lay their hands on, knowing that someone, somewhere, would buy them. Now the parrots are protected from export but their habitat is being destroyed from under them.

The cloud forest fascinated me: it was so verdant. Every inch of every branch was covered with mosses, lichens and bromeliads and other parasitic plants. Any colour but green would have seemed out of place. The track was very narrow. We passed a beautiful canyon with a river running through it. There was only just room for the twice-daily bus from the nearest town. On one side of the road there would be a sheer drop of at least 50ft to 100ft (16m to 33m): the vegetation was too dense to see the bottom. Santiago told me that few tourists come to this national park and that most of those turn back after three miles (4-5km). I had the feeling he wished he had done the same! No sun penetrated the mist-shrouded trees.

Twice we encountered a feeding flock of one dozen squawking Mitred Conures. They made enough noise for fifty! From the monument at 5,500ft (1,700m) we descended through the clouds to the tiny village of San Francisco. Our destination was a small concrete building, euphemistically described as a "hotel" in my itinerary, owned by Luci and Freddi. I sat by their "fire" outside, where a pot boiled eternally for the *maté* – the tea so beloved of the Argentine people. The view was of the forest still shrouded in cloud. Luci was very pleasant. I explained to her that I had come to this area to see parrots, which I am sure she thought was very odd.

I breakfasted on cheese, banana and Luci's excellent home-made bread. With Santiago, I departed early. The weather was even worse and little was visible through the clouds. The car windows, open in the hope of hearing parrot calls, let in the cold and the mist. No bird in its right mind had stayed at that altitude. We encountered only the occasional hawk.

Back on the highway, Yellow-collared Macaws watched us near the roadside. I could hear, then see, that an adult was feeding a young one. Santiago set up the telescope where they were feeding in an introduced chinaberry tree. The young one was reaching for the yellow or green berries and taking them without transferring them to its foot. It had yet to learn how to do this. Observing the family for nearly half an hour was the best part of the day.

Blue-fronted Amazon chick

We drove off road for an hour or so, encountering a few Toco Toucans. How I enjoyed watching them feeding on the immature fruits of, said Santiago, *Urea baccifera*! When I asked him what they were eating he replied: "Leaves". Strange! Toucans are not known to eat leaves.

Not long after, as we headed back towards Salta, we reached an orange grove where we were able to talk with Reuben, one of the workers. Blue-fronted Amazons were until recently considered pests by orange growers. Now they were not so common. Reuben told us that in January and February people used to stand in the groves to scare them off or they used gas bombs that exploded on a timing device. Local people obtain 15-20 pesos (£20 to £30) for each chick taken from the nest, he said.

This formerly common and widespread Amazon has declined dramatically throughout its wide range. The trade in it has always been enormous. Take the years 1981 to 1989, for example, when more than 280,000 were exported from Argentina to countries that were members of CITES. The government authorised the collection of half a million Blue-fronted Amazons between 1983 and 1991. Nestlings were removed from trees in the Chaco forests and trapping occurred in the citrus-growing areas of Tucumán, Salta and Jujuy. Santiago saw nothing wrong with this trade. His interest in conservation appeared to be non-existent.

We drove back to San Lorenzo. Santiago collected me at 8.30am next morning to visit the nearby Huayco (pronounced *wayco*) reserve at about 5,570ft (1,700m). Eighty or so Mitred Conures were feeding and flying. I love to see these birds in large flocks as, sadly, today few parrots in the neotropics can almost invariably be seen in such groups. For half an hour I enjoyed watching them eating lichen and the flowers of bromeliads. One was gnawing at the end of a dead branch. Three Maximilian's Parrots were sitting in the same tree as the conures. They were quiet and still and one occasionally nibbled at something. This behaviour was such a contrast to their noisy long-tailed cousins!

After unsuccessfully trying a couple of locations for the *Loros Aliseros* (Tucumán Amazons) we went to Las Costas National Park – an alder forest at 6,000ft (1,840m). Cattle, chickens and even turkeys were all over the place. Some national park, I thought! There was not a sign of parrots but a wrinkled woman on horseback, leading another horse laden with packages, assured us that this species visited the area. I tasted some of the alder fruits that the parrots feed on. They were bitter. Lots of small birds were active, also striking Plush-crested Jays, with blue-black and yellow plumage and yellow eyes. "Plush" refers to the mound of velvety black feathers on the top of the head.

Thus the sunless, rather uneasy, interlude in the forests came to an end. It reminded me how dependent on sympathetic company are one's experiences and memories of a certain place.

Update
The legal export of Blue-fronted Amazons from Argentina is still permitted. Adults and chicks (ostensibly all-but-one chick from each nest) are captured. The fact that taking of young from nests involves making a hole in the cavity (the hole is seldom repaired properly) is a serious problem as it reduces the number of nest sites available.

Species not previously mentioned:

Alder Parrot or Tucumán Amazon (*Amazona tucumana*)
VULNERABLE
Plush-crested Jay (*Cyanocorax chrysops*)

Chinaberry tree (*Melia azedarach*)
Red quebracha (*Schinopsis quebracho colorado*)

20. Colombia 2005:

Yellow-eared Parrot – Conservation Success without Parallel

It happened like this. I was asked by Loro Parque Fundación (LPF) from Tenerife to help publicise their conservation work. I was enthusiastic. I had followed for several years the reports of the projects concerning the endangered parrots of the Andes. There is a sad statistic connected with Colombia's 50 plus parrot species: at least 12 are in imminent danger of extinction. Paul Salaman, an English ornithologist based in Bogotá, co-ordinated the LPF projects in Colombia. When he was next in England, could we meet? I asked. Back came an e-mail: "I am unlikely to be in the UK in the foreseeable future. Why don't you come out to Colombia and I will take you to some of the project sites?"

The prospect was so exciting that I lost no time in booking a flight to Bogotá for eight weeks ahead. This city, Colombia's capital, is situated in the Andes at an altitude of 8,660ft (2,600m). Eighty per cent of the population of Colombia (approximately 44 million people) live in towns and pueblos in the Andes, because much of the country elsewhere is uninhabitable. In extent, Colombia is about four and a half times bigger than the UK with two-thirds the human population. After more than a century of cutting down forest, even on gravity-defying slopes where coffee and other crops are cultivated, most of the natural vegetation of the Andes has been destroyed. No wonder then, that the endangered parrots are mountain species, living either in the Andes or in the Santa Marta mountains to the north.

I was due to arrive in Bogotá at 8pm on January 27. Two delayed flights meant that it was 3am on the following morning when I landed. Paul was there, waiting, cheerful and confident as ever. Next morning we left Bogotá at 6.30am, on the first leg of an eight-day trip that was to take us to remote Andean locations where some of South America's rarest parrots live. First we

COLOMBIA

This is the only South American country with a Caribbean and a Pacific coast. Its main exports are cocaine, oil, diamonds and coal. The new millennium marked a fresh period in Colombia's history: significant progress was made in controlling social unrest, after a decade of strong economic growth. Great strides were made in conservation. Pro-Aves established a network of 12 reserves covering 25,000 acres and protecting 60% of Colombia's threatened bird species. **Yellow-eared Parrot**

spent an hour crawling through the traffic, dominated by the brightly painted buses belching acrid grey smoke from a pipe at roof level. It seemed that all of Bogotá was on the way to work.

As we drove to Ibagué, Paul told me how the Colombian bird conservation organisation ProAves formed a partnership with LPF with the initial Loro Parque project that commenced in 1999 to save the Yellow-eared Parrot. The population was declining so fast it seemed inevitable that it would be the next parrot to suffer extinction. This did not happen – and the story that unfolded was little short of incredible. ProAves is young in years – and so are its researchers. In the next few days I was to meet some of the enthusiastic people working on various projects and I was deeply impressed by their dedication and knowledge. They spent countless hours in the field in difficult conditions. I soon gained the impression that Colombian bird conservation would make gigantic strides in the next few years – and I was right.

Fundación ProAves had an office in Ibagué. We picked up Alonso Quevedo, a renowned ornithologist, a talented bird photographer and, above all, a wonderful person. Spending time with him was one of the highlights of the trip. His colleague

Roberto came with us. His job was to document altitudes and vegetation in the project areas, in order to produce detailed maps of the habitats of the endangered parrots. These maps will be crucial to their survival.

While at the office I heard the calls of a Yellow-fronted Amazon – and I went to investigate. I found a wing-clipped parrot in the garden on a long perch under shade, with a stick thoughtfully provided at right-angles without cover where she could rainbathe. A confiscated bird, she was being cared for by ProAves staff. She soon became chatty, telling me over and over: "*Quiero cacao! Quiero cacao!*", her voice rising crazily on the second *a* of the second *cacao*. Fortunately, there was no sign that anyone was answering her plea of "I want chocolate!"

We drove for several hours through spectacular mountain scenery to reach Roncesvalles in the Central Andes, located 233 miles (373km) west of Bogotá. A wooden house rented by Pro-Aves was our residence. At 6.30am next morning we set off into the mountains. After crossing a river by means of a couple of slender saplings, we went on horseback up the steep tussocky slopes, to a height of over 9,000ft (2,800m), where we left the horses and climbed higher. For a while I was having trouble breathing in the thin air. All that changed when the first Yellow-eared Parrots appeared! Few outsiders had ever seen this Critically Endangered species.

First I saw two on a distant palm stump far below, and then a pair flew from their nest to a nearby tree, isolated on the hillside. They perched in the sun, unconcerned by our presence, and gorgeous, their plumage gleaming gold and green. The large black beak gives them some resemblance to a small macaw, with a similarly endearing manner. I could see that this charismatic parrot could be to Colombia what the giant panda is to China. But it has more personality and vitality than a lumbering panda!

Here the steep meadow-like mountainside was dotted with wax palms with slender grey trunks banded with silvery-grey, some living, some dead, interspersed with low deciduous trees. The pair was breeding close by. Two holes, normally covered, had been made in their dead palm nest, for inspection and for photography. Uncovering one hole admitted a camera lens and uncovering the other provided sufficient light. Inspection occurred only when the parents were absent. An extending ladder was placed against the trunk and a member of the ProAves team climbed the 33ft (11m) to inspect the chicks and to take photos. He came down and reported the presence of three young.

How could I let the moment pass without asking if I could have a look? Yes, of course, was the reply! I climbed up and looked through the hole, at first seeing nothing in the darkness. Then I made out three large chicks, with feathers on the head but still with soft white down, their insulation against the cold nights. They looked so cosy and appealing! The impact of that moment is difficult to describe. I was enthralled, scarcely able to believe that this was happening to me! Then I climbed the ladder to another nest that held three eggs. I could see only one as the female had covered the eggs when she left.

There were several pairs in the vicinity, incubating, sitting quietly or flying overhead. As I watched them I was aware of small figures swarming up the mountainside. They came closer and deposited themselves noisily at our feet. Local children were making a Sunday morning outing! Nearly all of them wore T-shirts depicting the parrot, painted by their own hands from a printed design. They

Inspecting the Yellow-eared Parrot nest

Young parrot-watchers

knew all about it and the wax palms from their lessons in school. But what they surely were unable to comprehend, was the importance of this parrot on a global scale.

Little was known about the Yellow-eared Parrot until the mid-1990s. Once abundant throughout the Andes, it gradually disappeared, unnoticed, as the wax palms were cut down. *In 1996 only 20 birds were known to survive.* In that year Loro Parque Fundación started to support the work of Dr Niels Krabbe in Ecuador. He was trying to protect the land on which the last remnant population existed. His education programme among the local people raised the profile of the species to the degree that they evicted a trapper who had caught these parrots. At the beginning of 1997 the roost site of the Yellow-eared Parrots was purchased and the planting of thousands of wax palm saplings commenced. In these two years LPF donated US$23,569 to the conservation of this parrot in Ecuador. Alas! It appeared to be in vain.

The final sighting occurred in September 1998. Ironically, this was the month in which participants at the international parrot convention hosted by Loro Parque in Tenerife saw a film of the last few survivors made by Niels Krabbe. I confess to being moved almost to tears by it – convinced that this wonderful parrot would soon be extinct. My worst fears seemed to be confirmed when searches carried out in Ecuador between 1997 and 2000 failed to locate a single bird.

What happened to those last few is unknown: possibly they were shot or trapped. Yellow-eared Parrots had little fear of man. It would be possible to catch a local population in one night as they congregated together. Such activities had tragic consequences - for the species and for the individual. There is a record of 40 being trapped together in the late 1980s – and all were dead within three days. Unlike many parrots, they seem unable to tolerate captivity.

Yellow-eared Parrots

Hundreds of posters bearing a picture of a Yellow-eared Parrot in a wax palm were distributed throughout the Andes of Colombia. In 1999, as the searches were about to end, a scientist working on mammals in a remote area noticed some parrots that resembled the species depicted on the poster. His identification was right!

The report came from a remote valley in central Colombia. In April 1999 project fieldworker Bernabé López-Lamús went to investigate. Suddenly, descending from the clouds above a breathtaking montane landscape, two flocks of Yellow-eared Parrots swooped down into palm-studded fields. After a year of soul-destroying searching, he was delirious with delight. Sixty-one Yellow-eared Parrots alighted and clambered down the fronds in chattering groups to feed on the palm fruits. I think if that had been me I would just have stood and sobbed for joy.

This flock in Colombia, the last on the planet, was located in the nick of time. The species would almost certainly now be extinct if it had not been sighted then. As I discovered, the areas it inhabited were so remote that the parrots could have died out, with only the local people noticing their disappearance. Mountain people who saw the parrots in their vicinity did not know that the species had a very limited area of distribution.

They do now! The Yellow-eared Parrot has an amazing presence in their small town of Roncesvalles. We ate in the two-storey, iron-roofed hotel/restaurant, painted dark green and white, which had five small wooden balconies on the upper floor. The side was a patchwork of corrugated iron. Its appearance was more interesting than the food it served! In the main streets, with their single-storey dwellings and unpaved surfaces, telegraph poles had been painted to resemble wax palms, each one with a hole from which a Yellow-eared Parrot was looking. A number of buildings were artistically decorated with huge murals of the parrot. They brought colour to a little town that is usually shrouded in cloud. No one could visit Roncesvalles without being aware of the parrot's importance, further highlighted with posters providing information about its conservation.

Bird life in the area was scarce but I was impressed by the close sighting of a Black-billed Mountain Toucan. This large,

Black-billed Mountain Toucan

gorgeously-coloured toucan has light blue and yellow skin surrounding the eye, dark red iris and black and red mandibles. The plumage is amazing! The underparts are skyblue, except for the white throat; crown and nape are glossy black, the back is olive-brown, under tail coverts are crimson and the flanks are chocolate-brown. The tail is grey, tipped with chestnut.

On the following afternoon we visited a roosting site of the parrot high above the town. On a piece of farmland, perhaps unique in the world, many wax palms still exist. When the late afternoon sun emerged and lit up the area, the palms stood with gleaming white trunks like sentinels, closely packed in a small area. I thought they were truly a wonder of nature that should have been preserved for posterity. But naturalists did not know they existed here until the parrot's presence was detected.

I sat on a steep slope on the tussocky ground for the best part of one hour, watching a pair of Yellow-eared Parrots at their roost a few feet away. They perched on the top of a dead palm trunk, the female occasionally appearing and the male boldly surveying the scene, keeping an eye on me but unperturbed by my presence. When the female emerged I was able to observe the affectionate behaviour that is apparently typical. They are such appealing birds, so devoted to their mates! As the pair preened each other (on the breast as well as the head) the evening sun caught a distant flock of about 80 parrots coming in to roost on the other side of the ridge. Nearby pairs made a few circuitous flights before finally landing for the night and entering their palm trunk, as the clouds rolled down and a chill came over the hillside.

I scrambled down, past the cows and the farm, wondering how the area must have looked before man wreaked such havoc on it. There would have been hundreds of Yellow-eared Parrots and thousands of wax palms. Now both are critically endangered. Buying this farmland, to safeguard forever the palm stands, was then being investigated. At the time the fate of this unique piece of land, so important for the parrots' survival, seemed uncertain.

Wax palm roosting site near Roncesvalles

The biologists had realised that few bird species have such complete dependency on a single species of plant as this one has on the wax palm – for feeding, roosting and breeding. Mature specimens, known locally as *cera* palms, are the tallest palms in the world and extremely slow-growing. It takes 50 years for the trunk to appear; until then it resembles a leafy plant. In

Colombia this palm, the national tree, is critically endangered. Although it had legally protected status, this fact was ignored until the ProAves researchers launched a big campaign to save it. Before Easter every year hundreds of palms were cut down for the fronds that were traditionally waved in the Palm Sunday procession. Even the police had participated. During my stay in the Andes I visited several locations where these palms and other food trees for the parrots were being cultivated under the direction of forward-thinking ProAves personnel.

Our next destination, after many hours on a winding road, was Jardín in Antioquia. A delightful little town in the Western Cordillera, it would be easy to linger there, especially in the neat square with shaded seats under spreading trees. We visited a restaurant – but I could not stomach the food, fried in grease an inch thick! My friends kindly fetched me a fruit salad from a nearby café.

This is the other area where the Yellow-eared Parrot occurs. The population there was also in the region of 300 birds, most of them on privately owned land. A scheme had been initiated to help the parrots. Landowners could register their land as a private reserve and receive tax relief for every hectare of mature forest conserved.

I had breakfast that first morning in Jardín with the ProAves team. Once again, as in Roncesvalles and Genova, I was deeply impressed by the knowledge of these young ornithologists – Jorge Velásquez, José Castaño and Pablo Flórez. Their enthusiasm (for all birds) and total dedication to parrot conservation was never in doubt. It was a pleasure to meet them and to know that the future of some of Colombia's most endangered parrots was in such secure hands. These young men were as united as a family – with a parrot at its head. They were so inspiring.

They took me to a school near a remnant patch of forest used by the parrots. The teachers, Isabel and Andrés, who were due to talk about the Yellow-eared Parrot on television that week, had woven it into all kinds of lessons. When I left Jardín, Isabel presented me with messages of goodwill illustrated with Yellow-eared Parrots, from some of the children. I was very

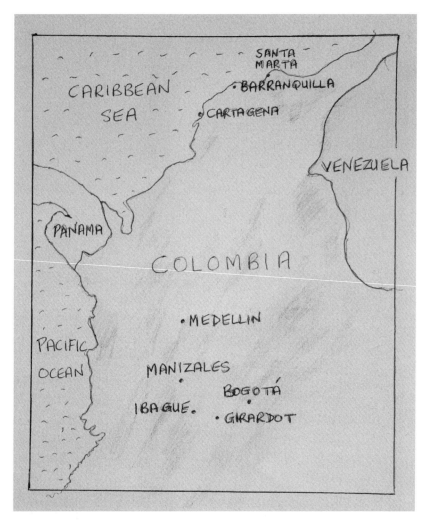

touched. There is no doubt that these youngsters are very aware of the psittacine treasure in their locality.

We spent the day visiting various areas used as corridors when the parrots fly down from their roost site. Again, birds were scarce but an inquisitive Squirrel Cuckoo, the widespread neotropical species, posed long enough to give me an excellent photo.

The next day we set off for the roosting site high above Jardín. An hour in a Landrover, a two and a half hour climb on steep rocky paths, a scramble across mud bisected with deep rivets, through swamp and across streams, lay ahead. Wagler's Conures, green parakeets with scarlet heads, were heard but not seen. The sun was going down as we reached the top. There were scarcely any living wax palms here; the area was a sad sight, with the landowner still cutting trees in order to survive; the pasture was so poor.

But my spirits lifted when a pair of Yellow-eared Parrots flew into the top of a dead palm to roost. They were the lucky ones who had claimed their own hole. It was not long before 33 more flew overhead in the fading light. They headed for two palms, located about 50ft (15m) apart. Pairs came in, fluttered into the top, then took off for a short fly around, or flew to the other palm. Here they roosted in the fronds. The air was shrill with their calls as the clouds above became tinged with pink. Further down the slope several parrots were perched in a tree, drinking from bromeliads and nibbling at the bark. Fifty parrots spent their nights here, with 60 or 70 more in a nearby roost.

The *finca* where we stayed was without electricity. Far below in the distance twinkled the lights of the town of Manizales. Up here, with no light pollution, the sky was the most amazing I have ever seen – a solid sheet of stars. Their brilliance was awe-inspiring. I reflected on the fact that most people, worldwide, are city dwellers, and will never observe this wondrous sight that somehow puts into perspective the insignificance of every individual.

We slept on the floor, four to a room in the pitchest-black I have ever known. Next morning we started the difficult downward climb before first light to be near the two roost trees before the Yellow-eared Parrots departed. Already, a few were moving on the fronds. They started to chatter, and then the synchronisation of their voices indicated that they were about to depart. With a whoosh of wings the entire flock was gone – and was out of sight in ten seconds.

For me, this visit was inspirational. It demonstrated very firmly what efficient partnerships can achieve in conservation: the on-the-ground skills of ProAves ornithologists and the funding from such focused organisations as Loro Parque Fundación and the American Bird Conservancy. Optimism for the future of critically endangered birds replaced the pessimism that I had previously harboured. To all those sceptics, I can say: "Look what has been achieved!"

UPDATE

The population of the Yellow-eared Parrot increased more rapidly than any parrot in conservation history, once action was taken. The original population of 81 birds in the Central Cordillera (Roncesvalles, Tolima) had increased to 312 birds by August 2003 and that in the Western Cordillera (Jardin) to 303 individuals! Furthermore, the survival of the Roncesvalles population was safeguarded with 6,560 metres of fencing protecting 1,255 hectares of habitat, plus another 3,300 hectares protected. In 2007, 52 active nests were found in the Roncesvalles population. In June there were 132 chicks in the nests! In 2008 Paul Salaman reported "a milestone of historic proportions". Eighty-eight pairs had nested, with two or three chicks in each nest. This was expected to bring the population in the region of one thousand individuals! The Yellow-eared Parrot was colonising new areas and its future was looking very bright, so bright that down-listing the species from Critically Endangered to Endangered was expected.

The Yellow-eared Parrot and the Wax Palm Festival had become an annual event. The fourth took place in July 2009 when ten years of conserving this parrot were celebrated.

Species not previously mentioned:

Yellow-eared Parrot (formerly called conure) (*Ognorhynchus icterotis*) **CRITICALLY ENDANGERED**
Black-billed Mountain Toucan (*Andigena nigrirostris*) NEAR-THREATENED
Wagler's or Red-fronted Conure (*Aratinga wagleri*)

Wax or cera palm (*Ceroxylon quindiuense*) **CRITICALLY ENDANGERED**

21. Colombia 2005:

Andean Parrots on the Brink

We set off from Roncesvalles on horseback at 6am, riding through the small town and up into the mountains of the Central Andes. I passed a flock of Bronze-winged Parrots who were out early to raid a crop of peas. They were not popular birds, especially when they descended on a field of maize. As they took off, as dark as rooks before the sun was up, I saw with surprise that there were 30 or 40 of them. The riding was hard and uncomfortable, up steep rocky tracks, some so narrow there was hardly room for the stirrups. I marvelled that the horse could keep his footing and that I (who had only ever been on a horse once before) stayed in the saddle. With such uncomfortable stirrups, a bag resting on my knees and my heart often in my mouth, it was challenging! I envied the young, fit local members of the team who ran up the slopes like mountain goats.

It took 1½ hours to reach the high oak forest where a little-known species lives. About three minutes before we reached the top a flock of 26 small parrots flew above us. Even although there was no sun, they made an unforgettable kaleidoscope of soft and varying colours such as I had never seen before in a flying parrot, let alone an airborne squadron! It was a very lucky sighting of Rusty-faced Parrots, greeting us on arrival. We glimpsed half a dozen a couple of hours later, flying in the distance, and underlining how fortunate our first sighting had been.

The genus *Hapalopsittaca* consists of four species of 9in (23cm) short-tailed parrots, confined to the Andes. It is one of the least known genera of parrots in the world; one species is Critically Endangered and two, including the Rusty-faced, are Endangered, due to deforestation. They are so rare that probably no photographs of live birds existed of the two endemic members of the genus, *fuertesi* and *velezi*, until Project

Hapalopsittaca commenced in 2001, again pioneered by ProAves with the financial support of Loro Parque Fundación.

The sub-species of the Rusty-faced Parrot found here, *velezi*, was first described as recently as 1989 and differs from the other two sub-species (the nominate race in the eastern Andes and *theresae* in Venezuela) by its golden-olive hind neck and nape. With its scarlet shoulder patch it is indeed a pretty bird. Occurring only on the western flank of the Central Cordillera, between 7,200ft (2,200m) and 9,800ft (3,000m) in the departments of Caldas and Tolima, it would be easy to overlook this quiet little parrot.

The area where it lives, in a remnant of forest surrounded by cattle pasture, is cold and cloudy. The oak trees are covered in lichens and mosses, and fallen branches disappear under a cover of these complex fungi and algae growing so prettily in symbiosis. The oak branches are heavy with epiphytes, the seeds of which are eaten by the parrots. Acorn Woodpeckers are quite conspicuous and perhaps make some holes suitable for parrot nest cavities. However, felling of trees for fencing in the nesting area, where we were, had occurred during the previous year, causing some pairs to desert their nests. That was highly regrettable. With such a rare species, every chick is important.

When the clouds parted for a while we could see Roncesvalles, a small patch of human habitation far below us, from where we departed the following morning. We drove the four hours back to Ibagué on dirt tracks full of holes and scattered with rocks, crossing little fords and somehow avoiding the dogs and chickens that wandered the streets. A white duck was sitting in a puddle in the middle of the road, enjoying the rain The scenery was impressive, despite the deforestation of even the steepest slopes more than a century previously. Some forest patches remained but the slopes were bare over large areas, or cultivated with food crops despite the gradient. Tall grasses grew on the roadside slopes, alongside houses of wattle and split bamboo, or shacks of wood or breezeblocks, usually with the roof of tin – more rarely thatched. Bougainvillea, *Cassia* and other flowering shrubs flourished around the houses, along with pink-orange busy-lizzies.

We stopped in the town while Paul's vehicle was repaired. Three hours later, the vehicle again roadworthy, we set off for Genova, a small town in the department of Caldas. Once again my heart was in my mouth. Paul seemed to get a buzz from overtaking on blind bends on narrow, winding roads.

On July 28 2002 Jorge Velásquez and Alonso Quevedo ascended over 10,000ft (3,000m) in the Colombian Andes through a mosaic of pastures to a small patch of cloud forest, shrouded in a dense mist that swirled around the forest canopy. Suddenly, a sharp cry pierced the gloom, immediately followed by a chorus of parrot calls. "The ghostly silhouettes of fourteen parrots tumbled from the cloud, drawing nearer, as if released from the heavens", said Jorge. They spiralled downwards in tight vortexes to alight in nearby trees. In those few seconds Jorge and Alonso thought they were witnessing a miracle, as one of the world's rarest birds – Fuertes' Parrot – materialised before their eyes. The moment would forever live in their memories.

Jorge and Alonso spent several days studying the flock, taking detailed notes, sound-recordings, photos and video to document the discovery and to provide vital information on the species' ecology. It seemed incredible that the 14 birds, which included

The team pose in front of a mural at Roncesvalles: Paul Salaman far left, next to the author, and Alonso Quevedo far right.

269

three juveniles, had survived in just a few dozen hectares of forest.

When I read about this I was thrilled to my core! So rarely is a believed extinct bird "rediscovered"... I could picture the elation of the two dedicated ornithologists whose months of searching had finally brought such joy after the parrot had not been reliably reported since 1911.

The rich soils and lush vegetation of this region long ago attracted colonists who used its natural resources and denuded its steep hillsides. What little forest remained was plundered for firewood and cleared for crops and pasture. It seemed impossible that the now famous Fuertes' Parrot could have survived here. In April 2002 Paul had said, "Our hope for this parrot is dwindling and we're all gravely concerned that it has been lost forever". This situation had long alarmed the conservation community but the harsh environment and difficult access had been a deterrent to searching for the parrot's possible range. Then a determined effort was made.

In 2000, Jorge Velásquez, then 20, was a student at Colombia's National University in Bogotá. He and Paul and a team from Fundación ProAves launched a series of searches throughout the Colombian Andes for this and for the Rusty-faced Parrot. Remarkably, Jorge (who I met several days later, quiet, unassuming and bearded) rapidly located several new populations of the latter and collected ecological data vital for its conservation. But Fuertes' Parrot eluded them until that unforgettable day in 2002.

In 2003 the ProAves/LPF team was elated to discover a Fuertes' Parrot nest containing young with the entrance 8ft (2.4m) from the ground. At an altitude of 10,500ft (3,200m), it was in a cut tree, in an area where felling had occurred. By 2005 three tiny populations of this parrot were known with total numbers perhaps in the region of one hundred birds. They occur only high in the Central Cordillera, above 8,500ft (2,600m), where most of their habitat has been destroyed.

The team identified an area of 700 hectares of good habitat for this parrot and ensured its protection under written contract with the local mayor. Not long after 1,500 hectares of montane forest were being managed as the El Mirador Nature Reserve. By forming a "friends of the parrots" group and giving talks to the local community, the team had taken important steps to secure Fuertes' Parrot's future. It will be successful only with the full support and commitment of the local people who unwittingly had been the parrot's greatest threat.

The critical requirements of the species appear to be tall mature trees, where they feed on berries, especially mistletoe, amongst the epiphyte-laden canopy branches, and where they search for nesting cavities. The latter were almost non-existent. The ProAves team therefore erected more than 200 wooden nest-boxes, covered with bark. In April 2004 came wonderful news! Five boxes were occupied by breeding pairs, which were then incubating eggs. The parrots had been desperate for somewhere to nest – so desperate that one box was occupied 15 minutes after it was erected!

In Genova it was very hot and close. We stayed at the home of Claudia, the education officer of the regional ProAves group. That evening the local children put on a wonderful show, using song and dance and puppets to tell the story of one of the most endangered parrots in the world that lives close to their town.

I was very moved when I first read the story of the rediscovery of Fuertes' Parrot in this remote and little-visited area. Never in my wildest dreams did I imagine that one day I would be in the same cool, moss-covered forest with Alonso, watching a pair of these extraordinary little parrots at their nest. Now here I was! We had left Genova in the dark, at 5.40am. For an hour we drove up a narrow, stony track, where clouds hung low over the mountains. At the El Mirador Reserve, the kindly forest ranger Don Gustavo met us with five horses. For two hours we rode up a steep track, so muddy, slippery and stony that the horses were stumbling. Finally we reached the house (derelict only a year previously) that the group had rented and renovated. It was of the usual rough construction of wood, with a brick wood-burning oven. Don Gustavo's wife welcomed us with hot soup and bread and cheese. After an hour or more, the horses were saddled again, this time for a short ride over even steeper ground.

271

The house below the páramo zone

We ascended into the páramo zone. This ecosystem consists of a dense growth of trees and shrubs that rarely exceed 15ft (4.5m) in height. It occurs *above* cloud and elfin forest; in other words, it is as high as you can get – and cold, often with frost at night. We dismounted not far from a nest-box. A little green head with blue crown and greyish beak looked out, totally unconcerned. It was a female Fuertes' Parrot! True, it had been tough getting here, but now I was watching one of the rarest parrots in the world from a distance of 6ft (2m)! She was incubating – and after a minute or so she went back down to her eggs. This species had had so little contact with man, in its remote habitat, that it knew no fear.

The team based at the house documented every sighting; they were in the field for 20 days each month. They knew that the male usually flew in to feed the female four or five times daily, and usually at about 11am. Half an hour after our arrival the male was heard and we hid in the undergrowth. He flitted in soundlessly, through the epiphyte-laden and lichen-encrusted trees. It was unreal, almost dream-like: we emerged and the male ignored us. Not as brightly coloured as the Rusty-faced Parrot, he was mainly green with the crown blue, forehead and cheeks dull yellow and a red patch on the shoulder. (This area is

272

duller, brownish-red, in the female.) We departed the scene quickly, when he was still present.

I could hardly believe what I had just seen! Here was one of the most critically endangered parrots in the world, glimpsed by only a privileged few, behaving with as little concern as a pair of lovebirds in an aviary! Another nest of this trusting parrot was located not far away and, on a nearby *finca*, there were five more active nests.

During the afternoon we returned to the same patch of forest to see another parrot species at another artificial nest. The contrast could not have been greater. The Bronze-winged Pionus is, understandably, so nervous of man (those that raid crops are shot) that it leaves its nest at the first hint of his presence. We reached a tree where a wooden nest-box hung from a bare branch, from which the female departed when she heard us approaching. One of the team ran up the tree as though it were a flight of stairs and brought down a chick for us to see. About ten days old, it was very noisy and had a crop full of seeds. A younger chick was also in the nest.

Bronze-wings are uniquely coloured parrots with navy-blue plumage and skyblue under the wings. This pair had apparently been as desperate for nest sites as were the Fuertes' Parrots. I was shown a former nest in a thick, decayed stump broken off at about 6ft (1.8m) high. It had proved to be unsuitable. The

Bronze-winged Pionus Parrot, above. Below, the chick.

two chicks hatched there in the previous year had died at the age of about three weeks, I was told, due to flea infestation. The cavity was not used again.

I climbed back down to the house and sat on a rock contemplating the extraordinary sightings of the morning. The sun emerged briefly then the clouds swirled in, obliterating the steep, rocky, tussock-covered mountainside, and the patches of oak trees with plumes of cloud flowing through them. We went in for lunch. It was delicious – rice and noodles (and chicken) with crispy rounds of fried banana.

I sat talking to Field Co-ordinator Nicolai Doran, about the Mercenary Amazon Parrot. I had glimpsed it briefly, high above, on a number of occasions. Nicolai had never seen this parrot perched. Then he showed me the skin of a Fuertes' Parrot that was illegally taken, alive, from the nest. This caused an uproar and the police were involved. Sadly, the parrot died after 15 days before it could be rehabilitated. It had been fed an unsuitable diet of bread and milk and rice. Taking of young had become a rare event, thanks to the educational work carried out by ProAves. Since they have worked with the local people, as well as with governmental bodies, locally and nationally, the vital steps towards securing its future have been taken. A lot more remains to be learned about this now iconic species.

The people now celebrate its existence. On National Parrot Day they parade in the street with banners, posters and children in parrot costumes. Ethics have changed. One banner bearing a colourful depiction of Fuertes' Parrot read: "*Prohibido meterlo en una jaula*". (It is prohibited to cage it.)

Early next morning in the smoky kitchen I watched Don Gustavo's homely wife preparing the food. She put the cooked white maize through an old-fashioned mincer while Don Gustavo was mixing the flour and water for tortillas, which he then placed on a grill over the wood fire. Outside Brown-bellied Swallows – a dozen or more – were collecting insects and entering their nests under the roof. Rufous-collared Sparrows, with their orange collars, were flitting around. The giant Great Thrushes were behaving just as our Blackbirds do, foraging on the ground.

After breakfast the horses were saddled to return to the páramo zone. The path was so bad that the horse behind me stumbled onto its knees. Finally the cloud came down and we had to turn back. Less than one year previously this area had been grazed by one hundred cattle. In the nick of time the cattle were removed and the stunted vegetation was regenerating, to the benefit of the precious Fuertes' Parrots.

After lunch we started back down the mountain. The way down was so steep and treacherous that as a raw novice I deemed it unsafe to ride. Three hours later, with legs reduced to jelly, I reached the bottom!

Before I left the country I had the opportunity to see one of Colombia's four parrots that are not found elsewhere (endemic). The Flame-winged or Brown-breasted Conure had survived in a few fragmented populations in the Eastern Andes between 5,600ft (1,700m) and 11,000ft (3,400m). Little was known about it until Ana Maria Gonzales started to study it for her PhD thesis. She was to be my guide on a wonderful sunny morning as we drove 44 miles (70km) north of Bogotá into the department of Cundinamarca. This parakeet occurs only at altitudes above 7,500ft (2,300m), which was where we left the car, negotiated a barbed-wire fence and climbed a hillside. It was covered in sphagnum moss and familiar-looking wild plants such as the yellow-flowering hawkweed (*Hieracium*). Then we came to a

Flame-winged or Brown-breasted Conure
Photograph: Alonso Quevedo/ProAves

small patch of forest that was very quiet and seemingly devoid of bird life. No one would have guessed at its importance.

One could search for months with little hope of finding this parakeet but with Ana-Maria's knowledge we waited only a few minutes to hear the calls of a *Pyrrhura*. It was not long before several Flame-winged Conures flew *towards* us and landed in a tree about 60ft (18m) away. Gradually, we crept nearer. Four-on-a-branch, they sat together preening in the sun, the yellow patches in their wings shining like little beacons when they stretched.

Beautiful, with their reddish ear-coverts and whitish nape feathers, they differ from other members of the genus in having the scalloped feathers of the upper breast soft brown. The edge of the wing is yellow. At last we moved too close and they took off. Then I discovered, to my surprise, that there were *ten!* We waited on a rock and they briefly re-appeared in the distance but we knew the show was over.

Ana Maria was studying the feeding and nesting habits of the Flame-winged Conure and showed me photographs of chicks. Nests were inspected once or twice every month and extensive notes were made regarding the individuals attending them. Observations were also made at roosting sites, attended by between three and 15 individuals. These sites are often woodpecker holes with the entrances well disguised by bromeliads. The trees at this altitude were lavishly bedecked with these plants with fleshy, water-storing leaves – and it was here that they drink. Even in the dry season the early morning mist brings enough moisture to secure their water supply.

In addition to studying their biology, ProAves carried out an education programme to teach people about the threats facing the 50 individuals that survive in this locality. What a joy it had been to see these unique Andean parrots and to meet the people working to save them! And a genuine privilege…

Updates
The projects go from strength to strength. In March 2005, not long after my visit, twenty-one active nests of Fuertes' Parrot had been found. This was the start of the long climb back from

extinction. In 2007, 1,500 acres of habitat had been purchased in Fuertes' Parrot's core breeding area to form a new reserve. The population numbered about 170 individuals and 30 pairs were using nest-boxes! In 2009, after five years of hard work to conserve it, the first Indigo-winged (Fuertes') Parrot Festival was organised. It ended with a parade with the participation of the entire community, many of whom were dressed up as parrots.

In December 2008 a camera installed in a nest-box of a pair of Flame-winged Parakeets recorded the absorbing sight of an adult feeding several young ones. ProAves had increased its land holdings to 39,000 acres in 12 reserves and 100,000 trees were to be planted in 2008. Furthermore, eco-tourism was increasing.

Colombian bird statistics (year 2000)
Critically Endangered 13
Endangered 24
Vulnerable 40
Near-threatened 52

Species not previously mentioned:

Fuertes' Parrot or Indigo-winged Parrot (*Hapalopsittaca fuertesi*) CRITICALLY ENDANGERED
Rusty-faced Parrot (*Hapalopsittaca amazonina velezi*) ENDANGERED
Acorn Woodpecker (*Melanerpes formicivorus*)
Brown-bellied Swallow (*Notiochelidon murina*)
Great Thrush (*Turdus fuscater*)
Flame-winged or Brown-breasted Conure (*Pyrrhura calliptera*) VULNERABLE

22. Brazil 2008

The Atlantic Forest: saved from oblivion

They were at the point of mutiny: soaking wet, covered in mud from repeatedly falling on the slippery trail, and hungry. After two hellish nights camping in the Atlantic Forest, without the compensation of seeing any birds, they had had enough. The organiser wanted to stay under canvas for another night, despite the persistent, drenching rain. Someone went off to check on the state of the river. His return brought the message that it was so swollen, crossing it had become impossible. That settled it. The eight "parrot watchers" who had seen not one parrot were adamant. They were going down. It took five, long, weary hours to get back to Guapi Assu Bird Lodge where welcome hot showers, dry clothes and warm food awaited them.

I cannot pretend I was sorry that I missed that part of the trip! I had flown to Rio Janeiro four days after the other members of the group where, in the early morning, I was met by the lodge's driver. The sun was shining – but I did not realise that was unusual of late. We left the city over a 10-mile (16km) long bridge, flanked by ports and industry, including hundreds of new cars waiting to be shipped. We barely missed annihilation when, to avoid crashing into the car in front, the driver swung suddenly into the oncoming lane. Luck was with us. It was empty for a few seconds. That was my reminder of the dangers of Brazilian roads!

Our destination was only 50 miles (80km) north-east of Rio but the journey took more than two hours, nearly half of it on an unmade road. As we neared the lodge, the driver stopped to point out to me a distant Campo Flicker (a handsome golden-headed termite-feeding woodpecker) and a Wing-banded Hornero (Ovenbird). Not far away were the forested slopes of the Serra dos Orgãos Mountains, so called because of their organ-pipe rock formations.

BRAZIL

The fifth largest country in the world, Brazil is only slightly smaller than the USA and 35 times larger than the UK. Its tally of 77 parrot species is larger than that of any other country. It has an incredibly rich avifauna in a wonderful diversity of habitats. Mainly tropical, with most of the Amazon rainforest within its boundaries, controversy has raged for years over deforestation, mainly to graze cattle, producing one third of the world's beef. It has a wealth of raw materials but mining them is polluting the rivers. Brazil's economy is the ninth largest in the world.

White-throated Hummingbird

The Atlantic Forest is a hotspot of biodiversity. Occurring mainly in Brazil, it reaches into northern Argentina and eastern Paraguay. About 93% of it had been lost by 1995. In 1500, just before the European onslaught on Brazil, these forests were connected to the Amazon and stretched from 5 degrees south to 30 degrees south, about 580,000 square miles (nearly 1.5 million sq km) of forest along a coastline of approximately 1,875 miles (3,000km). Extensive forest clearance to exploit Brazilwood occurred in the 16th century and vast areas were cleared and burned for cattle pasture. Deforestation accelerated at the start of the 20th century when Brazil's population numbered only 17 million. Now at 180 million, this is the world's fifth most populous country.

The Atlantic Forest was contributing nearly half of all the timber produced in Brazil as recently as the 1970s. By the end of the century saving the forest remnants had become desperately important. That included the 6,700 hectares which now form REGUA (Reserva Ecológica de Guapiaçu), founded by Nicholas Locke, an Englishman whose family had owned land there for several generations. Nicholas and his wife Raquel have dedicated their lives to conserving the forest and its inhabitants.

Extremely friendly and hospitable, they have made Guapi Assu Bird Lodge a home-from-home for enthusiasts who have the potential to see an amazing 83 Atlantic Forest endemic bird species, plus countless endemic plants. Nestled on a small hill overlooking the forest, close to restored wetlands, birdwatchers come here to see species that have small ranges, some endangered and nearly all difficult to find.

Nicholas gave us a presentation with images dating back to 1915 when it was a farm belonging to his great-grandfather. Swamps stretched from there to Rio; yellow fever was endemic. Slaves worked in the cane fields to supply sugar for the European market. In the previous century Brazil had imported more slaves from Africa than the whole of the US, until slavery was abolished in 1888. Now most Brazilians are dark-skinned, due to their African ancestry. The original Brazilian inhabitants could not be enslaved. Men hunted and women did all the work.

The Lockes' enthusiasm and determination to save part of the *Mata Atlantica* (the forest's name in Portuguese) was impressive. They started the reserve in 1996, planting one thousand trees per hectare, with a 95% survival rate. Gathering the seeds from native forest trees and plants, they started their own nursery. Volunteers are still planting. Reintroduction of one bird species from captive-bred stock has also occurred. This is the endemic, turkey-sized handsome black Red-billed Curassow, wiped out by hunting. Only 250 survive in the wild. Formerly widespread in lowland forests of eastern Brazil, it now occurs only in half a dozen protected sites. Who knows? Perhaps one day the endangered Red-browed Amazon Parrot, long gone from these forests, might also be reintroduced.

The Lockes employ the local people and help them to understand the concept of conservation. "We can do this only very gradually", explained Nicholas, "because the whole idea of conserving the forest is alien to them. Their belief is that forest is there to be destroyed." Local teenagers from families with hunting backgrounds visit REGUA to learn about the unique environment and the importance of saving it.

The lodge opened in 2004. Built around the original farmhouse, there are seven or so bedrooms, each with its own bathroom. It has a spacious and comfortable lounge / dining area with a large verandah next to the lawn where Nicholas encouraged us to play croquet before lunch on the Sunday. It was like a tiny slice of England apart from the hummingbirds at the feeders on the verandah, whatever the weather – and yes, that was also rather British! The glossy Black Jacobin Hummingbird (confined to the Atlantic coast), with its contrasting white tail panels, was always present, from first light onwards. The large Swallow-tailed was usually in evidence, also the widespread Rufous-breasted or Hairy Hermit. The Atlantic Forest region can boast of two dozen hummingbird species.

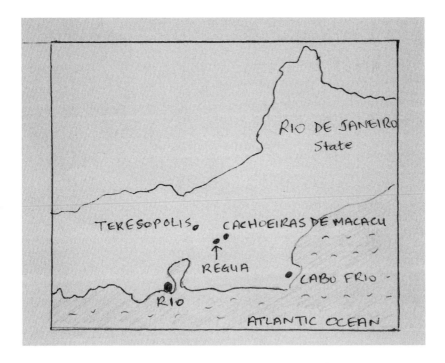

The lodge was perfect, small and friendly – and that also applied to our group. An interesting mixture of nationalities, three were Dutch, including a young couple, one French girl, one American girl and four British, including Steve and Linda, plus the organiser. Brian, a friend of long-standing, kept us amused all day long. He ate spontaneity for breakfast and was never short of a witty remark. In more serious vein he told me: "We bonded very quickly. Our experience in the forest brought us all down to the same level." In fact, a relationship developed rapidly and unexpectedly between two members of our group. We were all people-watchers as well, of course, and when bird sightings were scarce a different topic of conversation was not unwelcome! We had another common interest. We were all there to see parrots rather than to increase a "life list" of species. None of us kept one.

Without the help of bird guide Adilei the list of birds observed would have been much shorter. Truth to tell, the majority of the forest species were seen as dark shapes among the foliage and Adilei's quick action in getting his scope on them, reversed what would have been almost birdless days. Adilei was a slim, pleasant young man who always wore a huge smile. The job was not easy for him as our organiser spoke no Portuguese and he spoke little English – yet he knew bird names in our language.

I was outside at first light (6.30am) every morning to savour the panorama of distant, jagged cloud-shrouded mountains, with the early mist swirling between the peaks. Green was the theme – achieved with a rainfall up to 984in or 82ft (2,200 to 2,500mm) of rain per annum.

When no excursions were planned it was pleasant to wander at leisure within the grounds. Often seen nearby, then flying to the roof of the lodge, were a pair of Masked Water Tyrants, who walked over the lawn much as Pied Wagtails might do at home. A few minutes on the path from the lodge to the wetlands revealed the most common and conspicuous species. Kiskadees, of course, and little Violaceous Euphonias, the male shiny deep violet above and yellow below, the female dull green, were not at all shy. A pair of Saffron Finches, the male the richest yellow, the female yellowish, lightly streaked brown, fed on the green seeds of grass by pulling at a stem, holding it down with the foot, and running the bill along its length to remove the seeds. They are common, yes! But I enjoyed them more than the rarer, skulking species.

Where the path turned right towards the wetlands, a group of eleven Guira Cuckoos were resting high up in a dead tree. Guiras are always fun to watch as they fly or walk in single file in their search for grasshoppers and termites, probing the ground and, if in long grass, suddenly appearing, head only, to look around. Their strange, shaggy plumage, brown, black and white, spiky crest and long tail make them instantly recognisable.

The wetlands consisted of a couple of lakes with a trail most of the way round and a hide with a good view of the lodge perched on the distant hill. Herons and egrets were present among the lake's reed-covered margins, including the unusually coloured Capped Heron – mainly white with cream-coloured neck and breast, black cap and blue facial skin that extended to the upper mandible. Swimming with the Brazilian Teal were uncommon Masked Ducks, the male with black head, the female's being black and white. Low in the water and favouring areas with dense aquatic vegetation, they were not easy to see. Among the water lilies stepped Wattled Jacanas and swam White-faced Whistling Ducks, calling their clear, high-pitched whistle. All the ducks were wary.

In the marshy areas the familiar Amazon Kingfisher and the large Ringed Kingfisher were frequently sighted, also the White-headed Marsh Tyrant, often perched conspicuously on a twig a few inches above the ground. New to me was the diminutive 4in (10cm) White-barred Piculet, tapping on a slender branch as befits a miniature woodpecker with a tiny beak. It allowed a close approach and I could appreciate its red crown, black and white barred underparts and brown wings. It really made my day! Generally, only hummingbirds and tanagers could be observed without the need to use binoculars.

The most eye-catching tanager was the Brazilian. The males, carmine with black wings and tail, are like red flames in the bush: so conspicuous. Females are brown, with dull red underparts and rump. This gorgeous tanager occurs exactly in the region once covered by the Atlantic Forests – and favours habitats near water. Another beauty was the Burnished–buff Tanager, with its near-gold plumage, blue wings, striking black mask and bold black line from throat to abdomen.

One of the most distinctive species, perched boldly by the lake edge, was the Fork-tailed Flycatcher, with its black head, grey wings and snowy-white underparts. Its tail sets it apart from other flycatchers, its black feathers being twice the length of its body with two long widely separated streamers. A common migratory species, it was present from September until April.

Wherever we went, the Southern Lapwings objected noisily to our presence and Black Vultures were never far away. Small groups of Smooth-billed Anis were a permanent part of the landscape and Roadside Hawks, perched high and watching the ground, were frequently encountered. A noisy pair of Yellow-headed Caracaras always returned to perch in the top of a bare tree. The smallest member of the family, they are buff-coloured with brown wings. But these are common birds of the neotropics. Parrots there were none. Even the Orange-winged Amazons, that often put in an appearance near the lodge, were absent.

Species found within Guapi Assu's varied habitats, ranging from lowland forest (little remains) and wetlands to unspoilt high altitude forest, include such interesting parrots as Purple-bellied and Red-capped – but you would need to spend a few days to observe them. We had the time but not the weather. It was the hope of seeing the Purple-bellied Parrot that had attracted me to this region. One of our group had filmed this unusual parrot (it sings like a thrush) there in the previous year, recording it eating an entire bromeliad – a valuable clip as so little is known about its habits.

In 2008 Alan Davies and Ruth Miller embarked on their "Big Twitch" – to beat the record number of bird species seen by anyone in one year. Four months previously they had visited REGUA and notched up 30 "new" species on the first day, including the Plovercrest, a tiny hummingbird with a crest like a Lapwing.

A series of excursions can be made from the lodge, mostly designed for those who want to add new species to their list and are prepared for a long uncomfortable drive. The main drawback of the location was that it involved three-quarters of an hour (that is, one and a half hours each day) of being bumped and shaken before one could reach the main road near the town of Cachoeiras de Macacu. The unmade track in the other direction took one through an area of *fazendas* (farmsteads) and rich cattle pasture. All these areas were fenced and each *fazenda* was indicated by a painted wooden sign and archway.

One morning, after an early start, we travelled through spectacular forested mountains, so lush and inviting. Just as I was drinking in their beauty, huge billboards appeared at the roadside, depicting scantily-clad girls and advertising lingerie. Their inappropriateness was like a smack in the face!

We had stopped in a small town at noon to eat lunch. Up a flight of ornate steps, near the main street, I watched two young Rufous-bellied Thrushes being fed by a parent, much as a Blackbird (same genus) might do near a busy shopping street in the UK. House Sparrows were also present. Two White-eyed Conures were playing about on the roof of a dwelling and entering a hole under the eaves. This was my first sighting of parrots since I had left home! Our American participant was thrilled! She had come on this trip in memory of a beloved pet of the same species, whose photo she carried with her.

Near a store a man sitting on the ground with his little grandson watched us bemusedly as we trained our binoculars on a tiny White-eared Puffbird. Only 8in (19cm) long, to me it looked more like a black, brown and white finch with a big red beak than a puffbird. The man must have been totally bewildered. Sadly, in every town or village there is evidence of the only aspect of birds in which most people have an interest – confining native species in tiny cages, no more than 12in (31cm) in length. Their quality of life was nil. I wished that I could open the doors when no one was looking. The tradition of keeping birds this way, for their song, is a very long one. But who am I to be critical? A century ago – and less – wild-caught Goldfinches and Bullfinches would be seen in tiny cages in millions of homes in Britain. Today, anyone who sells wild-caught native birds can expect a prison sentence yet, ironically, the importation of wild-caught exotic birds was not banned until 2007 – and then for health reasons, not moral ones.

For me, the most exciting part of the day was glimpsing the gorgeous Blue or Swallow-tailed Manakin. It belongs to a family of birds that I love to see, one of the most exciting groups in South America. Alas, the views were brief of the turquoise-blue body and glowing scarlet head of the male – but they were dazzling, when we stopped by shrubby roadside vegetation. I wish I could have seen the lightening-fast display of this wonderful creature as he whizzed about on his perch in the hope of attracting a mate. An olive-green female or immature bird was also present. Brazil is home to 36 of the 60 or so species of manakins.

At Sumidouro, on the other side of the Serra dos Orgâos, are remnant patches of dry forest where a rare bird is found. After an hour of walking on the tortuous, red earth mountain road, passing the bank in which the Three-toed Jacamar burrow in order to nest, we found one. Five hours on the road was a long jaunt to view its silhouette, high above us, its dagger bill pointing skywards. If it had five toes I would have been none the wiser!

Very common 50 years ago, this jacamar is believed to have suffered substantial declines and much diminished range. It is now restricted to small patches of dry forest in the states of Rio de Janeiro and Minas Gerais. Sumidouro is its best-known surviving location. We were told that a nest tree of the Illiger's or Blue-winged Macaw was nearby. We briefly saw a pair of the macaws flying overhead but, alas, the tree (a palm) had gone!

One of the most charismatic birds of the Serra dos Orgâos region is the Saffron Toucanet – observed feeding on fruit at a bird table. Brown above with a long brown tail and saffron-orange head and underparts, it is one of those birds with an extraordinary colour scheme that only nature could have invented. The bill is mainly pale bluish but marked on both mandibles with psychedelic pink – and this colour extends onto the bare flesh surrounding the light yellow eye. Boldly perched in the open – unlike the

Saffron Toucanet

manakins – a couple of these toucanets posed on a telephone wire for our cameras!

The fair weather did not hold. We drove back through the darkness in torrential downpours that continued throughout the night. The British Friday evening tradition of having a few drinks was not neglected. Here it was a seemingly benign mixture of fermented sugar cane, lime and a little rum. There was a hilarious joke-telling session at dinner that night in which Nicholas participated with relish. But the menu told us we were definitely not in the UK. Some really simple dishes (always served buffet style), such as sweet potatoes cooked with onion, my favourite cheese empanadas and fried fresh sardines, indicated we were far from home. The cooking was skilful with only the subtlest hint of spices.

Next morning was spent walking trails, often steep, in the secondary forest – not a habitat that enthrals me. The upper storey consisted of spindly trees, palms and a few mature trees. The understorey of ferns, tiny palms and swathes of pink and orange *impatiens* ("busy lizzies") existed in a deep layer of leaf litter. Literally the only bird sighting I had was the backside of a pygmy owl through Adilei's scope. Adilei said he heard a Golden-tailed Parrotlet fly overhead. Now this rarely observed little parrot would have been a phenomenal sighting!

The monotony was broken when Chris caught with his bare hands a fer de lance – the most venomous snake in South America. Chris, a reptile enthusiast from Cambridge, was spending four weeks at REGUA at his own expense to document the species he found there. We all liked him, with his long curly hair and air of needing a good meal. Where snakes were concerned he had no fear (except, he said, of cobras, which were not to be trusted) and we watched in fascination as he expertly handled the snake. "You'll be as famous as Steve Irwin, one day", I told him. "Just make sure you don't suffer the same painful end."

The easy-looking downhill part of the trail was even worse than the slippery, stony uphill part. After four-and-a half-hours the muscles at the top of my legs ached and my knees turned to jelly. Twelve of us packed into the Landrover for the return journey, with Chris hanging on to the spare wheel at the back.

After lunch I went with Adilei and two others to a nearby location where the group had seen several parrot species four days earlier. Sheltering from the now torrential rain under a large tree, in an area of beautiful forest, I did see one Blue-winged Parrotlet – a sparrow-sized member of the parrot family. My "most wanted" species, the Purple-bellied Parrot, could sometimes be seen here – but not that day.

It was worth the soaking, though, because I was able to observe one of the world's most beautiful hummingbirds – the Frilled Coquette. The male sat still in the rain for several minutes, high up on a bare twig protruding from the top of a tree. Through the scope we could see his 3in (7cm) long body that weighs 3g, his fan of green and white feathers protruding from the cheeks, glittering green forehead and throat and broad rufous crest. In display the male erects his crest, also the feathers of his back, to reveal a white band across his rump. The little green and white female, with spotted throat, must be mesmerised! The coquettes (genus *Lophornis*) are well named – simply gorgeous, ornate little creatures of almost unparalleled beauty. Five of the eight species occur in Brazil.

It rained all through the night so our leader decided we should drive to Cabo Frio on the coast where (despite its name) he promised us sun and warmth. The rain stopped just before we reached the first area of wetland where excitement was provided by a single Roseate Spoonbill. The next wetland was even less notable – just a few egrets. The distant Kelp Gulls looked very handsome – huge with jet-black wings.

Four hours after we set out everyone started to raid the lunch box. Nearby was a pretty little cove – the ideal spot for a picnic, I suggested. But no, the driver – possibly with thoughts of the commission he might earn – took us to a gaudily painted bar on the beach front where we sat on yellow plastic chairs under yellow Skol umbrellas. I shivered as we looked over the grey sea and the sunless beach! The men were happy: a beer session was just what they needed. I watched the House Sparrows hopping around the bar area and the little Ruddy Doves on a nearby patch of grass.

After lunch most of the group were led away at the prospect of seeing turtles in the sea from the top of the cliffs. This did not sound very exciting to me! Adilei and I had a more serious mission. We would look for the Restinga Antwren. Restinga is the term given to beach-scrub habitat with a high incidence of cacti (one area looked exactly like Bonaire!) and bromeliads growing on sand dunes. This rare bird (total estimated population fewer than one thousand) proved ridiculously easy to find. We walked a couple of hundred metres to some scrub along the road leading away from the beach, and Adilei got out his tape. He played a recording of the antwren's call and within a minute there was one skulking in the undergrowth. It was true it was not easy to see it but I managed to get a photo of a male when it showed itself for a split second. He appeared mainly black with some white dots on the wings. The female looked rather different with her black mask, brown upperparts and cream-coloured underparts. Adilei was thrilled with his excellent photos which were the first he had taken of this neat little bird.

There were several antwrens there. They darted around at speed, here one minute, a few feet away the next. I paid dearly

Restinga Antwren male

The sweeping bay of Cabo Frio

for my sightings of them. In my attempt to get a better view, I knelt in the long grass in front of the thickets. This was the day I had forgotten to apply insect repellent. Later I discovered that my back was covered in nasty bites that irritated for twelve days. That night my skin was on fire! Thereafter I took great care to protect myself in every possible way but insects have always had a liking for my blood.

The Restinga Antwren has the misfortune to live in areas coveted by beachfront developers. Its range, in the area of Cabo Frio, is small and severely fragmented and its habitat is declining rapidly. Fortunately, it occurs on Ilha do Cabo Frio (an offshore island), access to which is restricted by the Brazilian navy.

From the top of the cliff we could see a few tiny islands, with Frigatebirds and gulls swooping above them. The curving bay and the gaudy bars looked quite attractive from up there. My thoughts returned to the Atlantic coast of Argentina, a long way south, where I had watched the beautiful Burrowing Parrots.

290

Here, apparently, there were Orange-winged Amazons who flew over at dusk to roost on one of the islets. But we departed at 4.30pm – too early to see them. We stopped, not far from the cliffs, to watch a group of 20 Roseate Spoonbills, glowing pink and swishing their necks as they fed in the wetlands. We arrived back at REGUA at 8pm after 12 hours away. It was too long, everyone agreed, and few birds had been encountered.

Next day there was blue sky! We drove upwards, visiting the well-sited Serra dos Tucanos Lodge an hour away in the Tres Picos State Park. Our hunger for parrot sightings was satisfied by thirty or so common and lovely little Plain Parakeets. I would have named them Perfect Parakeets. Their unadorned light green plumage is so immaculate and their small, slender form so lovely to my eyes. They visited the bird table which was loaded with papaya and other fruits. A few Maroon-bellied Conures were also feeding there but, so typical of *Pyrrhuras*, they were more elusive. Tangers, especially the colourful Green-headed (whose head is turquoise), were numerous. A bright green Brassy-breasted, with golden throat and upper breast and

Plain Parakeets feasting on papaya

291

turquoise "spectacles", sat and watched me from 4ft (1.2m) away.

Most striking of all were the Spot-billed Toucanets. I gasped with pleasure at the sight of them. The zebra-striped upper mandibles, green wings and tail and striking bare green skin surrounding the yellow eyes and chestnut under tail coverts are common to both sexes. The male's head (apart from the orange ear coverts), neck and underparts are black and his abdomen is yellow. The female is brown in those areas. These charismatic characters were not shy so we could enjoy them taking beakfuls of banana from the bunches hanging there. The toucanets breed nearby and their young, with unstriped bills, are sometimes observed. This was my sixth day in Brazil and at last I had long observations of one of the most showy of the great country's birds.

The owners of Serra dos Tucanos, a young Englishman called Andy Foster and his vivacious Romanian wife, had arrived six years previously and set about clearing the banana plantation near the house and putting up bird tables. A concrete hide close to the latter gave intimate views of the avian visitors. It was surrounded by vegetation, against a backdrop of verdant trees stretching high into cloud-obscured mountains. At last the sun had come out. I sat by the pool and enjoyed the warmth and the surroundings, listening to the faint sound of the boulder-strewn river, the twittering calls of tanagers and the hum of hummingbirds. Palm trees, set in the lush green lawn, were decorated with layer after layer of bromeliads and small ferns and orchids – just as in the forests.

Our minibus took us further up the mountain, with a brief stop at the hanging nests of Red-rumped Caciques. A distant bellbird (his calls were clear) appeared as a white spot in a far-off forest tree. It seems that the British have quite a strong presence in this part of the world. We visited David Miller, originally from Ireland, who had dwelt in his mock-Tudor house there for 40 years – half his lifetime. An authority on orchids, his third book on the subject was in production.

The great attraction here was the number of hummingbirds that attended his feeders, sometimes between 50 and 100 individuals.

He told me: "The buzzing is like being in the middle of a beehive."

The hummingbirds were so tame they would settle on the hand of someone they knew. I admired especially the male Brazilian Ruby, a long-bodied species with an iridescent throat that flashed magenta or violet, a glittering dark green crown and sparkly green-brown underparts. The pretty little White-throated Hummingbird was abundant here. Mr Miller kindly went inside and brought out a copy of Ruschi's classic book on hummingbirds to show

Brazilian Ruby Hummingbird

me the plate of the species. At that moment it started to rain again! While I had been mesmerised by the little nectar feeders a couple of others had walked down the road and seen the display of the Blue Manakin. I was envious!

After dinner one night, encouraged by a couple of really keen English birders staying briefly at the lodge, the others went out to look for the Giant Snipe, whose location was well known. Nowhere common, it is hunted and shot throughout its range. Being nocturnal and extremely secretive, this species is highly sought-after and the night-watchers returned happy. I didn't go. I did not need to add to my array of insect bites!

On our final day we arose at 2.15am to catch the 6am flight from Rio to Sao Paulo. We nearly missed it! We were eagerly looking forward to the Pantanal where parrots abounded. Despite their scarcity in the Atlantic Forest, partly due to an unseasonal cold front, it had been interesting to experience this unique habitat. The knowledge that the wealth of endemic bird species is bringing tourists to the region, which will hopefully encourage their conservation, is very pleasing.

Update 2009

As part of the BirdLife Preventing Extinctions Programme, funding became available to study the Restinga Antwren during the 2008/2009 breeding season. Of 15 nests located in the study area, only three were successful. Introduced common marmosets were found to be responsible for the poor breeding rate. These were to be removed before the next breeding season. In 2009, when the antwren population was believed to number between 250 and 1,000 birds, plans were in hand for a new reserve in the Restinga de Maçambaba.

Brazilian bird statistics (year 2000)

Critically endangered 22 (20 endemics including two parrots)
Endangered 36 (32 endemics including 5 parrots)
Vulnerable 54 species (26 endemics including 6 parrots)

Species not previously mentioned:

Campo Flicker (*Colaptes auratus*)
Wing-banded Hornero (*Furnarius figulus*)
Black Jacobin (*Florisuga fusca*)
Red-billed Curassow (*Crax blumenbachii*) ENDANGERED
Red-browed Amazon (*Amazona rhodocorytha*) ENDANGERED
Swallow-tailed Hummingbird (*Campylopterus macrourus*)
Masked Water Tyrant (*Fluvicola nengeta*)
Burnished-buff Tanager (*Tangara cayana chloroptera*)
Brazilian Teal (*Amazonetta brasiliensis*)
Masked Duck (*Nomonyx dominica*)
White-faced Whistling Duck (*Dendrocygna viduata*)
White-barred Piculet (*Picumnus cirratus*)
Brazilian Tanager (*Ramphocelus bresilius*)
Yellow-headed Caracara (*Milvago chimachima*)
Purple-bellied or Blue-bellied Parrot (*Triclaria malachitacea*)
Red-capped Parrot (*Pionopsitta pileata*)
Plovercrest (*Stephanoxis lalandi*)
Three-toed Jacamar (*Jacamaralcyon tridactyla*) ENDANGERED
Rufous-bellied Thrush (*Turdus rufiventris*)
White-eared Puffbird (*Nystalus chacuru*)
Saffron Toucanet (*Baillonus bailloni*)
Golden-tailed Parrotlet (*Touit surda*)

Frilled Coquette Hummingbird (*Lophornis magnificus*)
Blue-winged Parrotlet (*Forpus xanthopterygius xanthopterygius*)
Roseate Spoonbill (*Ajaia ajaja*)
Kelp Gull (*Larus dominicanus*)
Restinga Antwren (*Formicivora littoralis*) ENDANGERED
 (since 2000 uplisted to Critically Endangered)
Plain (All-green) Parakeet (*Brotogeris tirica*)
Brassy-breasted Tanager (*Tangara desmaresti*)
Green-headed Tanager (*Tangara seledon*)
Spot-billed Toucanet (*Selenidera maculirostris*)
Brazilian Ruby Hummingbird (*Clytolaema rubricauda*)
White-throated Hummingbird (*Leucochloris albicollis*)
Giant Snipe (*Gallinago undulata*)

Brazilwood (*Caesalpinia echinata*)
Fer-de-lance (*Bothrops atrox*)

23. Brazil 2008

The Pantanal

The contrast was extreme – and so wonderful! Within twelve hours we were launched from a dripping, green, forested environment into the searing heat of a Pantanal cattle ranch. The ten of us had been longing for the sun – and the wealth of parrot species. Our wishes were granted – and how!

As the parrot flies, our lodge in the Pantanal, near Miranda, was about 900 miles (1450km) from Teresópolis, the nearest large town to our previous location in the Atlantic Forest. We caught the 6am flight from Rio to San Paulo and the 9am flight to Campo Grande, just south of the Pantanal. At the airport our group was met by a smart small coach from Caiman Lodge. We nestled into the seats, appreciating the luxury (after the discomfort of the minibus) for the four-hour drive westward. The almost straight, flat road, flanked by palm trees, led past one *fazenda* after another where angular white zebu cattle grazed peacefully, contained by fences of short pale posts. The zebu or Brahman cattle, probably originally from India, are robust, droopy-eared animals reared for meat, which do well in hot climates.

Enthusiastic cries heralded sightings of shaggy-plumaged Greater Rheas and showy Toco Toucans. At last a sign read *Refugio Ecologico Caiman 30km*. We were getting close! A painted board indicated we had arrived. We turned right off the main road and reached the main lodge – but we were not there yet. We drove on a few more kilometres and finally came to a halt outside Pousada Baiazinha. Shaded by palm trees and a large *Caesalpinia*, with its mass of spectacular flame-coloured blossoms, the lodge itself was nearly invisible under neatly tiled roofs.

Lunch awaited us in a pleasant airy dining room-cum lounge.

The Pantanal

This is the world's largest freshwater wetland, a mosaic of lagoons, savannah, swamps and forest. It extends over an area of 54,000 sq miles (140,000 sq km) in southern Brazil, in the states of Mato Grosso and Mato Grosso do Sul, with its borders reaching into Paraguay and Bolivia. Two-thirds of this region is flooded annually, from about December to May. For 200 years huge cattle ranches have covered the area, almost all of which are privately owned.

Hyacinthine Macaw

The rear part was formed by glass doors, leading to a boardwalk by a serene lake where birds abounded. The food was as good as the view! The sun was fierce and I was contented. My room was excellent – high, brick-built, with ceiling fan and air-conditioning, very comfortable beds and a first-class bathroom. In the intense heat of the Pantanal these "luxuries" were essentials for the American tourists who are an important part of the clientele.

Attached to my room was a small deck that looked out, view unimpeded, over the lake and wetlands. It just got better and better! There was nothing more I could ask for. On the boardwalk not far from my deck, but separated by a marshy area, was a large cecropia tree. At once I found Quaker Parakeets eating cecropia fruits and a pair of pretty Golden-crowned Conures sheltering from the sun. These were just two of the five species of parakeets we saw daily.

At the front of the lodge was a wooden observation tower. I climbed its steps to view the landscape. Looking towards the main lodge, it was flat as far as the eye could see. A reddish earth track snaked its way across the land which was partly arid now, at the end of the dry season, with a few patches of green. To the right were a couple of small white-painted dwellings with neatly tiled roofs that matched the colour of the track. Not far beyond was a low fence with double gates. A few palm trees dotted the landscape of this open area. To the left was woodland with, just visible, another tiled roof. It was here that the horses were saddled. On the horizon more woodland stretched into the far distance.

Turning to the left, I could see a Jabiru Stork feeding in the wetland. I descended the steps of the tower and down more steps to the water's edge to watch it fishing. Just as I had done in Australia some months earlier, I marvelled at the grace and power of these huge storks, as tall as a man. The one here is the "original" Jabiru. The Australian species, also called Black-necked Stork, was named Jabiru by those familiar with the South American form – but the two are unrelated. Which is the most impressive? Possibly the South American form as its wings and body are pure white and the lower part of its neck is bright red – or most of the neck when in breeding condition. Its head is dark grey and bare of feathers. Slightly larger and with, perhaps, a more stately air, the strange bill almost gives it a Disney

The Caiman ranch

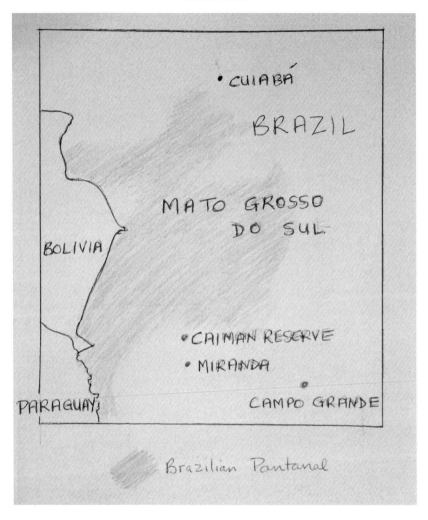

appearance. On the other hand, the Australian form has bright red legs and the female has yellow eyes that contrast with its glossy iridescent green head. Both have black dagger bills, the neotropical species' being slightly concave. In the wetland areas of both continents Jabirus are icons, symbols of the complex havens of wildlife that they inhabit. Both storks seem to focus intently on the ground beneath them, waiting and listening and watching, before suddenly plunging the bill into the marsh or the water to pull out a struggling frog or fish.

At 3.30 on that first afternoon we climbed into the safari vehicle, lorry-like with seats around the edges, closed top and open sides – perfect for moving around and taking photographs. It was our transport every day in the company of bird guide, Victor. When we descended to walk across a marshy area with mosquitoes, the heat was overwhelming. We encountered a well-named Gilded Hummingbird – unique in its bronze coloration and coral-red bill. Separated from us by a fence were two young Burrowing Owls, looking fluffy and innocent. They disappeared down their burrow if we approached too closely, then popped up again to see if we had gone.

Conspicuous and noisy – their metallic calls were one of the most characteristic avian sound of the reserve – were the Buff-necked Ibis. Walking around in pairs and prodding the ground with their long, curved bills, they could be approached more closely than the three other ibis species we saw. I found them all very appealing and always enjoyed watching them, with their long-legged gait and their slow, flapping flight with head and neck outstretched. In the vehicle we passed close to Green Ibis feeding in the roadside swamp, one with wings extended. On another occasion, a small group of Plumbeous Ibis with their ruby eyes, shaggy crests, mottled grey plumage and red legs, was probing into the long grasses.

That night, after an excellent dinner, we listened to a presentation by two members of the Ara Azul Project, Chagos and Monalyssa. *Ara Azul* means blue macaw – the imposing Hyacinthine, of course. Its biggest population, of approximately 1,500 individuals, is in the Pantanal. It also occurs in north-eastern Brazil and eastern Amazonia.

The largest and arguably the most spectacular of all parrots, what happened to it in the 1970s and 1980s illustrated how quickly a species' numbers can be decimated by trappers and exporters. These macaws proved so easy to catch that thousands were exported to the USA and to Europe, leaving only perhaps three or four thousand in the wild. The tragedy was that supply was greater than demand and hundreds of these magnificent birds died within a few weeks of being captured. Habitat destruction quickened their decline. Then, in 1990, a young lady who was to be their saviour arrived on the scene: Neiva Guedes, a recent biology graduate.

She was determined she would make a difference to the survival of this magnificent macaw. But how? She founded *Projeto Ara Azul* with great determination. For eight years she worked in the Pantanal without an official field team, enlisting the help of family and friends. An American biologist trained her to climb trees. She studied the macaws on 47 farms in Mato Grosso do Sul and realised that shortage of nest sites was inhibiting recovery of the population.

Every year, 3% to 5% of nest trees were lost as a result of storm damage or felling. Ninety per cent of the nests were in the large, smooth-barked trees known locally as manduví. They do not form cavities until they are 60 years old! A metre-long macaw needs a large cavity – and there were just not enough available. In 1995, Neiva erected the first nest-boxes. A

Chagos inspecting a nest-box

tremendous success, they were quickly occupied. By 2008, she and her team had observed 232 Hyacinthine nests in the artificial sites and 390 in natural cavities.

The macaws start to breed in July and several pairs on the ranch had chicks. Our group was very fortunate. On our first day we were able to accompany project members (Neiva was not there) on their "rounds". We followed their vehicle to the first nest in a large manduví in the middle of a field. The parents, who had been sitting atop the box, flew to a nearby tree and watched the proceedings, occasionally growling and yelling but seemingly not unduly concerned. Using ascenders (equipment favoured by mountaineers – a harness around waist and thighs attached to a pulley), Chagos reached the first nest-box at a height of about 40ft (12m) in a couple of minutes. He opened the door, took out a large chick, covered its head with a cloth, placed it in a bucket and carefully lowered it to the ground.

Hyacinthine Macaw chick

We all crowded round as petite Monalyssa took out the feathered chick. There were gasps at its large size, glossy violet plumage and huge dark eyes accentuated by the yellow bare skin surrounding them. What a beauty! At about eight weeks old, its upper parts were almost feathered, only the nape and mantle showing the dark grey down. It was quite calm. It was used to being handled; regular inspections were made at many nests. Chick mortality is high and these dedicated workers save the lives of some young macaws by removing ticks and other parasites and, if necessary, patching up the nest which might otherwise be flooded or hazardous for its occupants. Usually two eggs are laid (occasionally three) but only one chick will survive. All those in accessible nests are banded and micro-chipped before fledging. Once identified, their life histories can be documented.

In 18 years of studying nests, Neiva had known only one instance of three chicks hatching. The team gave supplementary feeds to the two smallest, and eventually moved one to a nest containing a single chick of the same age. Sadly one died from infestation by fly larvae but the other three fledged successfully.

Not all the nest-boxes are used by Hyacinthine Macaws. Seventeen other species have taken advantage of them and this can make more natural cavities available to the macaws. An unexpected treat was our visit to another nest-box, not far away, where a pair of Green-winged Macaws was rearing two young, probably about seven weeks old. Nests of this macaw are less common here and, again, we were privileged to see the chicks. Their red, green and blue plumage was in perfect condition with an area of greyish-white down on nape and mantle. The tiny lines of feathers on the otherwise bare facial area, typical of this macaw, were already well marked. The tails were half-length but their beaks were already huge. Again, their parents sat in the large manduví tree, watching us, occasionally taking off to circle around, their long red tails so prominent in flight.

That morning had been unforgettable. On our way back to lunch we stopped at the main lodge where a yellow armadillo was rooting around in the earth like a miniature prehistoric monster. Covered in scales, from its arrow-shaped head to its long, tapering tail, it was oblivious to our presence. Close by was a nest of Buff-necked Ibis in the crown of a palm tree. Shaded from the midday sun were two young, almost fully grown. I was grateful to Victor for pointing them out.

Victor was tall, dark and good-looking in a brooding sort of way. He seemed quiet and serious, probably because he had to concentrate hard to understand us. That was not surprising – the regional accents and those of the four members of our group for whom English was not the first language, all sounded rather different. Victor was an outstanding guide – not only because of his knowledge of birds, and his love for them, but because he was so attentive to our needs, constantly filling our water mugs and handing out fruit and biscuits. And making sure everyone had seen or photographed the species for which we had stopped. His presence was a large part of my enjoyment of those four memorable days.

At 3.30pm we went out again to meet Chagos and Monalyssa. Before we reached the main lodge our vehicle came to a sudden halt as Victor spotted a group of parakeets in a tree at the roadside. Well camouflaged among the leaves and wary, like all members of the genus *Pyrrhura*, they were Blaze-winged Conures. It was my first sight of the species but a good look eluded me. They were little more than silhouettes.

That afternoon we visited another nest-box. Its occupant was a Hyacinthine chick not yet feathered, aged about two and a half weeks. There were plenty of parakeets around. I walked down the road with Victor looking at Nanday Conures perched on a fence and a small flock of little Canary-winged Parakeets, well-camouflaged among the leaves of a large tree. Golden-crowned (or Peach-fronted) Conures were also observed. A pair of White-eyed Conures flew over, then a pair of Blue-crowned Conures, less common at that time. The Nandays, with their jet-black heads, perched in conspicuous spots in the open, watched us with interest and then flew off noisily. Maximilian's Parrots and Blue-fronted Amazons flew over in pairs.

There was nothing to compare, however, with unexpected sightings of Hyacinthine Macaws. We chanced across them feeding on their principal food – the nuts of the acurí palm with its feathery fronds – and here was a pair feeding only about 5ft (1.5m) from the ground on the fruits close to the thick trunk. They took off hastily on seeing us. When a palm fruit is opened with a machete, three round nuts are revealed within brown fibrous material, surrounded by white pulp like that found in a young coconut. In each cluster there are about 80 fruits. Some of these will fall to the ground, where they are swallowed by cattle who cannot digest them and pass them out in their pats. The macaws search for these softened nuts which they consume with relish. Once we saw a pair feeding in a grassy patch. They had probably found some nuts: I saw one pick up some vegetation to wrap around the item it held. They do this to obtain a better grip, making the nuts easier to crack.

A vivid memory concerns a single macaw drinking. Parrots find water in different ways, the most common being in bromeliads in rainforest and from streams in open country. Here these options did not exist. The macaw had walked across the muddy ground, interspersed with clumps of grass, to reach a large dirty puddle. At the end of the dry season this was all that survived of a larger extent of water. The macaw drank its fill, lifting its head time after time to let the water trickle down its throat.

It was always exciting to see Hyacinthine Macaws flying. Often they gave their deep throaty growl when in the air. Large macaws on the wing inspire awe in me, none more so than this species. Their flight is a slow aerial ballet, the synchronisation of two pairs of violet-blue wings. In dark silhouette, the large size, huge bill and long, sword-shaped tail in flight made them instantly recognisable.

We stayed out late for a session of "spotlighting". As we drove back to our lodge in the dark, Victor sat at the front of the vehicle, sweeping a spotlight from left to right, then from right to left. I was not optimistic enough to believe we would see a jaguar but smaller mammals, such as crab-eating racoon and crab-eating fox, were revealed in the beam of the light, along with countless bats.

Next day I was outside, close to the swamp at 5.30am, doused in insect repellent and with only my face exposed. I was there to watch the birds' dawning day. Half a dozen large ones left their roost and flew overhead. In the half light their long curved bills identified them as ibis and their metallic calls as Buff-necked. Grey clouds were hanging over the forest that skirted the lake and, as I watched, the sky above the trees lit up with an orange glow beneath a strata of light and fluffy clouds. Seven whistling ducks flew over, circled briefly and headed off. Kiskadees were shrieking their onomatopoeic calls and a thrush-like song came from an unseen songster. By 5.45am Blue-fronted Amazons were starting to leave their roost; five flew over silently. The loud, unmistakable sounds of the brown, pheasant-like Chaco Chachalacas rent the air intrusively. The clouds were becoming greyer.

I moved to the observation tower. From my lofty viewpoint I watched two Southern Lapwings dive-bomb a caracara; they had eggs or chicks nearby. A herd of capybara slowly made its way from the swamp, across the landscape from left to right. It intrigued me that in a herd there is every possible size, from tiny babies to big, heavy adults, 4ft (1.2m) long and 10 stone (65kg in weight). The largest rodent in existence, they look like giant brown, long-legged guinea pigs. Here they are protected but elsewhere they are killed for their meat. Chopi Blackbirds were feeding at the feet of the capybara and even riding on their backs. I grew rather fond of the Chopis, so busy and noisy, with a swaggering gait like our Starlings. About the same size, they were all glossy black and hung around the lodge, hopefully investigating my deck. The late Helmut Sick (in *Birds in Brazil*) describes them as having "one of the loudest and most melodious" songs of all the nation's birds. Even their whistled calls were a pleasure to the ear.

More Amazons were leaving their roost in pairs – and just one trio. By now a rosy-pink glow decorated the sky. The sun rose quickly; in five minutes it had gone, swallowed up by the clouds. More capybara were moving across the landscape, flycatchers were active and a pair of Green Ibis flew past. Four Maximilian's Parrots landed in a tree close to the lodge. Two handsome Rufescent Tiger Herons flew into the swamp and a stately Cocoi Heron, tall and grey, was fishing. Wattled Jacanas, with red frontal shields and chestnut wings, were stepping carefully among the water hyacinths. A young one, with white plumage from chin to vent, looked like a different species. Not far from the tower, a group of Nanday Conures quartered the ground in their search for seeds. A dozen or more, they disappeared the instant they landed, appearing again as flashes of blue (wings and tail) with an occasional glimpse of their scarlet socks. The search for breakfast had begun! As I turned to descend the steps I noticed a light blue Sayaca Tanager perched inside the tower. His agitation led me to look into a dark corner where his female was feeding chicks.

Breakfast was at 7am – mango and papaya, cereals, hot dishes including a rich cheese tart, and toast and jam awaited us. Half an hour later we climbed into our safari vehicle at the start of another day of surprises. The first was three Hyacinthine Macaws perched on a thick branch of a manduví tree. The middle bird was a full-grown offspring. Young of these long-lived birds are fed by their parents for six months after they fledge and experience parental care for 18 months in all.

Next came a dramatic incident: a Toco Toucan raided the nest of a Rufous-fronted Thornbird. There was no sign of the owner, a

306

small brown bird. It builds a pendulous nest of small sticks. The toucan inserted his long bill and felt around inside. First he threw out some feathers. It took him several minutes to bring out an egg. He held it between his mandibles, tossed it and then swallowed. A second egg followed suit – a tiny snack hardly worth eating. Poor thornbirds! Did they ever rear any young, I wondered? We had numerous sightings of Tocos, bizarre, yet beautiful. They moved around with such confidence, and their unique silhouette in flight (the bill so prominent) always caused excitement.

When I asked Brian what he liked most about the Pantanal, he replied: "The wide open vistas that allow us to see Toco Toucans, Hyacinthine Macaws and others in flight. To me, seeing birds flying is so much more rewarding than watching them skulking about in a bush". I knew exactly what he meant. It gave a feeling of satisfaction, of really experiencing the bird life, a feeling that is missing from the glimpses that you are lucky to get in rainforest.

When it was all over Linda said the same thing: "I was thrilled by one far-away sighting of a Toco Toucan in the Atlantic Forest but here the Toco Toucans blew me away! They made it for me – together with the macaws which were the birds I most wanted to see. The Hyacinthines were just wonderful and the initial sighting was unforgettable".

Another highlight was a flock of Yellow-collared Macaws feeding in a woodland tree, a *taruma-do-cerrado*. These small macaws were absorbed in consuming the grape-sized dark ripe fruits and peered down at us with interest. Mainly green with a golden collar, they were often observed in flight but here we had the opportunity to watch them for ten or fifteen minutes. The more we looked the more macaws we found. At first I saw only three or four but finally realised there were at least 20 and possibly 30! Later Victor pointed to a tree covered in small spiky cones, nearly black in colour. This was *chico-magra*, and the small seeds inside the cones were favourites of the macaw. A valued tree, it grows from even a cut stump and its leaves and fruits are consumed by the cattle – of which there were 20,000 on the ranch! These too were zebu, humped white animals brought from India during the 1920s .

Yellow-collared Macaws

There are four species of deer in the Pantanal – and we saw them all. The daintiest was the pampas deer, in decline due to loss of grassy areas. One little doe, with cinnamon coat and white chin and underparts, stopped nervously to look at us, big ears pricked. On the other hand, a large dark brown buck marsh deer ignored the passers-by as it grazed among the grasses.

Three-quarters of an hour before dusk we arrived at the roosting site of hundreds of Blue-fronted Amazons. Biting insects were making themselves felt and the evocative laughing calls of the Amazons were filling the air. The parrots were coming in pairs, almost wing-tip to wing-tip, from every direction. They sailed down into their roost site, a group of large mango trees, calling excitedly and occasionally taking off again to circle around, shouting. Half an hour earlier a small group of young people had been playing football on the grassy area in front of the trees. Just beyond the football pitch, a pair of Hyacinthine Macaws sat on top of their nest-box attached to a large manduví. They took off, to return some minutes later. I photographed them as they swooped low over the field. When I looked at the photo I was surprised to find that each bird was carrying a palm nut in its bill!

I sat on the bench used by the football spectators and watched the Amazon show. Victor came and sat beside me. When I asked him about this roost he told me: "I've lived here all my life. I'm

37 and I've been watching them as long as I can remember." He used to drive a tractor on the ranch. Now, without moving off it, he meets people from all over the world and helps them to enjoy the wildlife riches that have resulted from their protection. In other parts of the Pantanal it's very different. There is only one small officially protected area. Elsewhere poachers take the Amazon parrots and their chicks and not long ago thousands of caimans were slaughtered for their skins every year, jaguars were (and still are) killed when they take cattle, large areas are set on fire during the season when birds are nesting, and the introduction of exotic grasses interferes with native vegetation.

The Amazons at their roost looked and sounded so happy to be alive. They didn't know it, of course, but they were the lucky ones. No grasping hands come to snatch their chicks from the nest. On September 19, just two months before my visit, more than two hundred Amazons parrot chicks were seized by police after they received an anonymous call. All but 16 were Blue-fronted, hidden in boxes of vegetables from Ivinhema, about 190 miles (300km) from Campo Grande, where they ended up in the wild animal rehabilitation centre (CRAS), bringing the total there to 400 confiscated Amazon chicks. Sadly, 53 in poor condition died soon after. Children, acting on behalf of the smugglers, illegally collected the chicks – or even the eggs – just a few of the many thousand young poached from nests in the state of Mato Grosso do Sul and sent to CRAS since it opened 20 years ago. The problem is worse than taking away future breeding stock. Often the tree is cut down to access the nest sites which are at a premium.

In 1997 Projecto Papagaio Verdadeiro commenced. Based at Caiman Lodge, its aim is to manage and conserve the Blue-fronted Amazons of the Pantanal and the *cerrado* (the term for dry woodland of small trees and shrubs amidst savannah). Again, its driving force is a woman, Glaucia Seixas.

On our third and last morning in the Pantanal we went riding on patient horses reserved for visitors. Distant views of groups of 30 or so Jabirus were tantalising. I wished I could approach more closely to watch this parliament of storks. But we had to stay on the track, within fenced boundaries – and rightly so. In this reserve you cannot go out without a guide or wander freely away from the lodges. The wildlife comes first. In any case, at night a wandering human might fall victim to a jaguar. On the plus side, a major advantage is that the birds and animals on the ranch/reserve live in proximity to humans and many allow a close approach.

An afternoon visit to a mango plantation was rewarding. At last I had my first and only good look at Blaze-winged Conures, due to Victor's speed at focusing his scope. I was treated to the view of a young one shivering its wings as it was fed by a parent. This was an unexpected piece of luck, enabling me to see the scarlet carpal edge of the wing. (Both of Forshaw's books* state of immature birds: "undescribed" – so little is known about this species whose small range is centred on the Mato Grosso.) The scarlet under wing coverts of adults give this species its common name; from what I could see this colour was much less extensive in the young one. Apart from the scarlet under the wing, it differs little from the Red-bellied Conure except that the upper surface of the tail is olive – intermediate between the two sub-species of Red-bellied, of which it might well be a sub-species. For me, this was my most important sighting in the Pantanal.

Among the thick foliage of the mango trees were hiding Maximilian's Parrots. I could see only four or five and, as so often happens, I was surprised to count many more when they took off – twenty at least. I nearly missed a very attractive sight. Victor called me. I hurried over to find a tree full of Yellow-billed Cardinals, quickly moving on, their red heads, dark grey backs and white underparts lighting up the tree as though it were covered in Christmas ornaments. "How wonderful!" I exclaimed. All too soon they were gone.

As cardinals are beautiful, so are caiman hideous to my eyes. On the other side of the road was a small *baia* (lagoon) inhabited by seven or eight of these lumbering (on land) grey crocodilians. To my surprise, they hauled themselves out of the water and headed in our direction. It seemed that the guides fed them occasionally so that the visitors could observe them on demand. I confess they were too close for my comfort. I turned away, wandered along the road and spotted a gorgeous male Blue-

* *Parrots of the World,* third edition 1989; *Parrots of the World, an Identification Guide,* 2006.

crowned Trogon, his head a shimmering blue and his underparts scarlet. Elegant and colourful, he delighted the eye.

Returning to the vehicle, our group had an excellent view of a gang of white-lipped peccaries. We watched them emerging from the woodland in twos and three and fours, from big dangerous males to tiny "piglets", trotting along like clockwork toys. They kept coming, running here and there, snuffling around for leaves and fruits, until I lost count.

Another animal that uses its snout to seek out fruits, as well as its grasping hands, is the coati. A small group of females and their young searched the forest floor, their long tails (banded in brown and white), held vertically. Males travel alone. Once they were called *coatimundi*, meaning lone coati, and males were thought to be a different species!

There were also brown capuchin monkeys, glimpsed briefly when a small group crossed the road in front of us. One female panicked, bounding about nervously. She was afraid to cross. Then realising that the troop had left her behind, she took a flying leap from a tree on one side of the road to one on the other. My camera recorded the leap in mid-air and only then I saw that a tiny dark baby was clinging to her back.

In the plantation area there were strangler fig trees. Initially without a trunk of their own, they use the support of a palm tree and grow downwards, enveloping the host tree in a mesh of roots of tortuous shapes. Eventually they grow so big that the host dies and only its shell remains. The plantation trees were loaded with ripe mangoes. Victor picked a couple and, later on, he cut them up and handed them out. Mango is a favourite food of many parrots. You might wonder why if you are familiar only with the hard, fibrous fruits that end up in European supermarkets. Those picked fresh off the tree are juicily delicious.

We drove to the main lodge where half the group went canoeing on the lake. I watched Blue-fronted Amazons, Maximilian's Parrots and Canary-winged Parakeets (I find it hard to use the newfangled name, Yellow-chevroned Parakeet) coming in to roost. There were lots of little Canary-wings and they were not shy of a close approach. They settled down for the night as the sun coloured the sky deep orange, with starkly contrasting black cloud above it. Did this herald the end of the dry season? That night there was lightening and a little rain.

I never expected to see a tapir, largely nocturnal and, with its elongated snout, one of the strangest animals in South America, related to rhinoceros and horses. It has three toes on the hind feet and four on the front. On our last morning we left the lodge at 5.30am for our drive to Campo Grande. Towards the exit, a shout went up: "Tapir!" In a field close to the road, hurrying away, was the largest terrestrial mammal species in Brazil. It was a fitting finale for four days that had overflowed with everything we could have hoped for.

Species not previously mentioned:

Greater Rhea (*Rhea americana*)
Quaker or Monk Parrakeet (*Myiopsitta monachus*)
Jabiru Stork (*Jabiru mycteria*)
Black-necked Stork (*Xenorhynchus asiaticus*)
Gilded Hummingbird (*Hylocharis chrysura*)
Wattled Jacana (*Jacana jacana*)
Green Ibis (*Mesembrinis cayennensis*)
Plumbeous Ibis (*Harpiprion caerulescens*)
Hyacinthine Macaw (*Anodorhynchus hyacinthinus*)
Blaze-winged Conure (*Pyrrhura devillei*)
Nanday Conure or Black-hooded Parakeet (*Nandayus nenday*)
Canary-winged or Yellow-chevroned Parakeet (*Brotogeris chiriri*)
Blue-crowned Trogon (*Trogon curicui*)
Chaco Chachalaca (*Ortalis canicollis*)
Southern Lapwing (*Vanellus chilensis*)
Chopi Blackbird (*Gnorimopsar chopi*)
Blue-fronted or Turquoise-fronted Amazon Parrot (*Amazona aestiva aestiva*) (nominate race not previously observed)
Sayaca Tanager (*Thraupis sayaca*)
Rufous-fronted or Common Thornbird (*Phacellodomus rufifrons*)
Yellow-billed Cardinal (*Paroaria capitata*)

Capybara (*Hydrochaeris hydrochaeris*)

Yellow armadillo (*Euphractus sexcintus*)
Paraguayan caiman (*Caiman yacare*)
White-lipped peccary (*Tayassu pecari*)
Coati (*Nasua nasua*)
Brown capuchin monkey (*Cebus apella*)
Tapir (*Tapirus terrestris*)
Zebu cattle (*Bos indicus*)

Taruma-do-cerrado tree (*Vitex polygama*)
Chico-magro tree (*Guazuma ulmifolia*)
Manduví (*Sterculia apetala*)
Acurí (*Scheelia phalarata*)
Bocaiuva palm (*Acrocomia aculeata*)

Glossary

Altiplano
High-elevation flat plain between eastern and western Andean ridges.

Chaco
Dry scrub and woodland found from the southern part of Bolivia and western Paraguay to northern Argentina.

CITES
The Convention on International Trade in Endangered Species of Wild Fauna and Flora (CITES), is an international agreement with more than one hundred member states (see www.cites.org). Appendix I lists the most endangered species which would be threatened with extinction if trade in wild-caught specimens occurred. Appendix II names the species that could become threatened with extinction if trade in wild-caught specimens occurred. All parrots not listed on Appendix I (with three exceptions) are listed on Appendix II because parrots are the group of birds most vulnerable to large-scale trapping.

Cloud forest
Montane subtropical rainforest which is perpetually shrouded in mist, with stunted trees and numerous epiphytes. In the Andes this habitat occurs from about 2,900ft (900m) to 8,200ft (2.500m). The wildlife and plants are, as yet, little studied there.

Col
A low point in a ridge of mountains, often forming a pass between two peaks.

Critically Endangered
A species that faces a 50% risk of extinction in the immediate future (in ten years or three generations)

Dry forest
A forest composed of trees of short stature that tend to lose their leaves during the dry season.

Endangered
A species that faces a 20% risk of extinction in 20 years or five generations. These species are characterised by rapid population reduction and small and fragmented populations and/or a small range.

Endemic
A species found only in one region or country.

Epiphyte
A plant that grows on another, such as bromeliads, orchids and philodendrons.

Igapo
Forest that floods with black water, such as the Pilchicocha Lake in the Ecuadorian Amazon. *Mauritia* palms are found here, along with smaller palms.

Lek
An area in which male birds congregate and dance or display to attract females.

Llanos
Seasonally flooded grasslands, such as those in Bolivia.

Mangrove
Major ecosystem along tropical coasts composed of trees that are tolerant of immersion in salt water.

Near-threatened
Species that are close to qualifying for Vulnerable status.

Neotropics
The American (New World) tropics.

Ox-bow lake
If a river adopts a new course, it can cut off part of the former channel, leaving a curved isolated body of water known as an ox-bow lake.

Páramo
Open grassy areas above the treeline, from about 10,700ft (3,200m) up to 13,300ft (4,000m), with a gradual reduction in shrubby growth as the elevation increases. Frosts occur often and brief snowfalls are known.

Polylepis woodland
Andean woodland at high elevation, typically above the treeline at 11,700ft (3,500m) to 14,000ft (4,200m), consisting of low, gnarled trees with flaky-bark of the genus *Polylepis*. Most of these slow-growing trees have been destroyed by burning or cutting.

Primary forest
Forest that has reached its peak of maturity, blocking much of the sunlight from the ground. There is little underbrush.

Puna
Seasonally dry, windswept grassland above the treeline in the Andes.

Quebrada
A steep-sided valley.

Secondary forest
Forest that has been disturbed by cutting or by storm damage, allowing the sunlight to reach the ground. Many species of plants grow rapidly forming a dense, bushy cover of vegetation.

Subtropical forest
Usually luxuriant growth between about 3,300ft (1,000m) and 8,300ft (2,500m).

Temperate forest
Forest above subtropical forest, usually between 7,500ft (2,500m) and 11,500ft (3,500m).

Terra firme
Ground that never floods with the tallest trees and roots that form huge buttresses to support them, such as kapok and fig trees, with root systems that can extend 150ft (50m) along the ground.

Varzea
Seasonally flooded forest with such species as *Scheelea* palms and *Heliconia* plants.

Vulnerable
A species which is not assessed as endangered but which faces a high risk of extinction in the wild in the medium-term future.

Yungas
Forest on the steep eastern slopes of the Andes of Bolivia and northern Argentina.

Epilogue

During the thirty years that I have been visiting the neotropics, terrible changes have taken place. Hundreds of thousands of square miles of Amazonian rainforest have been destroyed and the Andean forests have been ravaged, so that this area has one of the highest numbers of endangered endemic birds in the world. Even while destruction of every type of South American habitat has progressed relentlessly, several dozen new bird species have been discovered – and usually immediately declared Endangered or Critically Endangered. During this period probably hundreds of bird species unknown to science have become extinct.

Oil is driving much of this destruction – oil taken from the ground and oil harvested from acres and acres of African oil palms, planted where once there were ancient forests filled with probably the richest diversity of animal and plant life on the planet.

We should remember that it is our own life styles, more so than the often seriously impoverished people in the area, who are driving this destruction. With our relentless, greedy consumerism and thoughtless use and disposal of plastic, we are killing the planet. Unless we stop and think and act, our own species will before very long, be on the endangered list. Despite increasing human population, the downward spiral has already started with disasters such as flood and drought that are the result of deforestation and other habitat destruction. Climate change and lack of water will also cause millions of humans to perish. This might seem implausible but it will be inevitable unless we change our ways. This also means producing fewer children so that the other creatures on this planet might survive.

One of my reasons for writing this book was to foster awareness of the problems facing wildlife and their habitats and to demonstrate how quickly the situation can deteriorate

within the space of 30 years. Within the next 30 years some of the species mentioned will be extinct unless there is more universal concern for their fate.

Many of us could help by donating to organisations working to preserve neotropical parrots and other birds. These include:

American Bird Conservancy www.abcbirds.org
Armonía (Bolivia) www.armonia-bo.org
BirdLife Internatioal www.birdlife.org
Fundación Jocotoco (Ecuador) www.fjocotoco.org
Loro Parque Fundación www.loroparque-fundacion.org
Parrots International (USA) www.parrotsinternational.org
ProAves (Colombia) www.proaves.org